CW01198162

IT'S (ALMOST) ALWAYS SUNNY IN PHILADELPHIA

IT'S (ALMOST) ALWAYS SUNNY IN PHILADELPHIA

HOW THREE FRIENDS SPENT $200 TO CREATE THE LONGEST-RUNNING LIVE-ACTION SITCOM IN HISTORY AND HELP BUILD A NETWORK

KIMBERLY POTTS

GALLERY BOOKS

New York   Amsterdam/Antwerp   London
Toronto   Sydney/Melbourne   New Delhi

G

Gallery Books
An Imprint of Simon & Schuster, LLC
1230 Avenue of the Americas
New York, NY 10020

For more than 100 years, Simon & Schuster has championed authors and the stories they create. By respecting the copyright of an author's intellectual property, you enable Simon & Schuster and the author to continue publishing exceptional books for years to come. We thank you for supporting the author's copyright by purchasing an authorized edition of this book.

No amount of this book may be reproduced or stored in any format, nor may it be uploaded to any website, database, language-learning model, or other repository, retrieval, or artificial intelligence system without express permission. All rights reserved. Inquiries may be directed to Simon & Schuster, 1230 Avenue of the Americas, New York, NY 10020 or permissions@simonandschuster.com.

Copyright © 2025 by Kimberly Potts

All rights reserved, including the right to reproduce this book or portions thereof in any form whatsoever. For information, address Gallery Books Subsidiary Rights Department, 1230 Avenue of the Americas, New York, NY 10020.

First Gallery Books hardcover edition July 2025

GALLERY BOOKS and colophon are registered trademarks of Simon & Schuster, LLC

Simon & Schuster strongly believes in freedom of expression and stands against censorship in all its forms. For more information, visit BooksBelong.com.

For information about special discounts for bulk purchases, please contact Simon & Schuster Special Sales at 1-866-506-1949 or business@simonandschuster.com.

The Simon & Schuster Speakers Bureau can bring authors to your live event. For more information or to book an event, contact the Simon & Schuster Speakers Bureau at 1-866-248-3049 or visit our website at www.simonspeakers.com.

Interior design by Julia Jacintho
Interior images © Adobe Stock

Manufactured in the United States of America

10 9 8 7 6 5 4 3 2 1

Library of Congress Control Number: 2024952122

ISBN 978-1-6680-0850-8
ISBN 978-1-6680-0852-2 (ebook)

FOR JOHN, AS ALWAYS

CONTENTS

Chapter 1: It's Always *Sunny* on TV — 1

Chapter 2: The Sun Always Shines on *Sunny* — 21

Chapter 3: And They're Off! — 37

Chapter 4: The Gang Gets a New Member — 55

Chapter 5: The Nightman Cometh — 79

Chapter 6: The House of the Rising *Sunny* — 131

Chapter 7: *Sunny* Dee — 141

Chapter 8: *Philadelphia* Freedom . . . to Get Real Weird with It — 169

Chapter 9: *Sunny* Stans — 191

Chapter 10: The Gang's All Here . . . Including the Mayor of Television — 217

Chapter 11: Still *Sunny* After All These Years — 239

Chapter 12: Into the Record Books, into the Future — 275

Acknowledgments — 293

Sources — 297

Index — 311

Chapter One

IT'S ALWAYS *SUNNY* ON TV

Rob McElhenney had a dream. Not a big-picture, life's-goal kinda dream, though he certainly had some of those, too. This was a literal, middle-of-the-night dream, a nightmare, really, about a cup of sugar and a friend with cancer.

The young actor/waiter had awakened, sweating, from a vision about a guy making a delicious pot of coffee, only to find his sugar bowl empty. When the man went next door to borrow a cup of sweetener, his neighbor greeted him with the news that he'd just found out he had cancer.

Wide awake now and shaken by the dream, McElhenney got out of bed. As he padded around his small Los Angeles apartment—actually a garage behind the house of its owner, who he'd found via an ad on Craigslist when he moved into town—he couldn't stop thinking about the somber scenario. It was terrible news for the man who had been given this life-altering diagnosis. He deserved the sympathetic ear of a buddy, someone to assure him it would all turn out okay.

And yet... the other guy was probably stressed out himself, trying to get ready for work. Maybe he was running behind. He desperately needed that jolt of caffeine. He really did just want to get some sugar and "get the fuck out of there," McElhenney reasoned.

And then he thought, there was something sort of funny about that, wasn't there? About acknowledging that part of someone's psyche, that part where one person's need for compassion and basic humanity bumps right up against another's desire to pretend they didn't hear this disturbing information and to flee home with sweet crystalline booty?

McElhenney had obsessed about this bit of dark humor past the point of any chance of a return to sleep, so he decided to head to his office (that corner of his West Hollywood garage apartment where he spent countless hours in a chair, balancing his Mac laptop on his knees) to write up his dream as a short scene. Maybe he would even film it. He knew two friends who would totally get the hilarity he saw in the situation.

☼ ☼ ☼

Most of Glenn Howerton's early TV work was in the comedy genre, which was unexpected for the Juilliard graduate. His plan after four years at the prestigious New York City training ground for dramatic arts included lots of theater, lots of Serious Actor roles. But while paying the bills with his day job as a bellhop at the Hudson Hotel, a gig he worked alongside comedian Rob Delaney, actor Matt Bomer, and fellow Juilliardian Lee Pace, theater audition after theater audition netted him few callbacks. No TV work was forthcoming, either. Howerton never even landed a guest role on the obligatory aspiring New York City actor résumé entry, *Law & Order*.

Then in 2002, the New York production of Denis Leary's ABC cop comedy *The Job* cast him for a small guest spot, playing a gay wedding planner. Later that year, he was offered his first lead role as the star of *That '80s Show*, a Fox sitcom about an aspiring musician working at a San Diego record store. An unplanned shift had begun. Howerton decided that since the world of New York City theater just wasn't that into him, he'd reciprocate and take the TV series job at Fox. He packed his bags and relocated to Los Angeles.

Meanwhile, on the West Coast, McElhenney wasn't having as much success as Howerton with landing TV work—there were one-off gigs as a teenage killer on *Law & Order* and an injured rookie firefighter on *ER*. But he and Howerton had met a couple of times back in New York, and their mutual manager, Nick Frenkel, reintroduced them as newbie Los Angelinos. They bonded quickly about their industry ambitions. And McElhenney was admittedly lonely. He had been pretty much on his own in this new city since his actor roommate Christopher Backus, the one he moved there with, went to a Hollywood party one night and met an actress. Less than a month later, Backus had moved out to Malibu to live with her. And less than a year later, he and Mira Sorvino were married.

Besides, McElhenney and Howerton had similar senses of humor. As predicted, Howerton loved the scene treatment McElhenney wrote about his sugar-and-cancer dream and encouraged McElhenney to expand upon it; both actors had been watching a lot of Larry David's irreverent comedy *Curb Your Enthusiasm*, particularly enjoying how David embraced the complicated nuances of interacting with friends and family and how the curmudgeonly TV version of Larry was often hoisted by his own petard. A favorite episode was from season 2, in which David had wrung laughs out of his character Larry's misplacement of a pair of plane tickets and a mistaken scene at a river, seemingly simple acts that led to Larry's sister-in-law canceling her wedding engagement.

Howerton thought McElhenney's dream scene had a lot in common with the spirit of outrageousness that made up some of the best stories on *Curb*, and saw it as worthy of development into a full script. Maybe a third person could be added to the mix, a mutual friend to the sugar seeker and the man with cancer? Maybe the third guy would be upset about the man with cancer choosing to share his news with the sugar seeker, whom he wasn't even that close with, instead of the third guy. Yeah, in fact, the third guy wasn't just hurt that he'd been left out of the loop—he was angry! How dare the man with cancer seek sympathy and compassion from the sugar seeker, when the third guy had been his friend for years? The third guy was completely pissed off!

And now McElhenney had the makings of an entire story—one that he and Howerton felt they *really* should turn into a video project.

Charlie Day had also met Howerton a time or two in New York and Los Angeles, their paths crossing at auditions, including the one landing Howerton *That '80s Show* (which led to an uncomfortable moment when the two happened to be in a car together as Howerton got the call informing him he'd won the role). Day met McElhenney during a flight to LA, when both of them were going to screen-test for yet another role, this one for a college-set sitcom called *Mather House*. Seated next to Day on the plane, McElhenney planned to psych his rival out a bit. He wanted that role very badly, and Day wasn't going to stand in his way. And then they started talking. By the end of the flight, McElhenney knew three things: (1) he genuinely liked Day, (2) Day was the funniest guy he'd ever met, and (3) there was no way in hell that he was going to land the *Mather House* role if Day was in the running.

As it turned out, neither got the role. The series, written by *Seinfeld* alums Alec Berg, Jeff Schaffer, and David Mandel—Harvard grads who named the series after the titular university residence hall that was once home to Conan O'Brien—was canceled before it ever began. McElhenney and Day would eventually have the chance to costar back on the East Coast, during the New Jersey production of the skippable 2001 horror movie *Campfire Stories*.

Charlie Day, who spent four years working at the much-respected Williamstown Theatre Festival in Massachusetts after graduating from Merrimack College, lived in a shabby East Village apartment with actor Jimmi Simpson, another Williamstown alum. The two had a reputation among their friends for making off-the-wall videos.

When they weren't holed up in their apartment at the corner of Delancey and Orchard Streets, helping each other prepare for auditions (including one that Day nailed for a *Law & Order* appearance), they could be spotted running around the neighborhood creating sketches, Simpson recalled. He was always stunned by Day's comedic skills, as the two and their buddies would don wigs, hats, and fake teeth for videos like "Drug Lord," in which Day, Simpson, and fellow Williamstown alums David Hornsby and Logan Marshall-Green are in a drug deal that goes bad; "Quit Smoking," in which Day goes cold turkey until he spots Simpson's cigarettes on a coffee table and murders his roommate after going through the whole pack; and the oddly mesmerizing "Speedwagon," in which Simpson and Hornsby earnestly lip-synch and then sing along with the REO Speedwagon power ballad "Can't Fight This Feeling." The videos are now posted on Simpson's YouTube channel; they are the kind of amateur videos anyone with an iPhone (and the wealth of talent contained among this crew) might do now, but Day and Simpson were doing hundreds of them before they had any huge forum to display them. And it earned them respect among their fellow actors for their creativity, eccentricity, and willingness to put their weirdness on tape.

"My God, those videos were everything," Simpson says. "[Since] there wasn't even YouTube yet, we were literally making them to watch with each other and our friends in the three-by-five-foot 'TV room' in our place on the Lower East Side. But we got to mess around with our instruments and creativity with zero stakes—essential learning time. Charlie was just so explosively hilarious; every choice he made slayed me. It was a joy to play straight man to him, plus my stories were just so fucking... bizarre. I got to do it my way."

When Day moved to Los Angeles a couple of years later, he reconnected with McElhenney and Howerton. The three, who all shared Nick Frenkel as a manager by this point, began spending lots of time together, drinking, watching movies and television (including Day and Simpson's home movies from back in New York), and talking about their work prospects. Common for most young people but downright an obsession for young Hollywood performers. They were unanimously frustrated with the lack of quality jobs coming their way.

They liked to hang out at Howerton's apartment and read the scripts McElhenney wrote when he wasn't slinging casual French American fare at Café D'Etoile in West Hollywood. McElhenney, unlike his buddies, didn't attend college, save the year he squatted in a high school friend's dorm at Fordham University while bartending and auditioning for TV commercials. When manager Frenkel met McElhenney's complaints about not getting acting jobs with the suggestion to write his own material, McElhenney did just that. He bought all the requisite books, like the Syd Field and William Goldman and Robert McKee classics on screenwriting, and taught himself the craft. One of his first efforts, a dark movie drama written while commuting on the New York City subway, was optioned by *Taxi Driver* writer Paul Schrader but got lost in development hell.

Without a formal education or training, McElhenney saw writing as lighting the path to his success in Hollywood, but he also began to think it wouldn't be enough. He didn't want to just write, anyway, but also act, direct, produce . . . make a whole project, tell an entire story. Howerton had talked to him about turning his expanded script for the sugar-cancer story into a video.

Day, with his own video experience, was a key factor in what would become, for the rest of McElhenney's career, a brand. He wouldn't just write a script—he would produce a proof of concept, a filmed version of his story, something that could be burned onto a DVD and shown to anyone who might be interested that not only could he write well, but also he could make it into a good movie or show. For this particular endeavor, he was looking to Howerton and Day to lend their ideas, their senses of humor, their acting talent, and Day's experience with a camcorder to help him bring the video aspect to fruition. Kevin Smith had done it with *Clerks*, Jon Favreau had done it with *Swingers*, and Edward Burns had done it with *The Brothers McMullen*. Now McElhenney saw this DIY project as his path to a career breakout.

☼ ☼ ☼

Two hundred bucks. That's what it cost to make the *It's Always Sunny in Philadelphia* pilot.

Well, maybe a little less than that. Videotapes for the camera, which McElhenney had purchased at Best Buy, opening a credit card account when he decided to start dabbling in homemade videos, ate up most of the informal budget. But there was also gas to get from location to location for the weekend shoots. There was the broom the trio of filmmakers bought so whoever wasn't on camera at any given time could use it as a makeshift boom mic pole. And there was a lot of cheap pizza, because the other actors who volunteered their time and talent to help film McElhenney's script deserved at least a slice or two. So while $200 is the unofficial official tally for what McElhenney and company spent to make what would become the *It's Always Sunny in Philadelphia* pilot, that is the sum most frequently cited as the cost of production. Sadly, there is no collection of receipts that could be framed and hung on the wall of RCG Productions—named so because it's the production shingle for Rob, Charlie, and Glenn—to mark some of the most consequential videotapes and pizza sold in Hollywood history. Various sources peg the pilot as costing anywhere from $85 to $100 to $200. Years later, Day would tell Stephen Colbert on *The Late Show* that the budget had definitely been less than $200, saying, "That's the number [the network] made up because people kept asking how much it cost." All that matters now is that it was indisputably one of the biggest bargains in television history.

To backtrack for a moment, the pilot wasn't yet a pilot at this stage. McElhenney, Howerton, and Day just wanted to get *something* on film that they would shoot together. In fact, though the trio has rarely talked about it outside their *The Always Sunny Podcast*, the cancer-sugar story wasn't their first take on filming one of their story ideas. Not only were they all watching *Curb Your Enthusiasm*, but they were obsessed with the original Ricky Gervais British version of *The Office* and the comedy series' mockumentary format. McElhenney, who looked so young that he was asked to audition for teen roles when he was in his twenties, was teased by his friends that he looked like Haley Joel Osment, the child star of the blockbuster film *The Sixth Sense*. So he came up with his own mockumentary, playing a twentysomething version of Osment and Day playing a twentysomething, post–*Malcolm in the Middle* version of Frankie Muniz. The two former child stars were "living in a shitty apartment together, fucked up on drugs, trying to get their lives together," Howerton said. He played their eccentric acting teacher, and though the effort was fun and allowed them to dip their toes into learning how to film a story as a group, they decided to go back to McElhenney's cup-of-sugar/revelation-of-cancer dream to continue with their videomaking efforts.

Except, at this point, no one had tagged the short as a pilot, or even as something they were making specifically for television. Howerton was happy creating a fun segment to show friends when they came to hang out at his place. He and Day were content to be doing *something*. While McElhenney would think of Howerton and Day as the on-camera talent—he was "just a scumbag waiter . . . Charlie and Glenn were real actors," he said—Day would tell friends that without McElhenney, the most ambitious guy he's ever known, he and Howerton "wouldn't have gotten off our asses" to make something happen for themselves.

Throughout the development of the project, the trio had added details and plotting to the story. All three would play struggling actors in Hollywood. That was the world they knew, and those jobs meant their characters had plenty of free time for various shenanigans.

Day would play "Charlie," the guy with cancer, while Howerton would play "Glenn," the sugar borrower. The third character, the one jealous about not being told about Charlie's cancer, was named Mac, and the filmmakers were doubling down on the initial shallow behavior from sugar-seeking Glenn. The characters were taking shape, and they all had epic journeys into selfishness and pettiness ahead of them.

Glenn, in an effort to cheer up Charlie, plotted to get Charlie's crush to go on a date with him, which would end with her sleeping with Charlie. Known only as "Waitress" (and played by Day's then-girlfriend, now-wife, Mary Elizabeth Ellis), Charlie's crush had eyes on someone else: Mac. And Mac was only too happy to sleep with her out of revenge for Charlie not sharing his cancer news.

Meanwhile, McElhenney's girlfriend at the time, actress Jordan Reid, was playing Sweet Dee, the female foil to the three fellas, and Mac was being played by... *not* McElhenney.

McElhenney had his hands full with writing, directing, and producing the film, overseeing the whole enterprise, and holding one of the cameras. (A second camera, owned by Howerton, was also in use, and would be held by whoever wasn't acting at the moment or one of the nearby friends.) David Hornsby, Day's pal from the Williamstown Theatre Festival and those wild sketches he and Jimmi Simpson filmed back in New York, had also made the move to Los Angeles and stepped in to portray McElhenney's namesake character.

The short film came together quickly. Just as McElhenney was learning to write scripts, he, Howerton, and Day trained themselves on how to make a narrative video by staging Howerton's and Day's and Reid's apartments as filming locations, carrying a boom mic on a broom to capture the film's sound, directing themselves and their friends, and editing footage into a cohesive few minutes of storytelling and character studies on their MacBooks. Friends like Jimmi Simpson, who had since moved to LA, also helped with broomstick boom mic holding.

Day's pithy review of the initial result: "It was not good."

The writing and acting were on point. But the sound and lighting left a lot to be desired, and these were things they worked on in a do-over shoot and reedit. Which they also deemed not ready for public viewing.

Take two was an epic improvement, the guys felt, but wasn't their best work, either. So back at it they went, even with all the complications that arose from the erratic scheduling they had to follow with so many costarring friends who had their own pursuits, their own personal lives, and who were, after all, working for pizza.

In what turned out to be a game-changing occurrence, Hornsby wasn't available to film round three because his girlfriend was in town visiting. Everyone else was ready for (another) repeat performance of their characters, so McElhenney agreed to jump into the role of Mac. Spoiler alert: it worked out well for both Hornsby's and McElhenney's professional futures.

The trio was happy with the third take, with the quality of the performances and the technical aspects of filming.

"We just knew . . . it wasn't any one thing. It was our process," Day said. "We hadn't refined it yet, and we said, 'Let's take another crack at it, knowing a little bit more about what [we were] trying to do.' And we made a much better version."

Along with all they had learned about camerawork, sound, lighting, and editing, the guys had also gotten a crash course in producing, and they all felt comfortable with the multiple roles they played in the project.

"We had the self-restraint to keep making it until it was as good as we thought it could be," McElhenney said.

Now, at last, it was time to get some feedback from someone they all respected.

McElhenney gave the movie to manager Nick Frenkel, who issued two thumbs up. He also told his clients he thought they had the makings of a television comedy. Never having imagined the story in that specific format or setting, McElhenney, Howerton, and Day nonetheless immediately started to see the possibilities. Frenkel had mentioned passing the potential episode along to an agent who might have additional thoughts about it, but the actors decided they wanted to produce an accompanying piece of work to go along with the first one and create a nice little package. They had another idea ready for these malcontents they were already starting to see endless storylines for, but there was something else that got the wheels turning in their minds. They had seen the payoff for the many hats they wore during production of the first episode. They now felt confident enough that their new skills provided them with the potential for more control over their acting futures. Frenkel had opened McElhenney's eyes to the power of writing one's own material, and Day's experience running all over his Manhattan neighborhood making offbeat homemade movies with his buddies had gotten Howerton and McElhenney excited to make their own. The guys had produced one episode that had wowed their manager . . . two, they thought, might really wow TV executives. Better yet, two episodes might be just the impetus that McElhenney, Howerton, and Day needed to prove they weren't ready to only act in a series; they were ready to star in it, write it, and be the executive producers and showrunners of it, too.

The second episode the guys and their friends filmed revolved around Mac, played from the beginning of this story by McElhenney. Mac was excited about Carmen, a woman he met at a party . . . until Glenn and Charlie informed him she was transgender. Carmen was played by Howerton's friend and Juilliard classmate Morena Baccarin, and though it had escaped Mac's attention that Carmen had a telltale bulge in her jeans, Charlie and Glenn pointed it out. Carmen confirmed the revelation to Mac, who was upset at what he claimed was her deception. Carmen countered that he had flat-out lied to her, telling her he was in pharmaceutical sales. When she told him she had seen him acting in an episode of *Law & Order*, her positive feedback on his TV performance made him confess his real profession and forget his anger toward her.

Production on the second episode, shot largely in the backyard of the two-bedroom apartment Day shared with Ellis on Franklin Avenue, went much more quickly, further boosting the trio's confidence in themselves, and sparking them to believe they just might have something special on the burned DVD they put into the hands of Frenkel and his agent friend Ari Greenburg, who liked what he saw, too. He got the humor and agreed it was a comedy made for TV. He offered to set up a few meetings around town.

The show was titled *It's Always Sunny on TV*, a nod to the characters' profession as aspiring actors, and inspired by the a-ha song "The Sun Always Shines on T.V." Howerton had heard the tune while at the Crunch Fitness gym on Sunset Boulevard, and he thought the adaptation *It's Always Sunny on TV* would make a fitting name for the self-absorbed characters he and his friends had created.

McElhenney, Howerton, and Day were certain the two episodes would show all the promise of the irreverent comedy they were determined *It's Always Sunny* would be: a deconstruction of the classic sitcom.

※ ※ ※

The whole project began with a dream and McElhenney's ambition pushing his friends toward a creative endeavor, the results of which he now carried on a single VHS tape. He was ready for the pitch meetings Ari Greenburg had arranged, ready to show TV executives what he and his friends had done and could do. The VHS tape as the delivery method of their creativity was certainly not going to make anyone in an executive suite see the *It's Always Sunny on TV* gang as fresh or cutting-edge, but it did have a well-thought-out purpose. Shiny silver DVDs, like the one holding the footage of the two *Sunny* shorts, copied directly from McElhenney's laptop, had a nasty habit of randomly refusing to play in DVD players. McElhenney had seen it happen on his own with a disc of the *Sunny* shorts he'd burned as a screening for friends at Howerton's apartment. Worst of all, he'd heard about such nonfunctioning DVDs ruining other Hollywood pitch sessions. Of all the things he could worry about going wrong at any of these meetings—though he was actually a confident, glass-half-full kinda guy by nature—a skipping or totally nonplaying DVD was not going to be one of them. Hence the VHS tape in its unlabeled original cardboard box, which he ferried to more than half a dozen meetings across a couple of days.

McElhenney had one objection to the idea of a pitch meeting: he didn't want to have to *pitch*. He didn't want to go into those network offices filled with television executives who thought they'd seen it all and try to persuade the skeptics that he and his inexperienced collaborators were going to bring something different to TV land. He and Howerton and Day made *It's Always Sunny on TV* to *show* they had something special to offer. So McElhenney intended to simply insert the tape into the VCRs, hit play, and wait for the laughing to commence.

It was a brash decision for someone who was lucky to get such a lineup of networks interested in the first place. Twenty-five-year-old actors, with little writing experience, no credits as producers or showrunners, and deleted minor performances in two movies (*The Devil's Own* and *Wonder Boys*) as their most impressive acting résumé entries don't usually/often/ever have the opportunity to sell their idea for a comedy series with no known cast members to MTV, VH1, Comedy Central, HBO, CBS, Fox, and FX, all in two short days. It was only the influence of Ari Greenburg that made those meetings happen.

Back in 2004, Greenburg, now the president of the William Morris Endeavor (WME) agency, was an Endeavor agent with an impressive track record of "packaging," or putting together the elements of TV series. He helped make *The Osbournes* a seminal reality program for MTV, and was also responsible for *Without a Trace*, *The O.C.*, *Prison Break*, and *Veronica Mars*—all series that became hits. Greenburg would go on to package dozens of other shows, including *This Is Us*, *Heroes*, *Supernatural*, *Westworld*, *Riverdale*, *Once Upon a Time*, *Bob's Burgers*, *Arrow*, and *The Flash*, and set up huge deals for the likes of Dick Wolf and Greg Berlanti, two of TV's most prolific producers.

Greenburg particularly connected with McElhenney on a personal level. Yes, he liked *It's Always Sunny on TV* and thought it was a very funny show with a lot of potential. But he also, like McElhenney, grew up in Philadelphia, and they both had dreams of making it big in Hollywood but were seen as underdogs to do so.

When Greenburg began interviewing for jobs after his Berkeley graduation, he was excited to land a meeting with a human resources executive at International Creative Management (ICM), one of the industry's biggest talent agencies. Greenburg's ultimate goal was to run a broadcast television network, and he was certain a spot in ICM's agent-training program would be an important first step to his dream destination as one of TV's top decision-makers. But before he could make it through the interview, the executive shared a crushing opinion: Greenburg didn't have the makings of a Hollywood agent.

Actually, that review would have crushed a less committed and ambitious young talent. Greenburg instead let it fuel him to become an agent at a different firm, working his way up from phone-answering assistant gigs to junior agent to TV packaging guru and all the way to president of WME. He saw that same kind of commitment and ambition and intelligence in his fellow Philadelphian, and that was a major factor in Greenburg's decision to take McElhenney and his homemade pilot around town to network development executives.

So, instead of making a formal pitch with a series bible, plans for episodes into season 5, and a big speech about why a prestigious cable network should let three twentysomething guys who spent $200 on a DIY pilot run a series with a multimillion-dollar budget, McElhenney, Frenkel, and Greenburg would walk into executive offices, shake hands, make introductions, exchange a few pleasantries, slide the pilot VHS tape into the office player, and watch along with the people who decided what was on the nation's TV screens.

Would they laugh alongside these newcomers, clearly getting the dark humor, and then say they wanted to be in the Rob McElhenney–Glenn Howerton–Charlie Day business? Or would they nod politely and shake hands once again as they walked the trio out the door—carrying the complimentary bottles of water and copies of *Variety* they'd been given—and have the assistant sitting outside the boss's office possibly offer to validate their parking?

For McElhenney—who was taking these meetings without his partners because his energy and confidence made him a born salesman ("He can sell you your own pants," Howerton said) and because Howerton and Day were more than happy to skip the business part of what went into a television show—it turned out to be a bit of a Goldilocks situation.

HBO and VH1 passed immediately, politely, in that showing-you-to-the-door kind of way.

MTV and Comedy Central liked the short videos enough to make offers, but neither of them were willing to let the guys continue on as the series' creative forces. That, of course, was a deal-breaker.

"'If you like what you're seeing, and you want us to keep doing it, then this is the process through which we did it,'" McElhenney said, explaining how he tried to reason with the executives. "Why would you change that? You know, [they] were like, 'We're not buying what you're saying. We like the show, but you're a waiter. With all due respect, we can't have a waiter step in and run this show.'"

CBS executives liked the show, but it was their opinion that the humor was not a good fit for the more buttoned-up demographic of the Eye Network.

And at the meeting with the Fox executives, there were no laughs whatsoever. Not a single snicker or snort in the room.

"They did not get it," McElhenney said. "It was the only room that did not laugh once. I was just looking over at an executive who had a stone face through the entire thing. When it was over, he stood up and said, 'Okay, thanks.' That was the end of it." Definitely no parking validation there, either.

And then came the inflection point: a meeting that brought together three talented creatives with fresh points of view that would fuel them to tell stories in clever new ways with a little-known but growing network anxious to build a brand. RCG had landed at FX, with its new president who wanted to shake up television programming and the way TV series were made. And who was the only executive open to the idea of allowing these three green would-be showrunners to learn how to make a TV series on his company's dime.

FX president John Landgraf thought he might have found the show that would allow him to start creating a signature comedy block at his new TV home. And just like Goldilocks, the *It's Always Sunny on TV* team thought they might have finally found their just-right.

Chapter Two

THE SUN ALWAYS SHINES ON *SUNNY*

One of John Landgraf's jobs before he took the reins as FX president of entertainment in 2004 was a five-year stint as the vice president of primetime at NBC, where, among his accomplishments, he shepherded the development of some of the network's biggest series ever, like *The West Wing* and, on the comedy side, *Friends*.

By the time Landgraf made his way to FX, one of his goals was to establish his new cable home as a prime destination for comedy.

So it might have been surprising that one of the first series he chose to help him build that brand was one touting itself as the deconstructor of traditional television sitcoms. In fact, McElhenney, himself a self-professed fan of *Friends*, would describe his comedy as: "We made the anti-*Friends*. That's what our mantra was."

So how did the executive who helped bring *Friends* to primetime TV, and the guys who made it one of their guiding principles to tear down that show's guiding principles, begin a partnership? It was a meeting of the minds when it came to what they found funny. And it made good business sense.

Launched only a decade earlier from leased space formerly occupied by a china showroom in Manhattan's Flatiron District and originally styled as fX, the network's early emphasis was on original, interactive live talk and entertainment shows (hosted by the likes of Tom Bergeron and Jeff Probst) that aired from a space that had been renovated into a functioning apartment. The network soon redesigned its logo and shifted focus to its primetime efforts. It spent millions of dollars on the rights to air hit dramas *NYPD Blue* and *The X-Files* five nights a week. FX continued to add other established series to its schedule—like *Buffy the Vampire Slayer* and *M*A*S*H* reruns—as well as NASCAR events and Major League Baseball games, and movie favorites like *The Green Mile* and *The Blair Witch Project*. Audiences grew, too, and in 2001, FX finally became available to cable viewers in New York City.

The cable network really began to hit its stride when then–FX CEO Peter Liguori again put original series in the spotlight. The premiere of *Son of the Beach*, a *Baywatch* spoof starring Timothy Stack and with Howard Stern among its executive producers, launched that initiative in 2000. The comedy ran for three seasons chock-full of double entendres, puns, and guest stars that ranged from Mark Hamill and RuPaul to (far, far at the other end of the talent gamut) Joey Buttafuoco. The edgy, dark dramedy *Nip/Tuck*, Ryan Murphy's series about the personal and professional lives of plastic surgeons played by Dylan Walsh and Julian McMahon, debuted under Liguori in 2003, and it was on his watch that the Denis Leary dramedy *Rescue Me*, which followed the personal and professional lives of deeply tested New York City firefighters post 9/11, was developed.

FX's first move to premium television land, though, came with Liguori's 2002 debut of *The Shield*, an intense, gritty crime drama created by Shawn Ryan that revolved around a group of Los Angeles cops working to crack down on some of the most violent, often gang-affiliated criminals while regularly using illegal methods to do it. *The Shield* received Golden Globe and Peabody Awards, and breakout star Michael Chiklis won the lead actor Emmy and Golden Globe for the series' first season. With standout performances by Walton Goggins, CCH Pounder, Glenn Close, Benito Martinez, and Catherine Dent, *The Shield* was not only FX's first major hit but it also has earned a spot on most lists of the greatest television series of all time, and its last episode in 2008 is widely considered to be one of the all-time best TV series finales.

Liguori and his executives had turned the latest iteration of FX into a hot new cable channel, but in a way that was equally as fresh and innovative as the launch team for fX had back in 1994.

And the future was only going to grow brighter for the network, thanks to the new executive who would earn himself the nickname "the Mayor of Television" and put his faith in three inexperienced friends who applied all their talents, and a bit of pizza money, to creating FX's history-making, most enduring hit.

When Landgraf (and his FX development executives Nick Grad, Eric Schrier, and Matt Cherniss) agreed to meet with RCG's manager, Nick Frenkel, it was as a favor to Frenkel.

And though all of his pitch-less pitch meetings had so far left him without an offer (or, at least, without an offer he and the "CG" portion of the trio of aspiring auteurs were content to accept), McElhenney stuck to his original plan. No pitch. Just the two proof-of-concept episodes of *It's Always Sunny on TV*, this time delivered on a higher-quality DVD, one that was guaranteed to play correctly.

"So I put in the DVD of the two episodes we'd shot and said, 'We made this. Check it out!'" McElhenney recalled in an essay he wrote for *The Hollywood Reporter*. "If FX worried about letting us do a show, they didn't let on. That they gave a waiter and his two buddies their own series is still pretty shocking to me."

Landgraf had his reasons for offering McElhenney, Day, and Howerton a deal, the biggest being he genuinely liked the pilot episodes. He thought they were funny, irreverent, unlike anything else he'd seen. Certainly unlike anything else he'd seen on cable. They had a distinct point of view and showcased the exact kind of humor he wanted to build the FX comedy brand around. And he liked McElhenney, who he would say was like a young Larry David, the now legendary *Seinfeld* and *Curb Your Enthusiasm* creator.

There could have been no better comparison to McElhenney, a huge David fan who would have some pretty, pretty, pretty interesting interactions with his industry exemplar a few years down the road.

"It was a good partnership, because they wanted to learn, and we wanted to kind of reinvent the model," Landgraf said.

So impressed was the FX honcho with McElhenney, Day, and Howerton that he offered them $400,000 to reshoot their pilot with a professional crew. And he agreed give them to what was most important to them: control. All three would star in the series, and all three would serve as executive producers and writers. McElhenney, officially credited as series creator, would also direct the new and official pilot, just as he had the two DIY episodes (which had cost a mere .05 percent of the FX-backed reshoot).

That pilot was not the end of the *Sunny* path to FX's schedule, however. To launch the Landgraf era of comedy on FX, *It's Always Sunny* was up against three other series pilots: a sketch comedy produced by Jamie Foxx (who was about to win a Best Actor Oscar for *Ray*, and received a Supporting Actor Oscar nomination for *Collateral*, in the same year); *Human Animals*, about a couple who makes wildlife documentaries, from *Married* producer Andrew Gurland and *The O.C.* producer Doug Liman; and *Starved*, about a group of friends in an eating disorders support group, created by and starring Eric Schaeffer.

By early 2005, *Sunny* and *Starved* were announced as the winners of seven-episode season orders, to air in a one-hour comedy block later that summer. FX scheduled both shows to premiere on August 4, 2005, with *Starved* leading the way at 10:00 p.m.

In return, FX had some demands for the *It's Always Sunny* pack. Though they didn't require tinkering with what the show was intended to be, they turned out to be significant changes.

First, the three main characters (more on that fourth main character we met in season 1 coming up shortly) were portrayed as actors living in Hollywood. That had to go. Landgraf felt there had already been a lot of shows about the industry in recent years—*Entourage*,

The Comeback, Curb Your Enthusiasm, and the soon-to-premiere *Friends* spin-off, *Joey*—and it wasn't a fresh topic or backdrop any longer. Los Angeles as the setting became redundant then since they weren't going to be actors; so say goodbye to Hollywood. But since the characters did need to be employed in a situation that would leave them with plenty of messing-around time on their hands, RCG came up with Mac, Charlie, and Glenn owning a bar. And how about setting it in Philadelphia, McElhenney's beloved hometown? Not only would it be a nice nod to the City of Brotherly Love, but it was where his family and so many of his friends still lived. Their South Philly pub, a dive bar if ever there was one, would be called Paddy's Pub.

The series needed a new name now that it was no longer a comedy revolving around the entertainment industry, so *It's Always Sunny on TV* morphed into *It's Always Sunny in Philadelphia*. Unwieldy, yes, as any media person who's covered the show for the past seventeen seasons and had to type that title frequently will concur, but it's a good adaptation of the original. One of the alternative names the newly appointed executive producers considered: *Jerks*. Succinct, accurate, but forgettable. And *It's Always Sunny in Philadelphia*, the title and the show, is anything but that.

In another knock-on effect of changing the characters' profession, new theme music had to be selected. A cha-cha version of "Hooray for Hollywood," the classic song first used in the 1937 Busby Berkeley musical comedy *Hollywood Hotel*, was no longer a good fit. *It's Always Sunny in Philadelphia* was running on a supertight budget, so the producers had to pick a new theme song from a library of moderately priced options. They wanted something peppy and upbeat, something that the characters might think was perfectly appropriate for who they are but which would actually be a rather ironic, feel-good introduction to a group that is given to rather appalling behavior right from the series' beginning. The winner: "Temptation Sensation" by German composer and big band conductor Heinz Kiessling. The *Sunny* crew were introduced to Kiessling's compositions by music supervisor Ray Espinola, and had actually chosen another Kiessling tune, "Off Broadway," as the theme song. But when Landgraf heard "Temptation Sensation," he was sure that was the way to go, a decision that Day has since said he agrees with (though he also said he thinks the song title sounds like something from a pornographic film). But "Off Broadway" survived on the series, along with a soundtrack full of instantly recognizable, oft-used (and oddly named) Kiessling tracks, including "Take the Plunge," "On Your Bike" (which includes the sound of a bicycle bell being rung), "Coconut Shy," "Captain's Table," "Hotsy-Totsy," and "Blue Blood."

Sunny composer Cormac Bluestone is another member of Day's talented circle of friends from the Williamstown Theatre Festival, and he points out that there are nearly twenty musical transitions used on the show. And because he has worked with that music for fourteen seasons and counting, he is probably one of the few people who knows each of those clips by title and songwriter. Bluestone, who plays multiple instruments and sings, has also worked as a casting agent, and an actor on shows like *Billions*, *The Blacklist*, *Veep*, *Blue Bloods*, and, yes, *Sunny*.

Finally, in a subject that has rarely been publicly addressed by the network, McElhenney, Day, or Howerton: before *IASIP*—a favorite shorthand to refer to the series—premiered on FX, a major casting change was made.

The original actress playing "Sweet" Dee Reynolds (so named because of her character's originally cheerier outlook, the opposite of what her male cohorts were portraying) was Jordan Reid Berkow, a willowy blonde who went simply by Jordan Reid. After college, she moved to Los Angeles to pursue an acting career. There, she reconnected with her ex-boyfriend, McElhenney, and they began dating again amid her involvement in the filming of the two pilot episodes.

In a 2016 blog post, Reid recalled one of the guys (likely Howerton) once scheduled a meeting in which she and RCG made a pact to stick together, no matter what, if FX wanted to make any casting changes. They all shook on it inside McElhenney's trailer; the network had to leave all of them in place, or none of them.

But while Reid said the professional relationship had been solidified during that pact meeting, her romantic relationship with McElhenney was not on track. Then she began to feel like her place on the show was on shaky ground, too. And when the network named the three guys as executive producers and provided office space and a desk for each of the three, she wrote that she began to feel like she "was welcome when I was the girlfriend of the creator—but once I wasn't, my role in creating

[FX's] new pet project was forgotten." Reid wrote that during a breakup conversation with McElhenney, he told her if she broke up with him, she was out of the show. She ended the romance anyway.

In a 2021 profile of McElhenney, *The New York Times* reported that after the foursome had finished the professionally reshot version of the pilot, FX asked the three executive producers if they would be willing to replace Reid in the role of Sweet Dee. Awaiting news of whether the pilot would be picked up for a series, the three friends agreed to hire a new actress as the female lead, and Reid was fired.

In her essay about the experience, which includes photos of her with her three costars, in a car with Day, and on the pilot set with Howerton and Artemis Pebdani, Reid wrote that she felt hurt and betrayed but was not sorry she hadn't agreed to remain in a relationship with McElhenney to continue her role.

She was given a small payment—the equivalent of one episode of the series, she wrote—but remained angry and did some things she wasn't proud of, like illegally recording "damning conversations." She also considered filing a lawsuit but was told it would be a long, expensive process that would also likely end her chances of casting agents hiring her for other projects because she would "always be known as 'the girl who sued FX.'" So she let it go, as much as anyone could.

And, though Reid wrote in the essay that she never again talked to Day or Howerton after she and McElhenney split, the aforementioned *New York Times* story quotes her as saying that she "no longer begrudges the men for seizing their opportunity." She and McElhenney each told the article's writer that they were once again friends.

※ ※ ※

After the drama of losing their leading lady—the only woman in the main cast—and with an order of a seven-episode season of television to create, McElhenney, Day, and Howerton had a lot on their plates. The opportunity that lay before them was, of course, an incredible break, but it came with no small amount of pressure. They wanted—demanded—that they be allowed to run their show, but the experience of writing a television series that would actually fill a time slot on a cable network once a week for at least two months was a huge leap from what they'd done before.

Their first order of business involved the search for an actress to play Sweet Dee. The likes of future *Saturday Night Live* star Kristen Wiig and Mary Lynn Rajskub, then playing Jack Bauer's analyst pal Chloe O'Brian on *24*, both auditioned, but the fellas had their minds set on an actress they already knew had the comedy chops and then some, thanks to her appearance on one of their favorite series, *Curb Your Enthusiasm*.

Kaitlin Olson was a member of the Groundlings (the influential LA improvisational and sketch-comedy group), had a recurring role on *The Drew Carey Show*, and did guest spots on *Punk'd* and *The Man Show*. But RCG remembered her best from *Curb*, where she played Becky, Larry David's sister-in-law. During the series' second season, Becky (whose boyfriend, on Larry's advice, had dumped her in season 1) was about to marry another man. "The Baptism" found Becky's Jewish fiancé agreeing to convert to Christianity, because that was a condition of marriage for Becky. But when Larry happened upon the river baptism, he mistakenly thought the fiancé was drowning and ran screaming toward the ceremony. The interruption gave the man time to rethink his conversion, which led Becky to issue an ultimatum: convert or no wedding. The episode ended with Becky, thanks to Larry, still a single woman.

Olson is brilliant in "The Baptism," showing off her improv skills—the series was largely ad-libbed, with actors working off outlines of the plot and subplots, then coming up with dialogue on the fly—as well as the physical humor she has become known for. And RCG wanted Sweet Dee to be able to go toe-to-toe with her Paddy's Pub cohorts, which Olson had proven she could do when getting in the face of *Curb* star David, as Becky yelled at him for ruining her love life.

"We wanted to find somebody who could be as funny as the guys," Howerton said. "And we felt a lot of times in comedies, girls are so often relegated to the 'Oh, you guys!' role."

Olson was excited about the audition. In fact, she went into the meeting so impressed with the scene she would be reading that she already knew she wanted the part. *Badly*.

"I remember it exactly," Olson said. "It was the scene in 'Charlie Has Cancer' where Dennis goes in and wants to borrow [sugar] from Charlie. Charlie tells Dennis that he has cancer, and Dennis says, 'Oooooh,' and just tries to back out of the room."

A look at Olson's audition video—available on YouTube—comes complete with the soundtrack of a room full of gigglers responding to her performance. No surprise, she was offered the role.

Then she was told that the scene she had read was not written for Dee Reynolds but for the part of Dennis Reynolds, Dee's brother. A more fleshed-out role for Dee had not yet been written.

"I was like, 'Are you kidding me?! Okay, but you know that I don't want to just be *the girl*,'" Olson said. "'You guys are going to be funny, and then I'm going to be *the girl*.' Rob had a long conversation with me, though, and told me that he would make me just as debaucherous as them."

※ ※ ※

The final cast was set, and with all the changes the network asked for made, Landgraf once again assured Rob, Charlie, and Glenn that they would enjoy almost total creative freedom. They penned seven season 1 *It's Always Sunny in Philadelphia* scripts that tackled such traditionally taboo television topics as abortion, racism, and child molestation. The Gang, as they refer to themselves and are known to fans, would encourage underage drinking as a business model for the bar, try to pimp out the Waitress (Ellis) to cancer-faking Charlie, and use the right-to-life debate and a dead old man (in separate episodes) to pick up women. Charlie quoted the N-word, Dennis shot Charlie in the head, and Dennis and Dee's Pop-Pop (Tom Bower) turned out to be a World War II Nazi officer who was still spewing anti-Semitic invectives from his nursing home bed. (In a later season we'd find out Pop-Pop's name was Heinrich Landgraf.)

Still, out of all that outrageousness in *Sunny*'s premiere season, network president Landgraf had just one objection to an episode: in the season finale, "Charlie Got Molested," the storyline had a figure from Charlie and Mac's elementary school accused of molesting some students. Initially, the accused molester was a priest. Landgraf suggested to McElhenney that the character not be a member of the clergy, so they made him a gym teacher instead (played by *Saved by the Bell* principal Dennis Haskins).

Landgraf truly meant it when he told McElhenney, Day, and Howerton they had autonomy in making the show they wanted to make, the one he'd been confident they could deliver. Not only did he not force edits on their more potentially divisive stories, he and his executives encouraged them to go further. Landgraf knew a middle-of-the-road effort wasn't going to draw audiences and pave the way to FX earning a reputation for great comedy. He had chosen what he felt were two strong, bold, funny series to launch a weekly comedy block. The network's job was to make it possible for the creators of *It's Always Sunny* and *Starved* to see their visions through.

"It's difficult to make gutsy decisions, because nobody ever knows [what will happen]," Landgraf said. "But if you're channel 258 and you choose a safe harbor, that's the riskiest decision of all."

Landgraf had multiple goals then, and obviously one of them was to keep the network's best interests in mind. He had a plan that would ensure FX and the *Sunny* producers would profit, handsomely, if the show became successful. His low-cost production strategy meant modest payment up front for RCG as producers, writers, and actors, but part of the eventual payoff for becoming a hit series would see RCG Productions (known as RCH Productions until season 4) having partial ownership of *It's Always Sunny in Philadelphia*. That meant when the series became profitable, the producers would have a share of that cash. That also incentivized the network (which would start its own in-house production company, FX Productions, to produce *Sunny* in 2007) and the producers to keep the production costs as thrifty as possible in order to minimize FX's gamble, and to reach that place of profitability as soon as possible.

With his first *Sunny* paychecks in mind, McElhenney kept slinging pecan-crusted racks of lamb and tiger prawn and papaya salads at Café D'Etoile throughout production of season 1. He didn't want to quit his server job without knowing if there would be a second season, and though his compensation for that first season was more than he'd ever made before, it was not an amount of money the then-twenty-eight-year-old could retire on in LA. As actors, the main cast made roughly $10,000 for each of the seven episodes. Overall, RCG split one million dollars for their roles as executive producers and writers (plus the added roles of showrunner and directing one episode for McElhenney). So, after full days on the *IASIP* set, McElhenney would change out of his Mac T-shirts and jeans and suit up in his Café D'Etoile uniform.

As for the series' finances, FX was spending around $500,000 to make each of the first seven installments—significantly less than half of what a half-hour comedy on network TV cost.

Of course, if that *Sunny* money sounds like low salaries and low budgets, even for newbie television creators, it's important to note that McElhenney, Day, and Howerton were being paid to learn how to write and produce on the job. They were literally learning how to make a TV series while creating it, surrounded by an experienced crew and with the full support of the network's president and his executives. Not to mention those promises of creative freedom, ownership, and big fat profits should their considerable efforts lead to sensational ratings.

Chapter Three

AND THEY'RE OFF!

Filming season 1 got underway with the reshoot of "Charlie Has Cancer," which would now be a mash-up of the two original DIY pilots. Another big change from the original work: Glenn, as Dennis, would not be going to Charlie's apartment to borrow a cup of sugar for his morning java but instead to borrow a basketball.

The three producers had written the other six episodes before filming began (without a writers' room to assist them), and during a review of all the scripts, FX decided "The Gang Gets Racist" should be the new series premiere. It was provocative, definitely showed a strong point of view, and would give viewers the chance to get to know who these characters were right away.

Well, all but Dee, who was not the focus of the writers' best efforts at this point. Kaitlin Olson had already elicited assurances from her costars that Dee would become anything but the voice of reason to their characters' escapades, as a condition of her signing on for *Sunny*. But it would take more practice writing for Dee, and getting to know Olson better, for RCG to really understand what she told them: don't write for a female; write for another character who would make sense as a member of The Gang. They would soon enough see how capable she was of infusing Dee with every shred of the outrageous selfishness and depravity they could pull off for Mac, Charlie, and Dennis.

The agreed-upon plan to keep the production as low-budget as possible was always at the forefront of strategizing for season 1, and factored into the design of how the set operated. The four cast members shared one trailer. Rob, Charlie, and Glenn had no official office for the season, so they often worked on scripts at home, or at the offices of their managers at 3 Arts Entertainment. Charlie didn't have his own computer, so he wrote scripts by hand on yellow legal pads. (He still has some of them, for *IASIP* fans hoping to spend some cash on premium collectibles someday.)

As for sets, there was no dedicated soundstage; production was centered in the former *Los Angeles Herald Examiner* newspaper building in downtown Los Angeles, at the southwest corner of Broadway and Eleventh Street. William Randolph Hearst developed the building for a million dollars in 1913, and after the paper closed up shop in 1989, the mission-revival structure became home to more than a thousand TV series and movies because it was budget-friendly and could house multiple sets in one location. For *Sunny*, the building was home to the sets of Paddy's Pub, Dee's apartment, and The Gang's favorite fancy restaurant,

Guigino's, where Charlie once tried to order boiled milk steak (with a side of jelly beans, raw).

Guigino's made its debut in season 1's "Gun Fever," and was named, Howerton said on *The Always Sunny Podcast*, after actress Carla Gugino, who he was thinking about when he was writing the episode.

The building was the main home of *Sunny* filming for seasons 1 and 2, but before it became home to portions of Arizona State University's journalism and film schools in 2021, it had also been home to the productions of TV shows like *Parenthood*, *Castle*, and *Brooklyn Nine-Nine*, and movies like Oscar winners *The Usual Suspects* and *Dreamgirls*. In fact, the bar set that was adapted as Paddy's Pub for *IASIP* was originally designed for the Robert Altman film *Short Cuts*. Full of media and Hollywood history (Arnold Schwarzenegger and LeBron James are partial owners of the building), the original Herald Examiner Building was designed by Julia Morgan, the first woman to be licensed as an architect in California.

Frugality for the cast, check. Budget-friendly sets, check. More production dollars were saved by making sure the filming schedule included no wasted time. Scenes were shot out of order instead of in a linear manner, so they could be grouped in ways that made filming more efficient. The cast and crew shot eleven to thirteen pages of scripts each day and completed an episode in three to three and a half days; most sitcoms complete an episode in five days.

One area where no expense was spared involved hiring staff, from the directors who helped steer the first season to the experienced crew who supported McElhenney, Day, and Howerton in running a show.

Half the season was directed by John Fortenberry, a veteran of Lorne Michaels's Broadway Video, who had helmed TV projects from *The Kids in the Hall* and *The Ben Stiller Show* to *Everybody Loves Raymond* and Comedy Central roasts of Denis Leary and Jeff Foxworthy.

The other half would be directed by the prolific Dan Attias, whose name every regular TV viewer of the last thirty years will remember seeing in the credits of their favorite shows, including *Melrose Place*; *Beverly Hills, 90210*; *Northern Exposure*; *Ally McBeal*; *Party of Five*; *Buffy the Vampire Slayer*; *Deadwood*; *Six Feet Under*; *The Sopranos*; *The Wire*; *The O.C.*; *Alias*; *Friday Night Lights*; *Heroes*; *Grey's Anatomy*; *Lost*; *The Walking Dead*; *Ray Donovan*; *The Americans*; *The Boys*; *Homeland*; *Billions*; and *The Marvelous Mrs. Maisel*. It's a massive, impressive list, and though the majority of Attias's experience has been with television drama, it was his experience directing ten episodes of HBO's Hollywood-set dude-comedy *Entourage* that caught FX's eye.

Sure, similarities to the comedy starring Adrian Grenier and Jeremy Piven had factored into FX's decision to ask RCG to change their characters' profession and setting before *It's Always Sunny* premiered. But the network also knew *Sunny* was still likely to be compared to *Entourage* because of the series' mostly male group-friendship premise. Attias's vast experience, especially with the success of the most recent example of that genre of TV comedy, was thought to be a huge plus.

Rob, Charlie, and Glenn met with the director at the Coffee Bean & Tea Leaf in West Hollywood. They all clicked right away.

Where some directors might have concerns about working with such inexperienced producers given the power to run the show they also wrote and acted in, Attias said it was actually one of the draws for him to collaborate with them.

"They were not at all giving the vibe that they were interested in throwing their weight around," Attias says. "They wanted to learn. They were humble about it. They were grateful for John [Landgraf] taking a chance on them."

With the production plan and staff set and the premiere episode chosen, the decision was made that part of the season would be filmed in Philadelphia, but most would be shot at the Herald Examiner Building in Los Angeles—again, budget. So McElhenney, Day, and Howerton went off to the City of Brotherly Love, and Olson soon followed with Ellis (the Waitress) as her flight mate. In fact, it was the first time the costars had met.

"We had a lot of cocktails together and were like, 'Okay, you're great, we're going to be best friends,'" Ellis said.

In Philly, they filmed parts of "The Gang Gets Racist" and "Charlie Has Cancer," among others, and gave the season a real Philly vibe, as if the whole run had been filmed on location. Several of McElhenney's friends and family hung out during filming. Some were even in scenes (two of his pals, both named Dennis, played construction workers in "Charlie Has Cancer"). And some even helped provide specific filming locations; McElhenney's childhood friend and future director of many classic *Sunny* episodes, Todd Biermann, lent his family's home for a few scenes in "Charlie Wants an Abortion."

Day's friend and future *Sunny* composer Cormac Bluestone took the train down from New York to play the part of Jimmy Doyle—the real father of Tommy (Spencer Daniels), the wild child whose mother tried to pin paternity on Charlie in "Charlie Wants an Abortion." Malcolm Barrett, who'd costarred with Day in the short-lived 2003 Luis Guzmán sitcom *Luis* on Fox, played Terrell, the scene-stealing friend of Dee who turned Paddy's into a gay bar and uttered the word that Charlie repeated, inspiring the title of "The Gang Gets Racist" for the series premiere.

The exterior of McElhenney's redbrick childhood home in South Philly, near Moyamensing Avenue and Dickinson Street, even made a cameo during season 1, and local media outlets excitedly covered this local boy done—or in the process of doing—good. One reporter referred to him as "Robbie Mac," and another got McElhenney to confirm he prefers Pat's in the local cheesesteak wars and he hoped his FX paycheck for season 1 would allow him to pay off his 2000 Toyota Tacoma truck.

Yet another Philadelphia writer chatted with McElhenney on set one day, and the actor (producer/writer/director) admitted his life had not been "going in the right direction for a long time," and that being part of this huge production, in his city, gave him a feeling of vindication. *Philadelphia Inquirer* television critic Jonathan Storm, who would soon coin the oft-repeated phrase "*Seinfeld* on crack" to describe *IASIP*, also chatted on set that day with Rob's father, Bob. The senior McElhenney was "beaming" watching his son at work, Storm wrote. Bob said there had not been enough dye to cover all the gray hairs he had during the days before his son found his way.

"But we weathered it," Bob told Storm. "I had this career path kind of laid out for him, but it didn't work out that way. He knew he was being called by other muses."

In a love note to his hometown that lives on in every single episode of the series, McElhenney and Day drove around Philadelphia one night with a handheld camera—back to their DIY ways one more time—filming the city landmarks that unfold in the opening credits. The Benjamin Franklin Bridge, Swann Memorial Fountain, Boathouse Row, South Street, and the Linc (home stadium of the Philadelphia Eagles), with "Temptation Sensation" as the soundtrack, have signaled another new misadventure for The Gang in every episode for twenty years.

In addition to Bluestone, and Ellis as the Waitress, season 1 introduced other characters who would become fan-favorite recurring faces in the *Sunny* family. Artemis Pebdani, who became part of RCG's circle of friends when she was Ellis's roommate and best friend in Los Angeles before Ellis and Day moved in together, was immediately unforgettable in "Charlie Has Cancer." She plays the very dramatic Artemis Dubois ("I was just looking for the most dramatic thing I could think of," Pebdani says about naming her character), Dee's friend and fellow actress. Artemis auditioned for Dennis to be a *Coyote Ugly*–ish bartender at Paddy's Pub by crawling across the bar and licking the side of his face, after delivering an enthusiastic monologue about what a small-town girl has to do to make it in the big city.

"Rob came to our house, and he was like, 'We need you to write a *Coyote Ugly* monologue. But it can't be from *Coyote Ugly*, because we can't have it be the exact thing,'" Pebdani says. "And there is nothing I love more than getting to be an actor playing a committed actor. It's just my favorite, and especially to get to commit to things that aren't good."

Artemis and Dee, like pretty much all pairings of a Gang member with any other non-Gang human, have a complicated relationship. Sometimes they're pals, pursuing their acting goals and hanging out at a club. Other times, they're romantic rivals. But for better or worse, season 1 sets up Artemis as truly the only person, outside of The Gang and Dee's short-lived love entanglements, who Dee can consider a friend even part of the time.

Jimmi Simpson, Day's friend and former roommate, made his *Sunny* debut in "Charlie Got Molested," the season 1 finale. Simpson and Nate Mooney, another Day friend and fellow Williamstown Theatre Festival alum, play Liam and Ryan McPoyle, the unibrowed, milk-loving, fist-bumping, incestuous brothers who were elementary school classmates of Mac and Charlie, and are often embroiled in fights with The Gang.

When longtime viewers of *Sunny* say they became fans during season 1, these frenemies are among the reasons why. As much as we began to know Mac, Charlie, Dennis, and Dee during those first seven installments, no small part of that came from their interactions with this collection of characters.

The Waitress, who works at a nearby coffee shop, is a great example. Not only is she the object of Charlie's obsession (stalking and restraining orders have been involved), she is also used by his friends to taunt him.

Both Dennis and, later, his father have sex with the Waitress, and Mac does "hand stuff" with her. They also take advantage of her alcoholism throughout the years, and in perhaps the most egregious act of all, they never refer to her as anything but "the Waitress."

In seventeen seasons, we have yet to learn her actual name, and it's unclear if that's because The Gang never bothered to learn it, doesn't remember it, or simply refuses to acknowledge her as anything but someone who used to serve hot beverages to them. We also eventually learn she went to high school with The Gang; she reminds Dee that they sat right next to each other in trigonometry.

Even Charlie, who seems to genuinely care for her, and who must know her actual name from the restraining orders she's taken out against him, refers to her only as the Waitress.

As for the McPoyles, they wreak their fair share of havoc on The Gang throughout the years, but in season 1, it's Charlie who sets the tone for their relationship. When Liam and Ryan falsely alleged that their elementary school gym teacher, Mr. Murray, molested them as children, Charlie tried to get them to retract the lie. They refused, seeing a big monetary payoff in the offing, so Charlie reported their scam to the police. But the ultimate culprit was Charlie: while drunk one night, he was the one who gave the McPoyles the idea to accuse Murray.

And just to wrap up this introductory season with no doubt remaining as to what every member of The Gang is capable of, "Charlie Gets Molested" found Mac upset not because he thought his classmates were sexually abused but because Mr. Murray didn't find him worthy of his attention. Then there were Dennis and Dee, who, believing Charlie had been assaulted, entered into a competition with each other to see who was more skilled at getting Charlie to face being victimized. They went so far as to tell Charlie's mom about the incident and then stage an intervention during which they encouraged Charlie's mom to make him show her, on a baby doll, where he was touched.

He had not been molested—by Mr. Murray, anyway—but far be it from any member of The Gang to let facts get in the way of a good scheme. It continues to be a defining characteristic for each of them.

The intervention featured two other characters who became all-time *Sunny* favorites: the Groundlings alum and *Pee-wee's Playhouse* legend Lynne Marie Stewart as Charlie's mom, Bonnie Kelly, and another Groundlings alum, Andrew Friedman, as Charlie's creepy uncle Jack. Jack was uncomfortably excited about having Charlie point out on the doll where he had been (allegedly) touched. It hinted at another ongoing storyline, one that would lead to the series' breakout episode.

Production on the six new season 1 episodes had gone smoothly. McElhenney directed the reshoot of the original pilot. And the series premiere was set for August 2005, with *It's Always Sunny in Philadelphia* following *Starved*, the kickoff shows for FX's block of half-hour comedies.

Landgraf and his FX executives were excited and optimistic about their new comedy duo, and to show them off to members of the media, FX hosted a celebration during the Television Critics Association press tour in 2005. The biannual Los Angeles–area event, held once during the summer and once during the winter, is a gathering of television critics and reporters from across the United States and Canada who attend panels introducing actors, directors, producers, and network executives from new and returning series they will be covering in the TV season ahead. Critics also conduct individual interviews with cast and executives, are shown series previews, and often visit sets of series in production at the time.

And the parties! Throughout the two-week-long press tour, individual networks host food-and-cocktail-laden soirees for their whole lineup, and sometimes for specific series. As *Starved* and *Sunny* were sharing Thursday nights beginning in August, FX took the opportunity to preview the comedy doubleheader with a July 17, 2005, premiere event at Trader Vic's at the Beverly Hilton, in Beverly Hills. Fried shrimp and shish kebabs aplenty were awaiting the guests, as was the legendary eatery's signature rum-infused libation, the mai tai, said to be originated by the tiki-themed restaurant's founder, Vic Bergeron.

There was just one detail the network might have overlooked, which threatened to leave a disastrous first impression on the press members in attendance.

Like *It's Always Sunny*, *Starved* had been selected for its spot in the FX schedule because of its strong point of view and its no-holds-barred moments, which were on full display in its first episode.

Starved revolved around a group of friends—three guys and one woman, like *It's Always Sunny*—living in New York City and bonded as members of an eating disorder support group.

One friend was a New York police officer named Adam Williams, who was bulimic. He shared during a group meeting that he had eaten 212 almonds very quickly the previous night, then threw them up just as fast, so they remained mostly whole. He washed them off . . . and *ate them again*. But telling wasn't showing, and there was more to come. While on duty later that day, Adam wasn't only binging and vomiting; he was also abusing his authority as a cop by extorting a deliveryman into giving him his bag of food. Adam scarfed down the egg roll and carton of moo shu pork, but as if his thievery and intimidation of the delivery person weren't enough, he found a spot on a sidewalk near a construction site and used his police baton to repeatedly punch himself in the stomach and spew its contents onto some garbage bags and a tarp on the ground . . . or what he thought was just a tarp. It was actually being used as a blanket by a homeless man sleeping beneath it. Adam had just barfed, graphically, on a homeless man, and a Trader Vic's full of media people watched it unfold, mai tais and shish kebabs in their hands.

There were some cringes, to say the least. And no one was running to load up their plate with the fried shrimp for a few minutes. But there were also some chuckles for Adam's malfeasance, and by the time the *It's Always Sunny* episode "The Gang Gets Racist" filled the screen, drinks, food, and laughs flowed freely.

One more thing about the link between *Starved* and *Sunny*, because Kevin Bacon and his six degrees of association with other actors has nothing on the *It's Always Sunny in Philadelphia* cast and their circle of Hollywood friends: the actor playing *Starved*'s troubled policeman was Sterling K. Brown, the future multiple-Emmy-winning star of *This Is Us*. He is also another alum from Day's time at the Williamstown Theatre Festival. And the two friends were about to become rivals.

Starved and *It's Always Sunny in Philadelphia* premiered, back-to-back, starting at 10:00 p.m. on Thursday, August 4, 2005. And the critical responses were overwhelmingly positive—at least for *Sunny*.

At *Variety*, the trade's television critic Brian Lowry wrote, "After years of futility, the search for a top-notch, 20-something slacker comedy is over, and it took a basic cable network to crack the code."

His fellow trade paper critic, Barry Garron at *The Hollywood Reporter*, noted how obvious it was that McElhenney, Day, and Howerton had spent a lot of time together, as friends, before working together on-screen. "Their ease with one another makes the onstage camaraderie genuine and natural," he wrote.

Albuquerque Journal critic Neal Anderson likened *Sunny* to *Seinfeld*—one of the gazillion times that comparison would be made—writing that the first three episodes provided for preview "[mine] genuine laughs from some hilariously provocative plotlines" that provide viewers with "edgier sitcom fare that thankfully lacks a moral."

For the *Los Angeles Times*, Paul Brownfield called *It's Always Sunny* a "small-scale gem . . . it's *Friends* . . . if *Friends* had ever cared to go beyond the clever clubhouse of the writers room and the glamorized unreality of the sets and casting choices and actually belong to the world at large." Brownfield even described the series' music as "breezy strings with a '50s feel, reminding you that there's a TV canon behind the show despite its slacker-cool milieu."

Boston Globe critic Matthew Gilbert celebrated the *Sunny* characters for their "romping through drunken nights and caffeinated mornings like indie movie heroes."

The Arizona Republic critic Bill Goodykoontz called out *IASIP*'s tackling of taboo topics like racism, homophobia, abortion, and underage drinking—all in the first three episodes. "I often found myself laughing at things one minute and feeling bad about it the next," he wrote. "Until I laughed again."

For *Starved*, it was a different story, one best summed up with the headline on a review by *The Washington Post* critic Ann Gerhart: "FX's 'Starved' Is a Bit Too Much to Stomach." Gerhart called the series "ambitious and accomplished, but ultimately unpleasant." And who wants to watch an unpleasant comedy?

As it turned out, more wanted to watch *It's Always Sunny* by the end of the seven-episode seasons for both new comedies. Though the *Starved* premiere had edged out *Sunny*'s series premiere (1.54 million to 1.42 million viewers), by the time both series wrapped their seasons in September, *Sunny* had averaged 1.14 million viewers per episode, while *Starved* had averaged 1.05 million per week.

To be clear, neither show set the Nielsen ratings on fire. Both started out with a decent amount of buzz, especially considering FX had such limited marketing resources for the new comedies that it split a marketing budget between *Sunny* and *Starved* (and according to *The Hollywood Reporter*, 99 percent of the budget went to *Starved*). But both stirred some controversy: the National Eating Disorders Association called for a boycott of *Starved* by viewers and advertisers, and McElhenney, Day, and Howerton shared in an episode of *The Always Sunny Podcast* that, despite having read the season 1 scripts ahead of time, Anheuser-Busch demanded their brands' signage be pulled from the Paddy's Pub set the day after the first episode aired.

Less than a month after both shows aired their finales, FX decided the network could not afford to move forward with both comedies for another season. Perhaps, Landgraf reasoned, it had been a mistake to launch both shows at the same time. Maybe the network would have been better off debuting one comedy series, putting all its efforts behind building its success, then using that hit to build a comedy block, and then a whole comedy lineup. That's how FX had developed its drama schedule, one series at a time— *The Shield*, then *Nip/Tuck*, then *Rescue Me*—until the network very quickly earned a reputation for premium programming, with frequent comparisons to HBO.

So the decision was made: *It's Always Sunny in Philadelphia* would be renewed for a ten-episode second season. *Starved* was canceled.

Sterling K. Brown had no hard feelings about the outcome of the competition between *Sunny* and *Starved*, and his friendship with Charlie Day continues. The two costarred in the 2018 crime thriller film *Hotel Artemis*, and when Brown was asked to host *Saturday Night Live* in 2017, he sought advice from Day, who hosted in 2012.

"[He's] the one person in my phone who has hosted *SNL*," Brown said of Day. "And so he said, 'Look, man, they got so many ideas and so many sketches that they've written, you just kind of have to sit back and enjoy the embarrassment of riches.'"

Landgraf had his reasons for continuing to champion *Sunny*, even with the lackluster ratings. First, and most importantly, he still believed in the show, as well as the talents and abilities of McElhenney, Day, Howerton, and Olson. He also noted the show had a high concentration of viewers in the all-important 18 to 49 age demographic, a key viewership statistic for FX and its comedy plans going forward.

And beginning with the third episode of *Sunny*, "Underage Drinking: A National Concern," FX moved the show's time slot, from Thursday nights at ten thirty to Tuesday nights at ten. Now *Sunny* was on its own night.

And it paid off. *Sunny* could use the entire marketing budget it had had to share with *Starved*. That was part of FX's plan as it began to think about *Sunny*'s second season. It wanted to strike hard while the show was still fresh in the minds of the viewers already hooked on the series, so there was talk of The Gang returning to the airwaves as soon as the following summer.

Landgraf also had something very special in mind to usher in season 2. Something that would change the future of *It's Always Sunny in Philadelphia*, and of FX itself.

Chapter Four

THE GANG GETS A NEW MEMBER

When Landgraf was hired as the president of entertainment at FX in 2004, *The Shield*, the network's first breakout series, was already a hit. Michael Chiklis had already won a Best Actor Emmy and a Golden Globe Award for the gritty cop drama's first season. *The Shield* premiered in 2002 with close to five million viewers, and for all of season 2, it dipped below three million just a couple of times. By season 3, Landgraf's first at the network, *The Shield* managed to reach three million viewers only once out of fifteen episodes. But Landgraf didn't panic. He planned.

His solution to the ratings spill: injecting some new blood into the Strike Team, the largely rogue and corrupt Los Angeles police division the series revolved around. But not just anyone would do—Landgraf envisioned A-list talent. At the top of his wish list: Emmy winner and, by then, five-time Oscar nominee Glenn Close.

FX was specifically concerned with the dwindling numbers for *The Shield*'s female viewership, and Landgraf and his team were certain Close could help bring them back. Not really expecting her to be interested in a lead role on a basic-cable television series, Landgraf's office nevertheless reached out to her representatives, who thought it was an interesting idea.

So Landgraf, Fox entertainment chairman Peter Liguori, and *The Shield* creator Shawn Ryan flew to New York, where they spent three hours at Close's Charles Street condo in the West Village, pitching her a lead role on the drama.

"She is as challenging and inspiring as you would expect, peppering us with questions," Liguori said of the meeting.

By the time the trio landed back in LA, they had gotten the news that Glenn Close was ready to sign on to play new precinct captain Monica Rawling. Her one year on the series earned her lead actress Emmy and Golden Globe nominations and increased the season 4 ratings by 21 percent over the previous year's numbers.

Which got Landgraf thinking . . . why wouldn't that work for *It's Always Sunny in Philadelphia*? Sure, it was a comedy, not one of FX's signature dramas. And *Sunny* was still a new show, with seven episodes in total to its name, while *The Shield* had thirty-nine episodes for viewers to get to know the characters and actors who portrayed them.

Still, Landgraf had the perfect A-lister in mind to add to The Gang, and unlike the blind shot he took with *The Shield*, his potential new *Sunny* star was already a close personal friend and former professional partner.

Landgraf's last job before joining FX was as a founding partner of Jersey Television, the production company behind, most notably, *Reno 911!*, the mockumentary-style spoof of *Cops*. The series, which initially ran on Comedy Central for six seasons, revolved around the outrageous, hapless officers of the sheriff's department in Reno, Nevada, and the equally outrageous, hapless characters they ran into on the job. One season 2 episode, called "Not Without My Mustache," included two sheriffs helping a teenager lose his virginity with a prostitute, a pair of incestuous siblings trying to dry hump in the back of a sheriff's car, and another sheriff losing a testicle, as had been predicted by a psychic the day before.

Reno 911! was created by Thomas Lennon, Robert Ben Garant, and Kerri Kenney (now Kenney-Silver). Its cast was a who's who of some of the best comedy actors working on TV, including the creators, Niecy Nash (now Niecy Nash-Betts), Cedric Yarbrough, Wendi McLendon-Covey, and Carlos Alazraqui, with a deep bench of guest stars rivaling several iterations of *Saturday Night Live* casts. Landgraf was an executive producer on *Reno 911!*, and therein lies a possible hint as to why he found *It's Always Sunny* so appealing from the first time he saw the DIY pilot. Just as McElhenney has often said a major motivation for creating *Sunny* was "desperation," as it was a way for him, Day, and Howerton to create work for themselves, Thomas Lennon and company were similarly driven. When a pilot Lennon,

Kenney-Silver, and Garant wrote for Fox was canceled as it was about to be filmed, they asked network execs if they could apply the unused portion of the budget to make a pilot for a new series, which became *Reno 911!* Fox passed on it, too, and it would be two more years before Comedy Central premiered it, in 2003. There is a commonality between the *Sunny* and *Reno* creators, of comedy sensibilities and of being proactive and making their own creative opportunities.

Other commonalities between *Sunny* and *Reno 911!*: the incestuous brother and sister in "Not Without My Mustache" were played by Day and Ellis, before *Sunny*, and before they were married in real life.

And Landgraf was a cofounder of Jersey Television with his good friend Danny DeVito, the A-lister he thought would make a great addition to the second season of *It's Always Sunny in Philadelphia*.

Landgraf knew the outrageous, taboo-poking comedy was right in line with DeVito's own comedy tastes and personal sense of humor, and he was just as confident that McElhenney, Day, and Howerton could write a character that DeVito would find worthy of his time and talents.

Landgraf sent DeVito the season 1 episodes and wasn't totally surprised to find his friend had already seen them. His kids with his wife, Rhea Perlman—Lucy, Grace, and Jake—were big fans and had turned their father on to the series. DeVito was interested in knowing more.

Landgraf's next step, a pro forma one he was sure, was to share his idea with RCG. Their reception to adding DeVito to the mix was . . . unexpected.

They said no.

Not because they had any doubt about DeVito's talent, obviously. McElhenney in particular was a devoted TV junkie throughout his childhood. He was especially a fan of classic comedies like *Family Ties*, *Cheers*, and *Taxi*. One of the greatest sitcom moments ever, he believed, was from the *Taxi* pilot, "Like Father, Like Daughter." DeVito's character, Louie De Palma, a dispatcher and supervisor for the Sunshine Cab Company, was arguing with his employees when he stepped from the caged office he worked in, revealing to the audience that this belligerent, aggressive man was a foot shorter than the five people standing in front of him.

DeVito had built up such a body of work on television (his Emmy- and Golden Globe–winning performance on *Taxi*), in movies (*One Flew Over the Cuckoo's Nest*, Golden Globe–nominated *Ruthless People*, and *Matilda*), as a producer (Oscar winners *Pulp Fiction* and *Erin Brockovich*), and as a director (*The War of the Roses* and *Throw Momma from the Train*) that he had earned a status as nothing less than a Hollywood legend.

In spite of all that, and somewhat because of it, McElhenney, Day, and Howerton told their boss that they were not interested in adding DeVito to their show. They knew his work but not his personality or his work habits. What if he came in and threw his experience, his accolades, and his connection to Landgraf around the set? What if he joined the cast and tried to interfere with the creative authority they'd established and sacrificed for? What if he came in and disrupted the chemistry that RCG and Olson had built so quickly during their brief first season?

That was just too big of a risk to take. FX executives had shown themselves to be pleased enough with season 1, and optimistic about the prospects for season 2, so as the executive producers saw the situation, it was best to leave the cast the way it was.

In that case, Landgraf told them, he was no longer interested in airing their series on his network.

Umm, wait . . . , they replied. *So when can we meet with Danny DeVito?*

"The only thing more important than chemistry on a TV show is *the TV show*," McElhenney explained of their abrupt reversal.

That's the version of events McElhenney has jokingly relayed throughout the years. And though Landgraf did not deliver his ultimatum so brusquely, it is an accurate summary of the situation that unfolded. Landgraf wasn't backtracking on the promises he'd made to RCG about offering near total creative control in exchange for the modest production and marketing budgets they'd have to work within for the series' early seasons. But he knew *Sunny* needed an injection of . . . *something* for season 2. Though *IASIP* absorbed *Starved*'s marketing money, it was still a fraction of what most television series had to work with for promotional efforts. Without a much more significant amount of cash to plan an attention-grabbing campaign for the series, Landgraf was sure DeVito's presence in the cast could bring a huge infusion of organic media coverage. And the only thing better than a bigger budget? Free publicity.

Landgraf also knew he could get FX parent company 20th Century Fox to sign off on additional cash to pay this all-star, the actor whose *Taxi* character had been named by *TV Guide* in 1999 as the most memorable television character of *all time*. DeVito said he was interested in talking more about Landgraf's proposition.

McElhenney, it was decided, would take the meeting solo. The chat would happen one afternoon at DeVito's home, a lavish estate in Beverly Hills that suitably impressed the young actor who had not so long ago lived in a garage.

"I was expecting him to live in a big-ass house, and that's what he does. He lives pretty well," McElhenney told the journalists assembled at the 2006 Television Critics Association (TCA) press tour panel, during which FX introduced DeVito in his TV comeback. "I was just really pumped to be meeting with him at all. To be honest with you, I never really thought that we had a shot at getting him anyway, even though I knew he was a fan of the show and hasn't been on TV for many, many years. I just thought it would be a good opportunity to meet Danny DeVito. I mean, shit, I grew up watching him, and it was an amazing experience, and then it seemed to work out. I was certainly nervous, but he's a really good guy, and he's a dude from Jersey, and we just get along really well."

DeVito was equally enthusiastic about his new gig, and equally complimentary about his new coworkers. "I got what I expected when he came in the door," he said during TCA about meeting Rob

McElhenney. "I really expected somebody who was very sharp, very smart, and had a handle on what he was doing. There's a certain thing that—a certain feeling that you get from people who are connected with what they're doing. Those are the people I really appreciate the most . . . their passion is so strong . . . there's going to be no limit to the amount that I can push them to get good work. They're so good about what they do. [McElhenney's] attitude was very giving and very open, and I think that's going to make for a good collaboration."

※ ※ ※

The first impressions between McElhenney and DeVito were key, as two confident, talented, smart, funny, and dedicated performers and businessmen immediately bonded. Game recognized game. That would benefit both men, their castmates, and certainly the future of *It's Always Sunny in Philadelphia*.

The mutual agreement that DeVito would transform the core cast from a quartet into a quintet wasn't without some negotiations, however. There was that extra cash Landgraf had to get Fox execs to approve for DeVito's salary. There were also smaller but still very important details, like budgeting for the A-lister's personal dressing room/trailer. DeVito, savvy entrepreneur that he is, had purchased his own trailer years earlier, which he leases—for his own use—to the productions he works for. Most important for securing the actor's commitment was the time he was willing to devote to season 2. *Sunny*'s filming schedule was just a few months for its inaugural run of seven episodes. But the sophomore season would expand to ten installments, and whatever amount of time that would entail for the production—it now averages around five months—DeVito wanted to work on filming no more than three *weeks*.

Three weeks to film a role that was going to be significant from the get-go. His character, Frank Reynolds, was never intended to be a very special guest star, someone to dip in and stir up hijinks in the name of stirring up some ratings. Frank was to be introduced as the father of twins Dennis and Dee. He had been an absentee parent, with all his time and focus on work while the siblings were growing up. Frank entered Paddy's Pub on the verge of divorcing his domineering wife, Barbara (played to perfection by *Fatal Attraction* Oscar nominee Anne Archer), and in hopes of finally connecting with his children. Very quickly, he made some major decisions about a new lifestyle, and after blackmailing his children and their friends so they allowed him to live among them, he spent the rest of the season—and no small amount of his wealth—trying to become a full-fledged member of their unrestrained assemblage.

It was a meaty role, and the evolution—or, more accurately, devolution—of the character was a big attraction for DeVito joining the FX series. But it was going to require figuring out a way to shoot all of his scenes for the entire season in under a month.

And that's how the *It's Always Sunny* cast and crew became the masters of block shooting.

Most television comedy productions are filmed in a straightforward, linear manner; the first episode of the season is shot from beginning to end. When that's finished, episode 2 is filmed, and that continues, in chronological order, until the entire season is complete.

Block shooting, in contrast, sounds simple, and as an overall concept it is. But in practice, it requires a whole production full of talent to be at the top of their game. Literally, it means scenes from different episodes are shot at the same locations, on the same days, in "blocks," which are later stitched together during editing to produce a seamless timeline.

For instance, a lineup of four or five *Sunny* episodes is grouped together, with a single director prepping them and schedules set to juggle details like locations, set design, props, wardrobe, hair, and makeup. One day's filming might include scenes in that block that take place at Charlie and Frank's apartment. Another day they might film scenes from that block's episodes unfolding at Sweet Dee's. Another chunk of time might be dedicated to that block's scenes that include Dennis driving around in his beloved Range Rover.

Efficiency in the production? Yes. Keeping the budget tight? Absolutely. But block shooting, with its compressed filming time and seeming chaos in scheduling, necessitates an unwavering attention to detail and continuity. Potential errors lurk everywhere—for instance, Mac might wear his *RIOT* T-shirt in one scene, but later in the same episode and the same time frame, shot on another day, he's switched to his *Kiss My Irish!* tee. If that goes unchecked until filming is complete, calling a mulligan to reshoot it will be costly in both time and money, negating one of the very reasons for block shooting to begin with.

Charlie Day described the process and the importance of continuity during a conversation on the *Life Is Short with Justin Long* podcast in 2020. "We kind of shoot [*Sunny*] like a couple of big movies. We used to do it in chunks of five at a time, so five-episode blocks," he said. "It's toughest on the crew. If you have a bruise in one scene and you're shooting an episode where you don't, then you go back, you've got to remember and plan it out so you're not in the makeup chair so long putting a bruise on, taking it off."

In the case of season 2 block shooting, continuity was even more pressing. DeVito was out after three weeks, so whatever they'd shot at the end of that block was what they had of the actor for the whole season—the season in which they were introducing the Frank Reynolds character with the intention of seamlessly integrating him into The Gang and their insane world.

At least RCG had the support of the entire production on that front. But what block shooting with DeVito's time constraints also required was that the entire season had to be written before they shot a single moment. And the majority of that duty fell upon the shoulders of McElhenney, Day, and Howerton, as *Sunny* had not yet assembled a writers' room. Episode 7 of the season, "The Gang Exploits a Miracle," was written by Day and the writing team of Eric Falconer and Chris Romano, who would go on to create the 2010 Spike TV comedy series *Blue Mountain State*. The season's eighth episode, "The Gang Runs for Office," marked the *Sunny* writing debut of Day's old Williamstown Theatre Festival buddy David Hornsby, who moved up as a regular writer, executive producer, and recurring actor on *Sunny*.

But the other eight episodes were all RCG, and though the guys had wanted—even demanded—that they be allowed to act in, produce, and write the show when they made the initial deal with FX, it's fair to say they've developed a love/hate relationship with the writing process throughout the seasons. That began with the incredible pressure of season 2, of having to lock themselves in a room together for hours at a time to come up with the stories that would continue to prove to the network that Landgraf and his executives had bet on the right team to help them build FX as a comedy hub. They also had the relentless pressure to make good on the promise McElhenney gave to DeVito during their first meeting at DeVito's mansion: that their team would create a character worthy of DeVito's big return to television.

They did just that.

Not only were RCG successful in launching DeVito as Frank Reynolds in the *It's Always Sunny in Philadelphia* universe, but they cleverly integrated him in ways that also allowed viewers a deeper dive into Sweet Dee, Dennis, Mac, and Charlie. And they introduced some of the series' first truly classic moments, the ones that became instant and still-quoted fan favorites.

In the season premiere, "Charlie Gets Crippled," sport coat–wearing Frank tracked down his children outside Paddy's Pub, where Dennis and Dee were trying to speed away in Dennis's car to escape their father's imminent arrival. He popped up so quickly that a jolted Dennis backed over Charlie, leaving him in leg casts and wheelchair-bound. At the emergency room, Frank explained he was seeking a relationship with his estranged twins as he was divorcing his wife, Barbara, telling them, "I hate the kind of person that your whore mother turned me into . . . the big house, the big car." Frank threatened to give all his money away, which frightened his children more than anything . . . until a raucous night in a strip club with Mac and Charlie (and strippers played by guest stars Tiffany Haddish and comedian Natasha Leggero in some of their earliest roles) strengthened Frank's resolve to leave his married life behind and join The Gang in the wild life he sees them living.

Meanwhile, the sympathy (and the free lap dances) Charlie got when the strippers saw him in a wheelchair gave Mac and Dennis an idea: with wheelchairs of their own, they would hang out at the mall and try to attract attention from women. But, as they would go on to prove time and again, no one could outscam someone in The Gang faster than another member of The Gang, and this time it was Sweet Dee who donned a back brace and a pair of crutches and preempted Mac and Dennis's plans of picking up a date with a sham shopping trip of her own.

Frank also tried the wheelchair ruse . . . at the strip club. Ultimately, as became a trademark of their many plans, the whole Gang found the tables turned on them. Dennis and Mac went back to Paddy's after

Dee blew up their spot at the mall, got completely drunk, then decided to drive to the strip club. On the way, they passed out, and the car, still moving at a high speed, crashed right into Dee and Frank, who were fighting outside the club. That's how they all ended up back at the ER, along with the poor soul who made the unfortunate decision to follow Dee out of the mall. The banged-up Gang, covered in various bandaging, slings, and casts, finally hobbled off to get ice cream, as Frank spoke of gratitude that no one *important* got hurt. Pan to the mall guy (played by another RCG friend, actor Kristoffer Polaha), bedridden with two broken arms, who expressed a different sentiment. "What a bunch of assholes," he muttered.

In just one episode, Day, Howerton, and McElhenney established that these characters really do belong together, for better or (usually) much, much worse. Despite Frank's uninvited arrival into the lives of his children and their friends, and their equally aggressive pushback against welcoming him into their fold, all they really proved is that they all have the same basic instincts toward selfish, often loathsome behaviors. The rest of the world is not safe from being dragged into their plots and schemes, but neither are the characters immune to the effects of their deleterious actions on one another. This could essentially serve as the logline of the series, the blueprint for most of their adventures. It's also what makes them a hilariously dysfunctional kind of family.

As for the rest of the stellar second season, it was more of the same, but even rowdier and raunchier. Frank officially moved into Charlie's grimy apartment, a multimillionaire trading his business attire for long johns and his mansion to share Charlie's hot plate and sofa bed. The senior Reynolds also officially declared himself a member of The Gang by buying the land Paddy's Pub is located on and coercing the others into Gangship, lest he have them sent to jail for blowing up the building next door. Mac had sex with Dennis and Dee's mom, Barbara, but Dennis was rejected by his pals' moms when he tried to seduce them in revenge. The Waitress, so frequently a pawn in The Gang's games, was used by an indifferent Dennis, so she slept with Frank in retaliation, which only served to crush Charlie.

In what remains one of The Gang's all-time worst—and still ongoing—offenses, "The Gang Exploits a Miracle" introduced viewers to Matthew Mara (Hornsby), a priest and former classmate of The Gang. Nicknamed Rickety Cricket because he wore leg braces during high school, Matthew was still traumatized by Dennis tea-bagging him when he passed out at parties and Dee using his crush on her back in their teen years to get him to eat a horse turd in public. When Cricket wandered into Paddy's to check out a Virgin Mary–shaped figure that appeared on the office wall (a water stain that became part of a moneymaking scheme, of course), Dennis and Frank saw a chance to get him to put a church-related stamp of approval on the stain. Dee was recruited to get him involved, which she did with a flirty session in his confessional, telling him she saw romance in their future. Cricket believed she was sincere, so he later rushed to Paddy's to excitedly share some news: he had left the priesthood and was now asking Frank for Dee's hand in marriage. She had told him she loved him and now was forced to admit she had done that only because she was sure, as a priest, he wouldn't do what he'd just done. As she told him he should just return to the priesthood, Cricket slowly realized the girl who ruined his high school years had become the woman who had now ruined his entire life. Charlie and Mac offered poor Cricket the tiniest consolation when the vainglorious Dennis, who had been fasting for days because he thought his face looked fat, passed out and fell off his barstool: they asked Cricket if he wanted to tea-bag Dennis, and scurried off to get the camcorder when Cricket said yes.

"What's fun about [the] show is the inventiveness, a kind of freedom to keep it surprising. It's not anything like the bar my wife was in," DeVito said about his debut season, referencing, of course, wife Rhea Perlman's TV bar in the classic sitcom *Cheers*.

Meanwhile, Cricket was not the only new recurring character to help The Gang unleash their naughtiness all over South Philly in season 2. Following papa Frank Reynolds, viewers were introduced to mama Mrs. Mac (the only name given to Mac's mother throughout the series), played by the hilarious Sandy Martin. A playwright, producer, and director also known for her roles in *Napoleon Dynamite* and *Big Love*, and a scene-stealing performance in the final two seasons of *Ray Donovan*, Martin's casting in *It's Always Sunny* was a literal walk in the park.

Martin and her friend, the late TV, movie, and theater actor Bruce MacVittie (*The Sopranos* and *Million Dollar Baby*), were walking Martin's dog in Los Angeles's Elysian Park when a couple approached from the other direction. MacVittie recognized one of the people as his friend Charlie Day; they knew each other from—where else?—

the Williamstown Theatre Festival. In 1997, Charlie's first year as a Williamstown apprentice, MacVittie was a visiting professional actor, and the two costarred in a stage production of *Dead End*, a 1935 crime drama written by Pulitzer Prize–winning playwright Sidney Kingsley. Day and MacVittie, who'd further bonded over both growing up in Rhode Island, were catching up while Martin was talking to Day's cute Jack Russell terrier.

Then, Martin recalled, "Charlie looked over at me and said, 'You're the mother in *Napoleon Dynamite*, aren't you?' I said, 'Well, I'm the grandmother, yeah,' and he said, 'Oh, that was so funny. I enjoyed that so much. Would you happen to be available to look at a little comedy script we've got going?'"

The actress said yes, Day emailed her the script he and Howerton wrote for "Mac Bangs Dennis' Mom," and she was soon making the trip to Philadelphia to film her first moments as Mrs. Mac, right on the front porch of McElhenney's real-life childhood home.

Sandy Martin, who also grew up in Philly, delivered one of the season's most memorable scenes, as Dennis visited her with fresh flowers and a box of candy, ready to romance Mrs. Mac, just as Mac had done to Barbara Reynolds. Mrs. Mac grumbled in his general direction but could not be wooed by florals and a box of drugstore chocolates, nor by Dennis sliding his hand onto her knee.

"Not interested," she told him. "Don't find you attractive. I think you're an ugly man."

Dennis was more horrified by this rejection than he was by his friend's hookup with Barbara. He told Mrs. Mac she was ugly, too, and she agreed. All in all, their back-and-forth was one of Mrs. Mac's most verbal exchanges of the series, as most of her communiqués come in the form of a series of grunts.

"That was so much fun," Martin says. "And then Rob McElhenney wanted me to always incorporate the grunts, so I just created my own little 'meh, meh.' They thought it was so funny and very nicely, comedically placed here and there. I mean, they liked those grunts so much I turned into the grunt queen of California."

Even though they didn't come face-to-face that season, Mrs. Mac was joined in The Gang's little universe by Mr. Mac, aka Luther MacDonald (Gregory Scott Cummins), a convict, husband, and tormentor of his son. Mac often slicks back his hair just like Luther does, and desperately wants nothing more than a crumb of his dad's affection. Luther has yet to proffer one to Mac, who in the season 2 finale, "Dennis and Dee Get a New Dad," took Charlie along with him to reconnect with his father during a trip to prison.

Since Charlie had never met his own father, Mac, in as unselfish a gesture as he is wont to make, thought he and Charlie could both become pals with Luther. On the other hand, Luther said he did have a "father-son type of thing" for his boy and his friend: he wanted them to smuggle heroin into the prison for him—in their anuses. Just when viewers thought Frank might win the Worst Father of the Year Award, a new contender emerged.

Except Frank wasn't exactly a father to Dennis and Dee—not a biological one, anyway. Also in the season ender, Dee was approached on MySpace by a man named Bruce Mathis (*7th Heaven* star Stephen Collins), who claimed he might be the twins' father, and had plenty of photos with Barbara as proof. When Dennis and Dee took Frank and Barbara to Guigino's—The Gang's go-to fancy restaurant—to confront them with this alleged paternity case, Frank and his kids got the shock of their lives. Barbara *had* carried on an affair thirty years ago with Bruce Mathis. The siblings were gobsmacked by their mother's confession, delivered oh-so-matter-of-factly, and Frank melted down in front of the entire eatery with a hysterical rant aimed at his ex-wife that resulted in him suffering a minor stroke.

Frank's unhinged freak-out at Guigino's—making it perfectly and loudly clear how he felt about having been cuckolded for three decades—is among the moments that made DeVito's debut on *Sunny* unforgettable. But many others helped cement season 2 as the first collection of episodes to pay off, undeniably, on the somewhat rough promise of the first season. In "Mac Bangs Dennis' Mom," DeVito also busted out "the move," a cringey gyration/dance, as a toupeed Frank tried to pick up younger women at a club. While filming the scene, no music was playing, but DeVito moved like there was while singing the words "Go for it, go for it." RCG found the whole package so hilarious that, while editing the episode, they selected a disco track for the scene and McElhenney and Howerton decided to sing "Go for it" repeatedly—which makes it look like Frank is getting his groove on to a song of the same name. (Day shared on *The Always Sunny Podcast* he was disappointed that his voice is MIA on the tune; he was on his honeymoon when it was recorded.)

Other classic moments from the sophomore run:

In "Dennis and Dee Go on Welfare," the twins quit their jobs at Paddy's when they realized they could get a bigger paycheck with unemployment. To celebrate, they spent their afternoons sitting on a stoop, drinking beer out of paper bags and singing along with Biz Markie's "Just a Friend." It remains one of the most indelible visions of the series, and the character pairing would become a signature in *Sunny*'s storytelling arsenal. Then, when their unemployment ran out, Dennis and Dee learned they could go on welfare if they were crack addicts, and proved without a doubt that any member of The Gang will go to any length to avoid labor.

In "The Gang Goes Jihad," Frank walked into the bar and happened upon The Gang randomly singing an a cappella version of "More Than Words," the 1991 power ballad by the rock band Extreme. The performance was good, and music went on to become yet another recurring element that plays a key role throughout the show. The funny part was how seriously Mac, Dee, Charlie, and Dennis took it. These are people who have done terrible things to other people and to one another. Their concern for the world outside their front door is relative only to how it impacts them at any given moment. They also are generally not fans of expending energy on anything that won't pay off in some big way. But here they were, each actually trying to make something good, giving the harmonies their best efforts, working well together, for the sake of making—"beautiful" might be too strong a word—at least pretty music together. A rare, charming moment for The Gang.

The episode, though now nearly twenty years old, sparked a bit of fresh reaction after the October 7, 2023, Hamas attack on Israel and the subsequent Israeli military action that followed. Some viewers—including new ones and longtime fans who had forgotten the early episode—were so incredulous that the series had done an episode where the characters blew up a building owned by a rival Israeli businessman that the urban legend fact-checker website Snopes.com actually did an investigation titled "Was 'The Gang Goes Jihad' a Real Episode of 'Always Sunny in Philadelphia'?"

In "Hundred Dollar Baby," one of the first of the series' clever movie homages (another *IASIP* trademark), "Frankie Fast Hands" (Frank's nickname in his younger days as a boxer) decided to teach Dee some self-defense. Along the way, they clashed with his old rival (played by *Laverne & Shirley* star Eddie Mekka) and his daughter. Dee began taking copious amounts of steroids to prepare for her fight with her new foe and became so aggressive she told her opponent, "I will eat your babies, bitch!" and later punched a hole in the wall of her own bedroom. Meanwhile, Charlie, training for an underground fight club match Dennis and Mac signed him up for, swiped handfuls of Dee's pills and washed them down with beer. The steroids led to mood swings, like when he ate a sandwich and went from sobbing to raging to laughing hysterically in a matter of seconds. It became one of the first fan-favorite Charlie memes, but far from the last.

Episode director Dan Attias said Day's performance in the scene was one of his favorites of the season. He also recalled it as a moment that left McElhenney overjoyed.

"I love remembering how Rob just thinks Charlie is the funniest guy he's ever met," Attias says. "It was hard for him not to laugh at Charlie doing takes while he was going crazy in that scene at Paddy's, when Mac and Dennis were worried he wasn't going to show up for his fight, and he was just out of it, he was just a maniac. Rob just laughed at Charlie, and he would be so delighted by things Charlie would come up with."

The jam-packed episode also included the first great Dee and Charlie moment. The two, who, along with Frank and Charlie, are the most reliable character pairing for pure over-the-top insanity, got into each other's faces when Dee discovered Charlie had used the last of her pills, right before her big fight. Both physically and verbally, the two actors went toe-to-toe in wringing every drop of humor out of the moment, threatening to beat the daylights out of each other. When they accidentally hit the car of a stranger, the driver confronted them. Big mistake: they turned on him instead and landed in jail together for beating him up in front of Paddy's.

But writers RCG, the cast and crew, and Dan Attias weren't done making this episode a pure gem. "Hundred Dollar Baby" spoofed *Million Dollar Baby*, the 2004 drama that starred (and led to Oscar wins for) Clint Eastwood, Hilary Swank, and Morgan Freeman, as well as earning Best Picture honors. Another sports-themed flick, the 1984 teen classic *The Karate Kid*, also got a shout-out in the episode, via its soundtrack song "You're the Best," sung by Joe Esposito and originally written for another Philly-set story, *Rocky III*. *It's Always Sunny* played the track over a sequence of Dee and Charlie training for their fights. Another fun little connection between the song and *Always Sunny*: the lyricist behind "You're the Best," late Grammy winner Allee Willis, also cowrote the Rembrandts' "I'll Be There for You," the theme song for *Sunny* inspiration *Friends*.

In "Charlie Goes America All Over Everybody's Asses," Mac, Dennis, and Frank adopted an "anything goes," freedom-loving atmosphere at Paddy's, where Frank's game of Russian roulette in the basement went as wrong as it could go. The McPoyle brothers had a family fun night out, showing up dressed in bathrobes and nightgowns with their equally unibrowed sister, Margaret (Thesy Surface), to pound glasses of their signature drink (milk) and make out—with each other—at the bar. Charlie favored a more literal form of patriotism, however, sporting a flag bandanna and an eagle-emblazoned denim jacket as he insisted everyone stop trying to "tread" on him as he sang passionately about how he was going to "rise up . . . kick some ass in the USA . . . climb a mountain . . . sew a flag . . . fly on an eagle . . . drive a big truck" in a little ditty titled "Rock, Flag, and Eagle." The song, which Day improvised, was inspired by a conversation he and Hornsby had about the jingoistic imagery used in a lot of truck and car commercials. "Rock, Flag, and Eagle" is one of the most enduring Charlie Day/Charlie Kelly *Sunny* scenes, memes, and images, adorning T-shirts, magnets, stickers, posters, and pretty much anything else a fan can buy or sell on a piece of merch on Etsy.

In "Dennis and Dee Get a New Dad," the big reveal of the Reynolds siblings' actual biological father wasn't the only shocking paternity storyline that wrapped up The Gang's second year. While Dennis and Dee had too many fathers, Charlie still had none. Or did he?

The audience was going to have to wait a while for the answer to that cliffhanger's question, and to see if MySpace had cost Frank Reynolds a set of twins but gained him a son after Frank's long-ago fling with Charlie's mom came to light.

But another question posed before the season certainly did not go unanswered: Would DeVito's return to primetime television rank as a creative success? Yes, by anyone's measure.

"When [they] added Danny, he was just igniting the whole thing," director Attias says. "He was using a totally different type of humor. He threw himself into it, just entirely dependent on the spontaneity, with no ego, and did anything. It just created the world."

Frank Reynolds arrived, dressed so un-Gang-like, a buttoned-up, successful businessman, ready to act as a proper father to his children. He soon gave way to the more rambunctious, wild Frank Reynolds, the one who wanted to live with, and like, Charlie, and let his freak flag fly higher than everyone else's.

The Gang as we know and love them (in spite of themselves) was now truly born.

Chapter Five

THE NIGHTMAN COMETH

Spoiler alert: The Gang did not open season 3 with a confirmation about Frank and Charlie's father-son relationship, the one introduced as a surprising possibility in the closing scenes of the season 2 finale. *Sunny*'s third season premiered on September 13, 2007, and drew 2.34 million viewers. "The Gang Finds a Dumpster Baby"—the title literally teases the story, though it's what Dee and Mac *do* with the little guy they nickname "D.B." that makes the story peak Gang behavior—featured not only the return of DeVito's Frank Reynolds but also an inherent acknowledgment by FX, with its fall premiere date, that the series was heading upward in ratings and popularity.

The season 2 debut, back on June 29, 2006, had drawn 1.64 million viewers for DeVito's first episode as Frank, an almost 50 percent increase in the average viewership numbers from *Sunny*'s first season. The season's second episode—the one in which Frank blackmailed The Gang to secure his spot in the group—had retained most of the premiere's audience, with 1.5 million viewers. FX continued to keep and grow the comedy's enthusiastic—and primarily young and male—fan base. College students, in particular, were already smitten with The Gang's shenanigans, but since social media was not yet the arbiter or tracker of how people were spending their tube-watching time, FX decided to move *IASIP*'s premiere to the fall for the first time. Back-to-school days for college students made it much easier and likelier that they'd get together to watch the show and laugh about these five lunkheads' misadventures, and the network was relying on word-of-mouth to draw even more viewers.

More firsts for the show: the season would finally have an official writers' room, and just in time, because season 3 was expanding from ten episodes to fifteen, and McElhenney, Day, and Howerton would need help keeping The Gang in a properly degenerate state for more installments. Directing duties for those episodes would be shared by three actors turned directors: *The Wonder Years* star Fred Savage; Savage's fellow former child star, Matt Shakman (*Just the Ten of Us* and *Webster*); and *Teen Wolf* and *Will & Grace* star Jerry Levine.

In the block shooting of it all, Levine was up first with an episode that would air ninth in the expanded season's lineup. It's an episode that led to one of RCG's biggest regrets of the series, but also one of their biggest successes: "Sweet Dee's Dating a Retarded Person." When the creators speak of the episode now, they refer to the slur as "the R-word." The episode, with the story credited to Howerton and the teleplay credited to the series' new writing team of Scott Marder and Rob Rosell, was one filled with outrageous and often hilarious moments, heavy on arrogance by and comeuppance for The Gang... all makings of an outstanding *It's Always Sunny* occasion.

The plot: Sweet Dee had a new boyfriend, Kevin, better known as up-and-coming local rapper Lil' Kev. She was excited about her new fella, in no small part because he bought her jewelry, and because, as "the next Eminem," Dee saw the prospect of a lot more baubles coming her way. But she made the mistake of bragging about him to the guys, so when she introduced him at Paddy's, they jumped at the chance to mess with her. Charlie wondered if Kev's "Lil'" moniker was some sort of reference to a tiny foot or hand. But Dennis dropped another thought on her: Lil' Kev was the titular "R-word" person. Dennis confirmed Lil' Kev's real name as Kevin Gallagher. He then said Kevin went to elementary school with them... in a trailer behind the school. Kevin rode the short bus, Dennis claimed, and while Dee immediately insisted there was no way she was unknowingly dating an R-word person, Dennis engaged her in an episode-long back-and-forth about whether Kev was developmentally disabled... or was just a rapper.

McElhenney—in the *Always Sunny Podcast* episode titled "Sweet Dee's Dating a [Redacted] Person"—says the idea for the Lil' Kev character was sparked not by Eminem but a couple of "low-grade Eminems," white rappers with a certain affectation that meant "you couldn't understand what the fuck they were talking about" when they would do interviews.

"We were like, 'Oh, they sound... [fill in the R-word],' and so let's have a go at them," McElhenney said.

And they did, and The Gang, especially gold-digging Dee, got as good as they gave in the end. It's one of the essential episodes for understanding the humor and the intentions of deconstructing the average television comedy, and creating a smarter "dirtbag sitcom," as Emily Nussbaum, Pulitzer Prize–winning TV critic for *The New Yorker* (and a *Sunny* fan) termed comedies like *IASIP*, *Archer*, *Wilfred*, and some that didn't air on FX, like *Angry Boys* and *Eastbound & Down*.

Back to those intentions: Howerton, who noted it was particularly regrettable that the R-word was used in the episode's title, went on to add "it was also a word that was abused by people who, you know, are awful people. And our characters are awful, awful people." On their podcast, McElhenney, Day, and Howerton agreed they cringe every time (which is often) the word is uttered.

Said Howerton: "Like, [you] just feel it go right up your spine."

RCG also pointed out the TV episode was made more than fifteen years ago, and the R-word was used more frequently back then. But without turning *The Always Sunny Podcast* into an "apology tour," McElhenney said, "This was one of the episodes where it deviated from the characters to the way that we were using it so casually... to me [that] made it feel like the filmmakers, us, at the time, were not conscious of what we were saying and how painful that could be for people, because it is a derogatory term. But we didn't know that at the time."

The heaviness of that one powerfully loaded word could have outweighed everything else that worked in that episode. But it didn't end up that way despite the insensitivity due to the great writing and some exceptional performances.

Lil' Kev, for instance, is played by Kyle Davis. Now a twenty-five-year Hollywood veteran, the character actor has starred in terrific, canceled-before-their-time series like the Fox comedy *Enlisted* and the Ray Romano / Andre Braugher / Scott Bakula TNT dramedy *Men of a Certain Age*, as well as hits like *Felicity*, *Monk*, *The Shield*, *ER*, *Dexter*, and *American Horror Story*.

But it's his performance as Lil' Kev that fans remember and recognize him for. Some of them are inspired to buy personalized Cameo videos from him, which he always performs and records as the Lil' Kev persona, often with a specific rap message. In some interactions, Davis says, fans are surprised to learn he has had other roles. Sometimes they think he really is a rapper (aside from the Beastie Boys songs he and his brother performed for their parents in their backyard when he was a kid, his professional freestyles are limited to Lil' Kev). Davis has appeared in just two *It's Always Sunny* episodes (he returned in season 6's "Dee Gives Birth")—less than an hour of screen time total—but his presence and portrayal of the guy at the center of the controversial storyline, the controversial word, earned him a beloved place in the *Sunny* canon. Fan convention appearances and spirited social media feedback await memorable guest stars who visit and return to the comedy.

Davis's experience as Lil' Kev began with a very personal greeting from DeVito. Davis had just completed a night shoot on the horror film *Resurrection Mary*, and the 6:00 a.m. wrap gave him barely enough time to make it to the *IASIP* set for an 8:00 a.m. call time. When he arrived, sleepless and unable to breathe very well because of a cold, the first thing someone asked was if he wanted to meet DeVito, who was already there filming another episode. Davis said yes, of course.

"And he was standing there with his robe open, and only a pair of tighty-whities underwear," he says. "He's just like, 'Hey, how you doing?'"

The actor had landed the role in the usual way, via audition. He says there was plenty of competition, including his best friend and writing partner, Devin McGinn. Day later told him he won the gig when, during the scene set in Lil' Kev's house, he stepped into the hallway to give Dennis (Howerton) a high five. But he was too far away, and as he leaned forward, the high-five motion turned into something mirroring a claw. RCG wondered what he was doing. But they couldn't stop laughing at the move, Day told him, and decided immediately to offer him the role.

"He was so good," director Levine said. "I had trouble determining whether or not he was really marginalized in that way, or if he was just being brilliant . . . he was being brilliant. And it wasn't until the turnaround at the end—because he stayed in that character for most of the time that I saw him—until the very end [Lil' Kev's rap scene]. Then I felt a different kind of power coming from him."

Aside from the episode's finale—which revolved around his rap earning a decisive victory for Lil' Kev in the battle of him versus the

Reynolds twins and becoming one of the series' classic moments—Davis says his favorite part of filming was the scene in Lil' Kev's bedroom, where Kev and Sweet Dee watched cartoons and ate popcorn. The rapper was just pounding kernels by the handful and chewing with his mouth open. Dee, her head freshly filled with Dennis's insinuations about her boyfriend, was watching him chow down with a look of disgust on her face, while the camera panned in closer and closer on Kev's gaping, snack-packed piehole.

"I actually almost literally choked to death eating the popcorn," Davis says. "Because we're doing all these takes, I just kept saying, 'Shit!' Like, they just kept running the camera, and saying, 'Okay, let's do it again. Keep doing it,' and I was just shoving mouthfuls of popcorn every single time, chewing, trying to swallow, spitting some out, chewing it . . . then I just got so much stuck in my throat, and I wasn't drinking. It started getting backed up and basically, I was almost throwing up popcorn. It was crazy, but super funny.

"I get the popcorn face sent to me, still, every day [on social media]. I've probably been sent it a million times. It's iconic. It's funny. I even started making some Lil' Kev shirts with me eating the popcorn on them."

Mostly the connections with fans are positive. Davis says he tries to remember that people discover or rewatch the show and specific episodes at different times and decide to reach out to him randomly. So the 999,999th time he receives a DM with a close-up photo of his face with popcorn spilling out of his mouth is one more fan's attempt to show how valued his work is, and to make a little human connection with a stranger who's brought him or her a moment of joy.

Davis says he has spent a not insignificant sum of his character actor's salary sending autographed photos to fans, especially during the COVID pandemic, to show appreciation for viewer support.

Since the aforementioned season 6 episode, Davis has yet to reappear on *Sunny*. He heard there was talk of bringing him back for "The Gang Wins the Big Game" in season 13, but plans fell through. He hopes to get a return invitation at some point, though. He thinks fans would love to catch up with Lil' Kev's career. And Sweet Dee *is* still single....

※ ※ ※

The Lil' Kev story alone would have been fodder enough for a memorable episode of most other comedies. But "Sweet Dee's Dating a Retarded Person" had an entire other storyline sparked by Lil' Kev's success as a local rapper. Mac decided that he and The Gang could start a musical act and find success, too. Never mind that they had no organized musical experience—save that a cappella rendition of "More Than Words" in season 2—but Mac convinced Charlie and Frank they could be a successful act because Lil' Kev had done it and, mostly, because The Gang members are just arrogant enough to think they can do anything successfully, even when there's very little evidence to support the ambition. In fact, the only reason Mac invited Frank to be a bandmate was because Frank could bankroll the purchase of instruments they could pretend to play onstage. Meanwhile Dennis, who Mac admitted had a great voice, wasn't allowed to join. Dennis liked too much of that "'80s glam-rock femme shit," Mac said, and that just wasn't the artistic direction Mac wanted to take the band in.

But when Mac, Charlie, and Frank hit Walnut Music, they were in for a huge surprise: Charlie, it turned out, was something of a musical savant (much like Charlie Day in real life). Charlie Kelly may not have been able to read or write (he definitely could not), but he was quite proficient in playing the keyboard. It just made sense to him, he said. Mac, meanwhile, was trying on guitars, staring at himself in the store's mirrored walls to see which one would look coolest onstage, and Frank was making so much racket at a drum kit that the sales associate wanted to call the cops. But with Charlie's talent, Mac thought they could be the next Sid Vicious and Johnny Rotten. Or maybe Axl Rose and Slash. Charlie suggested they might compare to "Holland Oates," who he believed was one guy. In addition to Charlie-style thinking, it was a nice shout-out to the beloved Philly duo.

The band practiced with their new instruments at Charlie and Frank's place; they were really bad. Frank suggested trashing a hotel room to get in a rock 'n' roll frame of mind. It worked until he found out they had used his credit card to secure the room, so he wanted them to start gluing everything back together. At Paddy's, with their instruments all set up on a stage, they couldn't agree on a costume or a band name. Frank wore a suit and his toupee and wanted to call the group the Pecan Sandies; Mac tried to rock eyeliner, tight pants, and a ripped shirt (sleeveless, of course), and wanted to call the band Chemical Toilet. Charlie emerged from the Paddy's office wearing his homage to Bob Dylan: black turtleneck, sport coat, fiddler cap, and a scarf. But it was what he held in his hand that would change the future of *It's Always Sunny in Philadelphia* as much as the addition of Danny DeVito did. Charlie's nod to Dylan as a songwriter went beyond fashions; on a lyric sheet decipherable only to himself (it can only be described as a page of modern hieroglyphics), Charlie wrote and presented to Mac and Frank lyrics for the song "Nightman." Mac thought it was a page from a coloring book.

When Chemical Toilet took the stage—Mac won the name game—Charlie, shy about sharing his singing and songwriting with others, began performing his song. He sang about how the Nightman fills him up, and he becomes the spirit of the Nightman. This was a good thing, Charlie intended to convey.

A sample of the lyrics he sang: "Every night, you come into my room / and pin me down with your strong arms / You pin me down, and I try to fight you / You come inside me, you fill me up / and I become the Nightman."

To Mac and Frank, it seemed like Charlie was singing about a man breaking into his bedroom and sexually assaulting him. Frank's look of perplexity was a masterful bit of facial acting by DeVito. Charlie was shocked by their interpretation of his musical storytelling. But Mac was so disturbed by the song that he went to Dennis and asked him to replace Charlie as Chemical Toilet's lead singer. Mac's initial rejection of his participation in the band stuck in Dennis's craw, so it was with utter smugness that Dennis agreed to front Chemical Toilet. But he warned that he would be wearing spandex. When he showed up for his first rehearsal with Mac and Frank, Dennis was wearing a gray spandex jumpsuit with a maroon codpiece and sash. He paired the '80s-rock-god look Mac had feared with the '80s-rock-god oooohs and ahhhhs and gyrations Mac had also feared. Chemical Toilet was quickly down another lead singer.

But that led to magic.

Flushed away from Chemical Toilet, Dennis went to Charlie's apartment, where he found his friend huffing spray paint from a sock while singing a sad little song about how "Nightman" had been stolen from him when he was tossed from the Toilet earlier: "They took you, Nightman / and you don't belong to them / They locked me in a world of darkness, without your sexy hands / And I miss you, Nightman, so bad. . . ." Charlie sat in the dark, with curtains over his windows and a blanket covering his head. Dennis let the light in, revealing Charlie's silver-paint-covered face, and proposed they partner up to make some music together, away from the Chemical Toilet twosome. Charlie turned on his keyboard and got a beat going. Inspired by the sunlight now flooding his home, he and Dennis started to sing about "Dayman, fighter of the Nightman, champion of the sun . . . a master of karate and friendship for everyone." Dennis added some "ah-ahs," inspired by Queen's "Flash," the theme song from the 1980 *Flash Gordon* movie. They stood side by side, Dennis in his spandex jumpsuit and jeans, Charlie in his long johns and face paint, and swayed together and clapped their hands above their heads. One of the most classic and joyous moments of the series unfurled.

Levine recalls this as the first *Sunny* scene he shot, and the first scene filmed for season 3.

"[It] opened up with a small, dark room, curtains closed, Charlie Day sitting with a blanket over his shoulders and a little piano in front of him, huffing glue, trying to create a song which grew into 'Dayman,'" Levine says. "Glenn Howerton shows up and Charlie says, 'I'm writing a song.' And this is just a rehearsal. Glenn says, 'What's the song?' Charlie says, 'Dayman.' And he goes through it a little bit, and then at one point, Glenn just goes, 'Ah-ah!' And they were off. And that's become, I think probably one of their anthems of the show.

"And so, that was my first day, and Charlie and Glenn created that right there. Well, I don't think it's the first time they did it. They wrote it together, so they probably said, 'Let's sing it like this.' But I had never heard it before, and it was too funny to even direct, just capture. Just capture it. Just try and capture what they're doing. That was the tricky part of it. It was clear very early on that they would just hit the ground running, and there wasn't anything more to do than catch up with them and get in with them and see if we can find a way to capture what's the funniest. And they use ideas, and they were very open, but they clearly knew what they were doing and what they wanted to do.

"It was very early on, and I think that was very important to the establishment of the show," Levine continues. "That they knew what they wanted, and they knew what they wanted to do with it."

Charlie and Dennis debuted their "Dayman" performance—as Electric Dream Machine—at Paddy's, attired in tight, silver, David Bowie–esque spacesuits and red boots. But despite the "ah-ahs" and the choreographed sway-clapping and the prominent black codpieces, the crowd turned on them quickly. The Paddy's patrons threw trash, just as Charlie always feared they would if he performed his music in public. He and his Electric Dream Machine bandmate fled the stage, with Charlie screaming his most Bobcat Goldthwait–like screams. The crowd didn't want to see Chemical Toilet, either. It was only when Lil' Kev stepped on the stage, and kicked Mac and Frank off, that the boos turned to cheers.

With no musical backing, Lil' Kev freestyled an answer, definitively in most viewers' minds, to the question Dee had asked him just moments earlier: Was he the R-word, like Dennis claimed he was, like the title of the episode claimed he was?

Kev rapped his way through a rhyming diss that decimated Dee, calling her "a broke-ass bitch with a gay-ass crew," describing Dee's looks thusly: "face beat up by the school of hard knocks, hair so fried and bleached by Clorox," and "it's like she's skinny, but fat in all the wrong places, mothers gotta cover their babies' faces." He finished with a literal mic drop, the one that answered the question Dee dared to ask with one of Lil' Kev's own: "Just one question, Dee, before you take your bow: this gravy train's leavin', so who's retarded now?"

Lil' Kev had taken his final bow (so far) on the Paddy's stage, but there was still lots of music to be made. The bar's crowd let Charlie and Dennis know they thought the world premiere performance of "Dayman" was garbage, but Dayman and Nightman were soon to make a return.

First, although Lil' Kev and The Gang's musical aspirations would have a game-changing impact on *It's Always Sunny*, there were plenty of other highlights that made the third season one of the series' best. Everything gelled—the cast had had a full season together with DeVito, who fit in as a costar and with his character from the minute he stepped foot on the set; the new group of directors brought fresh ideas to the fifteen episodes; and the newbie multi-hyphenates were settling into their many roles as RCG, now with the creative addition of an official writers' room, and had more minds helping with juicing up their storytelling.

All of those factors contributed to the busy, Levine-directed season opener "The Gang Finds a Dumpster Baby," in which Dee and Mac used shoe polish to paint a baby boy they found in the Paddy's dumpster so they could exploit him as a minority model. Charlie and Frank bonded over their love of dumpster diving (with Charlie Day climbing a real mountain of garbage to retrieve discarded treasures); Charlie learned the disturbing news that Frank had impregnated his mother and forced her into an abortion that "didn't take" (it would be many more seasons before Charlie, and viewers, found out the whole truth about his father); and Dennis slept with the girlfriend of a hipster who publicly humiliated him and his newfound interest in saving the environment after he saw the movie *An Inconvenient Truth*.

In "The Gang Gets Invincible," Dennis, Mac, and Dee (posing as a man named Cole) aspired to NFL stardom when the Philadelphia Eagles held open tryouts. Eagles quarterback Donovan McNabb was supposed to make a motivational speech to the hopefuls. Instead, they got a McDonald's sales pitch from a guy who looked like "Alvin," as Mac and Dennis called him, from *The Cosby Show*. Because it was: actor Geoffrey Owens, who played Elvin on *The Cosby Show*, began a recurring stint on *Sunny*, in which he was an actor who later also pretended to be Tiger Woods and Don Cheadle. Frank, more concerned with "trippin' balls" than football, hung out in the parking lot with Charlie during tryouts, where Frank took LSD and secretly dropped some into Charlie's beer. The two got into a skirmish with an army of McPoyles, who spilled out of an RV, each more unibrowed than the last. They were there to support their brother Doyle McPoyle, who earned a spot at Eagles training camp during tryouts... until Frank, still trippin' and playing with his ever-present gun, accidentally shot Doyle in the knee. It was a five-star effort for Fred Savage's *Sunny* directorial debut.

Charlie, while still quite high on Frank's supply, debuted his spandex-clad mascot Green Man in "The Gang Gets Invincible." The character, who appeared in a full-body, Eagles-green spandex costume and danced with abandon with the McPoyles, has become a favorite for fans to imitate at all kinds of pro and college sporting events everywhere... he's become "the sports world's version of Waldo," as ESPN.com writer Toby Mergler called him. But *Sunny*'s Green Man was himself an imitator of a McElhenney friend who celebrated a 2006 Eagles win versus the Dallas Cowboys at the Linc in Philly. Postgame, McElhenney watched his friend—a buddy from high school—take off his clothes in the parking lot of the stadium, slip into a green spandex full-body suit, and run around, slapping high fives, taking photos, and generally sharing his merriment about his beloved team's victory with fellow Eagles devotees.

"Everyone started chanting, 'Green Man! Green Man!'" McElhenney told Mergler. "It went on for several hours, and all I could think was, 'My god, there has to be a way I can take advantage of this on the show.'"

Which he did. After convincing Day and Howerton they needed to experience Green Man and the reaction he inspired from fans, RCG decided to order a suit similar to the one worn by McElhenney's pal, and Day agreed to put it on and dance around. They were sold—Charlie Kelly's Green Man made his debut on *Sunny* the following season, and the rest is sports and television comedy history.

In another impactful episode, "Dennis and Dee's Mom Is Dead," Frank glided into Paddy's with an announcement: his ex-wife, Barbara, died during neck-lift surgery, and the only thing on his mind was a bottle of celebratory champagne and the upcoming reading of Barbara's will. At the office of her attorney—the debut of a recurring character who would be known only as the Lawyer, played by former *The Daily Show* correspondent and producer Brian Unger—Frank and Dee were left nothing but insults from Barbara, which prompted them to yell at the Lawyer as if he were Barbara, and him to remind them that he (a) was not her, and (b) could not deliver their messages to her. Frank was especially furious that Barbara bequeathed all her money to Bruce Mathis, the twins' already wealthy biological father, and that Barbara, even in death, reminded Frank that Bruce was more handsome, kinder, and better endowed than Frank. Dee was most upset that Barbara decided to be buried with all her jewelry, and that she had called Dee a disappointing mistake before leaving her nothing.

In the *Sunny* directorial debut of Matt Shakman, a protégé of *Sunny* director Dan Attias, Frank plotted a ruse for himself and Dee to right Barbara's slight: he would pose as Dee's fiancé, Seamus; she would call philanthropic Bruce, and tell him she and Seamus wanted to adopt a bunch of kids but needed her mom's moolah to afford that. Too bad for them that Bruce, unbeknownst to Frank, knew who he was and what he and Dee were up to.

As for the other grieving Reynolds, Dennis had inherited Barbara's massive house, which he, Mac, and Charlie decided to turn into a party mansion. Except they realized they had no other friends outside The Gang. Nothing that a bicep-shaped flyer inviting random guys at the gym to the house wouldn't solve... until everyone pointed out the bicep held upside down looked like a penis, and Mac's repeated insistence that they were seeking nothing sexual from their party guests made everyone think they absolutely were looking for something sexual. In stories that merged in a *Seinfeld*ian bit of tidy comeuppance for The Gang, Bruce said he couldn't give the money to an unmarried couple, so he would perform a wedding service for Dee and Seamus; in a wink at actor Stephen Collins's signature role as Rev. Eric Camden on the family drama *7th Heaven*, Bruce noted that he was, after all, a licensed minister.

The next day, Seamus and Dee (in a wedding gown, because she's never one to pass up the opportunity for drama of any kind) joined Bruce, Dennis, Mac, and Charlie at Barbara's house for the ceremony. Bruce pronounced Dee and Seamus man and wife, and then congratulated Frank for marrying his daughter. Bruce knew they were scamming him all along. But he wasn't done. After calling Frank the "little asswipe" who raised his children to be "animals . . . monsters . . . who contribute nothing to society," Bruce dropped a bombshell on Dennis, who was giddily videotaping Bruce's bashing of Dee and Frank. Bruce asked Dennis for the camera and videotape, then told him he was turning it in to the Lawyer. Dennis was going to lose the party mansion, because Barbara stipulated in her will that Dennis could not allow Frank onto the property, lest it be taken away from him. Before fleeing in a huff, Bruce had one more parting shot to The Gang: "You're the most horrible people alive!"

And apparently Bruce's disgust with his children was permanent. The 2007 episode was Collins's last appearance on *It's Always Sunny*, and is likely to remain his final one. In 2014, Collins admitted to incidents of sexual misconduct with three underage girls across a two-decade period, from 1972 to 1994. Despite his public admission about the abuse, Collins was never criminally charged for the acts because of statute of limitations issues. He was fired at the time from the movie *Ted 2*, was dropped by his agent, and resigned from his position on the board of SAG-AFTRA. He soon thereafter effectively retired from Hollywood and relocated to Iowa, where he lives with his third wife.

"Dennis and Dee's Mom Is Dead" also, of course, marked the end of the road for Anne Archer, who bid *Sunny* adieu (her only previous on-screen appearance was in the season 2 finale), much to the disappointment of fans who enjoyed Barbara's deliciously wicked ways.

Years later, Howerton admitted he still second-guesses the decision to kill off Barbara. "Because that was a really funny character," he said. "And I find the longer we go on, the more we have a desire to do at least a few episodes here and there that feel grounded in the emotional reality of the characters, and when you want to do that it's nice to have family members to draw on."

<hr>

But the introduction of the great Brian Unger into the series' universe would pay off in memorable ways for years to come, even though the actor has, as of the most recent season, appeared in just six episodes. Unger was brought into the *Sunny* fold, no audition required, by McElhenney, who had met Unger nearly a decade earlier when the two costarred in a 1998 Yoo-hoo commercial. Unger was the chocolate drink's spokesperson, and a baby-faced McElhenney (who was about twenty-one at the time) played a teen whose love triangle with his best friend and his best friend's girlfriend was settled with a bottle of Yoo-hoo. During the lunch break on set, Unger was sitting at a table, and McElhenney approached, carrying a tray of food from craft services and a request to join Unger. They shared a pleasant conversation, the specific contents of which Unger says he doesn't really remember. But he recalls that McElhenney was charming and funny and smart, and he was left with the impression that his costar was going to go off and do great things.

Cut to *Sunny* season 3. Unger and the showrunner had not kept in touch post-Yoo-hoo, but Unger received a personal call from McElhenney, who asked him to come hang out with The Gang for an episode. Unger was working on more documentary, journalistic sorts of series at the time on Discovery, History, and the Travel Channel. He was curious about *Sunny*, which he knew about, but had never seen.

"So I got to set, and even in that very first episode, it was kind of like being shell-shocked," he laughed. "I didn't know who these characters were.... Danny [DeVito] was so outrageous that much of my performance is rooted in the actual experience that's happening in the scene. Danny, Rob, and Charlie, their characters are all being so disgusting and repulsive. The absence of manners and protocol, all of that, was just like, much of my reaction is kind of like, 'Oh, so this is the show?' Then, once I did the show, I went and watched everything and I, still to this day, think it was the most important preparation for doing a show. It's not knowing the show."

Unger says each time he's been asked to return for another episode, it always comes as a surprise, and he delights in the things the writers ask of the Lawyer, though RCG's notes for his performances have been few and far between. "There's never been a moment on set with them that felt labored," he says. "I've always had to contain my enthusiasm, and enjoy being on set with them. They've done it a million times. I've only done it six. So when I'm on set, it's just such a thrill, and so fun. I mean, it sounds so clichéd, but it's all on the page, and it's just so great."

As a foil for The Gang, much of his humor comes in playing his scenes a bit more grounded in the face of what is often insanity from his scene partners. And that doesn't just include The Gang. By his fourth episode, season 6's gem "Dennis Gets Divorced," the Lawyer went up against The Gang again when he represented Maureen Ponderosa (Catherine Reitman), the high school sweetheart Dennis married and almost immediately wanted to either strangle or divorce. Dennis's legal rep: Jack (Andrew Friedman), Charlie's uncle, who is obsessed with the size of his and everyone else's hands, and who maybe, probably, almost certainly is the pedophile who inspired his nephew's song about the Nightman. Also not really in doubt: Jack is a terrible attorney, which is how Dennis ended up on the business end of alimony to the cat-obsessed Maureen. In the episode, Jack met the Lawyer, and instantly became smitten with his legal competency, and more so with his generously sized hands. He asked the Lawyer if they could take a photo together, with the Lawyer's hands covering his own. Uncle Jack was giddy when the pic was snapped, and he looked into the camera to exclaim, "We're lawyers!"

Brunch, after the episode first aired, has never been the same for Unger. Especially since he moved from Los Angeles to a farm outside Atlanta, *Sunny* fans get giddy themselves when they spot him in public. And be it at brunch, the supermarket, or Home Depot, they always ask for a photo with him, with his hands covering theirs, just like Uncle Jack's hand photo.

"Little did I know this would become an iconic thing," Unger says. "But the show has this intensely devoted following. I was eating in a restaurant, and there was a table of four next to us, and one of the guys was whispering to one of the others, 'I think that's the lawyer from *It's Always Sunny*,' and he said it in what he thought was his indoor voice. [It had] gotten to the point where I just turned to him, and I went, 'Yes, I am.' They all just erupted."

※ ※ ※

Sweet Dee's reunion with a high school pal—and fellow outcast—in "The Aluminum Monster vs. Fatty Magoo" brought another fun guest star to the season. Dee was the titular former back-brace-wearing Aluminum Monster, and her formerly overweight BFF Ingrid Nelson, played by fellow FX star Judy Greer (*Archer* and *Married*), had been nicknamed Fatty Magoo. Dee ran into Ingrid in a clothing boutique and saw that her friend not only had lost weight but also owned the store and her own fashion line. She was inspired by Dee's constantly shared high school vow to become a famous actress/model/lawyer/fashion designer. Dee is, of course, not at all happy about that, especially when Ingrid asks how her dreams turned out. Dee shared a new vow: "I got a fatty to take down." She decided to design her own dresses, and if one of The Gang dares to dream, the other members of The Gang assume they can do that dream, too. So Frank taught Mac how to start up a sweatshop, to make the dress Dennis designed (skimpy amount of shiny fabric, significant emphasis on breast enhancement) to sell to Ingrid (who didn't want it). Charlie, who's got sewing skills because he's been mending his meager wardrobe his whole life, was, as usual, called upon to perform the actual labor of the latest group scheme. Which, as usual, was not a success.

"It was hard to not laugh a lot, because they are so funny, and they play around so much," Greer says. "In some ways, I felt like I was the straight [man], so I just got to enjoy all of their antics. I think that happens with a lot of guest stars on that show, but it was definitely hard not to laugh with them. Those people are such great people, and they're kind and fun and funny. It was really fun to be on their set. I just can't imagine anyone not loving doing an episode of *Sunny*, because the whole group just wants to have a good time. It's really hard sometimes when you go on a show as a guest star . . . sometimes they don't give you the time of day. But they were a really special cast. You could tell there was something special there, more than just your usual group."

In the back-to-back "Mac Is a Serial Killer" and "Dennis Looks Like a Registered Sex Offender," the titles again were quite literal in setting up the storylines: Mac's friends thought Mac might be the local serial killer on the loose, because he was being uncharacteristically evasive. But he was killing no one; he had started dating Carmen, the transgender woman he was seeing in season 1, and didn't want his pals to know. The possibility of crime afoot did allow Charlie to engage in his obsession with *Law & Order*, especially when he and Frank interviewed Mrs. Mac about whether she thought her son could be killing people around the city. Mrs. Mac sold him out, but there's a good chance it was because she wanted them to leave her house so she could watch television. In the end, The Gang did find the real serial killer, who was still pretty close to home for one of them.

And in "Dennis Looks Like a Registered Sex Offender," overcrowding at a local prison resulted in early release for some inmates, including Dennis-look-alike child molester Wendell Albright (Howerton with padding and facial prosthetics) and Luther, Mac's dad. Luther wanted his son's help in making amends with some people from his past, but The Gang assumed he really wanted to do them harm. Dennis had his own problems… not only did his friends think the depiction of Wendell on the flyers looked like him, so did everyone else who saw the flyers (including Luther, who knew Wendell from lockup). Dee used this information to mess with her brother's head when she took him to a park and told a group of dads the shirtless man doing exercises and talking to their children was a convicted child molester (obviously she was still upset about the way Dennis messed with her head about Lil' Kev). Dennis was on the business end of an ass-kicking, but Dee helped him make it right in the end, thanks to a favorite from The Gang's get-out-of-scrapes arsenal: they blackmailed Wendell to leave town.

Elsewhere, Charlie and Frank were involved in a domestic dispute. Frank was as anarchical as ever, but he craved the cooking and cleaning and sexual fulfillment of a "bang maid" (exactly what it sounds like in Frank vocabulary), so he moved in with Charlie's mom. Viewers were in for a rare treat: dinner at Mrs. Mac's home, with four Gang parents, as chef Charlie wanted to get his mom drunk so she would alienate Frank and send him back to the sofa bed he and Charlie shared at Charlie's apartment.

Mac, meanwhile, was trying to get another couple together: his parents. Mac even tried to gussy up his grunting ma by slapping a Christmas bow on the top of her head. But Charlie's need to break up his mom and (maybe) dad was more powerful than Mac's matchmaking—besides, Bonnie and Luther were super flirty with each other—and the dinner party ended with Mac blaming Charlie for ruining his childhood dreams of his parents reuniting.

But there was one more Mac fantasy to be decimated, tying up his childhood torments into a package as neat as Mrs. Mac with a bow on her head. Mac and Charlie called the cops on Luther when they reviewed his list of people he wanted to redeem himself to, mistaking it for his hit list. They were both on it. But when they arrived at Bonnie's house to see Luther being led away in a cop car, they found out the list was a collection of people Luther wanted to make amends to. He had been arrested only because the officers caught him violating his parole when he bought three airplane tickets to New York ... because he wanted to take Mac and Charlie to the Baseball Hall of Fame in Cooperstown, another dream turned into a nightmare.

"You weren't going to kill me, of course you weren't going to kill me! I'm your son!" Mac said.

"No," laughed Luther. "I wasn't going to kill you. But I'm going to now. As soon as I get out, I'm gonna kill ya."

It was that rare television season that didn't have a clunker in its lineup, and *It's Always Sunny* was on such a creative streak that the final four episodes—in the show's longest season—were all among the series' best.

"The Gang Gets Whacked (Part 1)" and "The Gang Gets Whacked (Part 2)" saw The Gang inadvertently indebted to local gangsters after finding and selling a stash of cocaine that belonged to the mob. Frank refused to get them out of this jam, so it was up to Charlie, Dee, Mac, and Dennis to come up with $25,000 for mob repayment. Charlie sold the coke for a few hundred bucks, which Dee used to buy pills, which Charlie sold to a bunch of crazy lawn jockeys at a racetrack, where he fell in love with a female horse named Peter Nincompoop. He and Dee then used that money to buy more cocaine, which they planned to sell and pay off the mob, until they got a taste for the coke and snorted all of it themselves. Mac donned a velour tracksuit and tried to join in with the gangsters threatening The Gang, and Frank, holding steadfast on not saving his Paddy's cohorts with his money, did agree to pimp Dennis out to cougars at the local country club (complete with a gold chalice for Frank's cereal, and Frank slapping Dennis and manipulating him to "do right" by Frank). Rickety Cricket was pulled into the drama when Charlie bribed him into selling what little cocaine he and Dee had left to his fellow "street urchins" in exchange for Cricket being allowed to move in with Dee. Unbelievably, this part of the plan worked, and they held in their hands enough money to pay off the mob. So they doubled down and gave Cricket money to do it again, and this time he used it to buy two old trash cans to use as drums and write a musical. This crazy, over-the-top-farce—there's a scene straight out of a Three Stooges clip where Frank and Mac took turns slapping Dennis—culminated at Paddy's, where the mob showed up looking for their money, everyone pulled guns on each other, and Frank ended up saving the day after all, sort of: Dennis sold his pimp chalice and raised the twenty-five grand to wipe out The Gang's debt.

And then it got really weird: in the tag scene, Cricket, his legs broken by the mob, who thought he tried to force himself on the mob boss's wife, was sitting in a busy Philly street, playing his garbage can drums, as Peter Nincompoop galloped by.

But they had plenty of weird left for season 3's penultimate episode, "Bums: Making a Mess All Over the City," when The Gang decided responsibility for solving the city's homeless problem fell upon them. Dee and Mac joined a citizens watch program (until they learned they weren't assigned weapons and struck out on their own), and Frank, Dennis, and Charlie bought an old cop car and an even older cat at the junkyard. Frank even shelled out money for cop uniforms so he and Dennis could enjoy perks from citizens grateful for the pair of Reynolds "officers" keeping them safe—i.e., free hot dogs from a street vendor. But when they left Charlie out of their uniform scam, and started actively harassing and stealing from the locals, Charlie whipped up a costume of his own, in honor of Frank Serpico, the famous whistleblower on corrupt NYPD cops portrayed by Al Pacino in *Serpico*, the 1973 Oscar-nominated movie. Charlie was also salty about Dennis prioritizing his junkyard cat (who he named Agent Jack Bauer after Kiefer Sutherland's counterterrorism agent on *24*), but mostly he adopted a decent Pacino imitation and took his duty to his (fake) badge seriously. He went so far as to blow up Frank's cop car (an explosion that Agent Jack Bauer survived) and record an accounting of Frank and Dennis's corruption, which he delivered on the sidewalk outside of city hall, in an envelope addressed to the "mare" (Charlie's spelling of "mayor").

As usual, The Gang's good—but mostly selfish—intentions accomplished almost nothing, but the episode included a couple of very special touches. In the opening scene, Mac wore a T-shirt that read *WHAT ARE YOU LOOKING AT DICKNOSE*. It was a nod to episode director Jerry Levine and a T-shirt he wore in the 1985 coming-of-age movie *Teen Wolf*. RCG had let Levine know they were huge fans of the movie and his performance as Stiles, the best friend of Michael J. Fox's titular teen werewolf.

"Rob wanted to wear a T-shirt that I wore in that movie, to pay homage to it," Levine says. "And he would, of course, cut the sleeves off of it. He was very sweet. He said, 'Would you mind if I wear this?' I said, 'Please.'"

And when Dee and Mac were confronted by a character named "Tweaker" while they were on patrol to make the streets safe from crime, the man pointing a gun at them was played by McElhenney's father—and Olson's soon-to-be father-in-law—Bob McElhenney.

For the capper of the stand-out third season, The Gang once again revisited the topic of Charlie's (alleged) illiteracy. "The Gang Dances Their Asses Off" was foremost simply a very fun episode. It was also the first time—but certainly not the last—The Gang would have occasion to see their enemies congregate for the sole purpose of sabotaging them. Charlie was excited to tell his friends he had signed Paddy's up to host a dance contest—a dance marathon, actually—but when they read the contract, the free publicity they thought they were getting turned into a desperate fight for the bar's survival. When looking over the document, Charlie mistook the "z" in the word "prize" for a "d" . . . he thought the word was "pride," and he had put Paddy's under "pride" because he was proud of it. "Your illiteracy has screwed us again!" Mac shouted at him. But with the bar on the line in this legally binding piece of paper, Frank said there was just one solution to the jam they were in: The Gang had to dance.

The endurance competition was broadcast live on local Q102 radio, hosted by the Q Crew DJs (played by twin brothers Jason and Randy Sklar). Paddy's was packed, so there was the potential to sell plenty of hooch to thirsty dancers, in a last-person-standing contest that could last for hours or even days. There was a bar full of people who each intended to be the next Paddy's Pub owner, but the biggest threats came from two particularly motivated contestants: the Waitress and Rickety Cricket. The Waitress wanted retribution for the many wrongs perpetrated against her by The Gang, and she was in a desperate cash crunch. Cricket came armed with newly enhanced legs, bionic-like according to Dee. He needed the souped-up pins, of course, because during his last interaction with The Gang, they'd involved him in a scheme with the mob, who broke his legs. And now he was consumed with a desire to use his magic limbs to dance his way to avengement.

As has always been the case for both the Waitress and Cricket, though, the event was a bust. The marathon was a long session (more than forty-eight hours) of squabbling among The Gang, and the Waitress's attempt to win Paddy's fell prey to Dennis's plot to get back at Charlie for dancing with a random contestant Dennis was trying to sleep with. Cricket's leg braces gave out early in the night and dashed his hopes, but Dee found a way to use him in her machinations to pit her brother and friends against one another to win the bar for herself… until one wrong step by Larry, the homeless man Frank had hired as his insurance policy to win the marathon, resulted in Cricket pulling a Jeff Gillooly and clubbing Dee's knee instead of that of his intended victim, Larry. Dee was left in agony in a heap on the floor, with her fellow losers Dennis and Mac (who had knocked each other to the floor while fighting), and Charlie (who had passed out after eating the cough syrup–laced brownie Dee gave him). Larry was the marathon winner as the last man (barely) standing, meaning Frank was the owner of the bar, still.

In addition to the treats of Mac breaking out his signature karate-inspired dance moves and Charlie proving himself to be a surprisingly graceful dancer, the eventful season ended with The Gang miraculously still in charge of Paddy's. And Mac offering an understatement of a recommendation for Charlie: "That kid *really* needs to learn how to read!"

As The Gang continued to build on its fan base with these defining season 3 moments, the episode that they now wish they could, at the least, title differently continued to stand out most of all. And not because of the political incorrectness of the R-word or the storyline of that part of the installment.

It was because of the song. *That* song, "Dayman," and its title hero's wish to challenge the Nightman to show that he was not only, as the lyrics went, the champion of the sun, but also the master of karate, and friendship. For everyone.

If those words sound like the guileless sentiments of a prepubescent boy, you're close: they were written by a pair of professional television writers, and they spilled forth from the top of their TV writer heads in about a minute.

The writers: Scott Marder and Rob Rosell, Syracuse University friends turned Los Angeles roommates and writing partners who joined *It's Always Sunny in Philadelphia* for season 3. The writing team quickly became so prolific at coming up with the kinds of fantastical tales The Gang likes to get up to that many a story RCG has told about the writers' room during interviews or on *The Always Sunny Podcast* begin with "Marder and Rosell," as they're referred to, though it's usually more giddily pronounced as MarderandRosell, as if they're one person, just like how Charlie Kelly thinks of Daryl Hall and John Oates.

Rosell, whose *Sunny* fandom was cemented with season 2's "Mac Bangs Dennis' Mom," says he and Marder submitted a writing sample that at first failed to sell RCG on offering them a position in the inaugural *IASIP* writers' room. A second sample earned positive feedback and a meeting with McElhenney, Day, and Howerton, and the quintet instantly realized there was a common comedy sensibility among them.

"We were kinda off and running," Rosell says, as he and Marder were hired into a writers' room where they were in some ways more experienced than their bosses.

While RCG had never been in any other writers' rooms before they began writing *It's Always Sunny*, Marder and Rosell were staff writers on *Cavemen*, the 2007 ABC comedy adapted from the GEICO cavemen insurance commercials. Though short-lived—only six of the thirteen episodes produced aired in the United States—*Cavemen* gave Marder and Rosell the basic how-to of working within a writers' room structure. And despite the fact that RCG had produced seventeen episodes before Marder and Rosell joined the fun, the series creators were missing some key operating information that the new duo was able to shed light on. Namely: lunch.

McElhenney and company were unaware that when it comes to the writers' room, there is such a thing as free lunch.

"They didn't get their lunches taken care of, which is, generally you get your lunches brought to you in the writers' room, because usually, you are working so much," Rosell says. "I remember Rob [McElhenney] being shocked about that, and calling FX about it, and them saying yes."

With lunch squared away, the writers delved into brainstorming mode for the critical season. Though the fan base had grown among enthusiastic viewers, and creatives in Hollywood, The Gang's ratings were not yet in such a position that the show was assured renewal. But with fifteen episodes to show their stuff and a staff of scribes to compose those escapades, *Sunny* had developed into its strongest shape yet.

The beginning of what would take the comedy to its next, and ultimate, inflection point (after the addition of DeVito) began in those early days of the new writers' room. Howerton shared with the other writers that his wish list included an episode in which The Gang started a band. It was one of the many stories on the series that was partially or wholly inspired by real life. In addition to possessing a fantastic singing voice himself, and having access to Day's imaginative songwriting abilities and multiple-instrument-playing skills, Howerton was part of a band. His actor friend and fellow Juilliard student Sam Witwer is the frontman of the alternative metal band the Crashtones, and around the time of the creation of "Dayman," Howerton had joined the Crashtones onstage for a few live performances. He recalled that they began every show with a cover of "Flash." The "ah-ahs" were stuck in his head.

Howerton had the idea for the story of the Lil' Kev episode, and it was assigned to Marder and Rosell to write the script. The "Dayman" song was a "total afterthought," Rosell said. "It was written in less than a minute. I don't think anybody really thought that much of it, especially that [it would] become this great quintessential thing in the show."

Marder and Rosell brought their draft back into the writers' room, and everyone liked the whole script, but they were cracking up when they got to "champion of the sun, you're a master of karate and friendship for everyone." No one could stop laughing at these tossed-off lyrics. One of the *Sunny* writers' room toys—every writers' room is stocked with various toys, be it Rubik's Cubes, games, LEGO bricks, cards, or Nerf accoutrements, to help keep anxious hands busy and blocked minds open—was a small musical keyboard, just like the one Charlie played in his apartment when he and Dennis crafted "Dayman" (it was, in fact, the exact one used in the episode). Charlie fired it up in the writers' room as they sat around reading the script.

"We started to write a little melody to the lyrics," Day said. "And then Glenn . . . [who] has a fascination with the *Flash Gordon* soundtrack . . . almost like it happens in the episode, Glenn starts adding these falsetto 'ah-ahs' to the melody that I'm writing. We're in the writers' room, and we're starting to laugh our heads off. So that actual discovery of the 'ah-ahs' got kind of re-created in the episode.

"The following week, the whole crew was still singing the song," Day added. "But then in the editing room, we weren't loving the episode, even though that scene was really funny. We sent it to the network, and they said, 'This is one of the funniest ones we've ever seen!' So we kind of stepped back from it and looked at it from the outside in and said, 'You know what? This is funny.' . . . [But] we truly didn't know that that episode or that song would be as popular as it was."

The "writing" for the rest of the lyrics in Charlie's music from the Lil' Kev episode—the "Nightman" portion that shocked Mac and

Frank during the Chemical Toilet rehearsal—was equally impressive and spontaneous: Day made it up on the spot. During the "Sweet Dee's Dating a [Redacted] Person" episode of their podcast, RCG recalled how Charlie took the stage in his Bob Dylan–esque getup, asked that the camera be trained on him, and said they should "just see what happens." What happened was that he not only improvised the rhyming "Nightman" riff on the spot, but he also had everyone, from the series' regular cameraman to McElhenney, unable to stop laughing.

"To allow ourselves the freedom for each one of our characters or performers to come on the show [and] be like, 'All right, just turn your brain off and let it rip,'" Day said. "We've gotten so much good stuff out of doing that."

In this instance, they ultimately got a musical out of it. And the pathway to a record-breaking television run.

Prepare to jump ahead in time for a bit, won't you?

The "Dayman" and "Nightman" songs were among the first things shot for season 3, and the earworminess of the tunes stuck with the *Sunny* crew the rest of that year's run. Viewers wouldn't see the Lil' Kev episode until a little more than halfway through the season, and though the cast wasn't immediately aware of it, the fans were belting out the songs, too, "ah-ahs," bonkers lyrics, and all.

By the time RCG and company were ready to return to the writers' room for season 4, they had decided to take the idea of the musical episode further; they wanted to write and perform an actual, entire musical that would form a *Sunny* episode.

But what would be the theme of this musical? And why would The Gang write and perform a musical at all?

"That was a point of contention and discussion, not only amongst ourselves, but also with the network," McElhenney told *GQ*. "At that point, we weren't at a place, as a show, where we were just doing whatever we wanted and then finding ways to justify it. We still felt constrained by reality."

Thankfully, they got over that quickly and realized the obvious answer: they should simply double down on the Dayman and Nightman storyline they had so memorably dropped on viewers back in season 3. Charlie Kelly would write a whole musical about the adventures of the Nightman and the Dayman, at odds with each other, until the Dayman—initially a boy-aged person—would battle the Nightman and evolve into the Dayman, who was in love with a princess who worked at a coffee shop.

Charlie Kelly—and Charlie Day, with the help of McElhenney, Howerton, and Day's pal Cormac Bluestone—did just that. To close out the show's fourth season, "The Nightman Cometh" would delight *IASIP* fans with another musical experience, complete with a formal stage, sets, props, costumes, a script, and a director (and, with the title, a cheeky nod to Eugene O'Neill's play *The Iceman Cometh*, about a group of alcoholics who waste their time at their local bar, trying to mooch free hooch and not progressing at all in their lives).

And when TV Charlie presented The Gang with his creation—the fact that he had written and planned to stage a musical—RCG cleverly worked into the plot that The Gang was also curious about why someone would write a musical for no good reason. The answer, just as clever, would be revealed at the end of the musical, and thus the episode tied up the story in a nice little bow of heartbreaking reality for TV Charlie. Real-life Charlie and the rest of the *Sunny* cast and crew were about to launch a journey that would be more fun than they ever could have imagined.

But again, why had Charlie written a musical for no good reason? The Gang assumed they were going to be part of the production, but they demanded to know why were they doing it. Whose face were they going to shove it into, who was the mark, what was the angle? Or as Mac put it so perfectly pithily: "Who are we doing it versus?"

They didn't believe Charlie had no ulterior motives, of course, but when he threatened to give The Gang's roles in his musical to other people, they calmed down . . . until they got to the first rehearsal at the "fine local theater" Charlie called his venue. It was actually the auditorium of a local elementary school. Artemis served as his assistant, and as soon as Charlie assigned roles—Frank as Troll, Dee as Coffee Shop Waitress Princess, Mac as Lead Boy/Dayman, and Dennis as the Nightman—there were issues. Frank wanted to play the troll naked. Dennis and Mac wanted to swap parts (because Mac wanted to be the Nightman, with cat eyes and karate chops as he walked across the stage). Dee didn't like that the story made it sound like her character was in love with a little boy. They aggravated Charlie to the brink; he was talking about himself in the third person.

One bright spot in Charlie Kelly's *The Nightman Cometh* musical production team: Gladys, the sweet, elderly lady who provided piano accompaniment. Gladys was portrayed by Mae Laborde, a bubbly actress who was ninety-nine years old when she made her first appearance on *Sunny*, and had celebrated her one hundredth birthday by the time she returned for another classic *IASIP* episode, season 5's "The D.E.N.N.I.S. System."

Laborde, a former bookkeeper for bandleader Lawrence Welk, began her career as an actress at age ninety-three; she earned her Screen Actors Guild and American Federation of Television and Radio Artists cards (SAG and AFTRA didn't merge until 2012) when she was in her mid-nineties. A popular presence in her Santa Monica community, the four-foot-ten whirlwind was known for driving her whale of a car—a canary-yellow 1977 Oldsmobile Delta 88—with speed and precision around her neighborhood. Her acting career started, in fact, after her former neighbor, bestselling author of *The Soloist* and Pulitzer-nominated *Los Angeles Times* reporter Steve Lopez, wrote an affectionate article in which he rode along with Laborde, while asking her for driving tips because his vision was being impacted as he got older.

Los Angeles talent agent Sherri Spillane, an ex-wife of crime novelist Mickey Spillane and the onetime agent for Tonya Harding, Joey Buttafuoco, and John Wayne Bobbitt, read Lopez's 2002 article.

After so much time spent working on behalf of the punch lines of the 1990s, Spillane saw Mae's charm and spirit as the chance to help guide a more positive, feel-good Hollywood career, and contacted Laborde. A star was born.

"She's got this way about her that's so endearing that everybody falls in love with her," Spillane said of her client and friend. "She's got that cute little face, and she's very funny."

Laborde, who outlived her husband, Nicholas, and her only child, Shirley, resided for decades in a little cottage near the beach, and in a constant effort to connect with people, she read tea leaves for them, and she graduated from the Santa Monica Citizens Police Academy. She supplemented her Hollywood money by growing tomatoes and selling them to a local restaurant. She kept a scrapbook with all the clippings she'd saved of press coverage on her prolific late-in-life career, and her advice for living a good, long life: she didn't drink alcohol or smoke cigarettes, she ate a very nutritious diet (which she prepared herself), and, most importantly, she said, she thought positive thoughts.

And those stories she told Charlie Kelly about Calvin Coolidge? She told them to Charlie Day and the rest of the *Sunny* cast, too, improvising part of her way through a brief but oh-so-memorable scene. "Nightman Cometh" director Matt Shakman said Mae was so happy to talk to the "beautiful people," as she called them in one of her spontaneous lines, that her stories about Calvin Coolidge sometimes preempted the scripted lines she was supposed to say. What was written as a small scene turned out to be quite possibly the longest one he ever shot for the show.

She was as delightful in person as she appeared to be to viewers, and as funny: Howerton said of her enunciation of The Gang's iconic, oft-used line "What is *happening*?": "No one has ever delivered it better than she did."

Sadly, Mae didn't have the chance to return to the series for a third appearance; she died in her sleep—at age 102—on January 9, 2012, in Santa Monica. She had lived there for more than eighty years.

☀ ☀ ☀

Meanwhile, Gladys, with her playful banter with Charlie Kelly, was the only person not going off script (in some cases literally) during the production of the musical *The Nightman Cometh* within the episode. Mac insisted on wearing contact lenses that gave him the very real look of a feline, and he did include many a karate move as he made his way across the stage. Sweet Dee was so displeased about her princess-attired coffee shop waitress singing about being in love with a "tiny boy, little boy, baby boy," that she wrote a follow-up song to assure the audience she was not doing anything improper with a child, and that she was considered a catch and available to mingle with interested gentlemen after the show. Frank was caught chewing gum during rehearsals, ignoring Charlie's instructions not to. Then there was Dennis, not making any demands but instead being annoying by being too agreeable with his musical director; Dennis's egomania was juiced up by the prospect of being front and center with a small crowd focused on him, so he was willing to do anything, sing anything, or move in any way Charlie commanded—anything to get some of that sweet, sweet attention trained on him.

Everyone—from Day, Hornsby, and Bluestone, who wrote most of the music for the songs and storylines in the musical; to McElhenney and Howerton, who helped write the lyrics and additional storyline details; to the *IASIP* wardrobe department, whose costumes have become perennial Halloween favorites and pop up routinely at *Sunny*-related fan events like comic cons and live podcast tapings; to production designer Scott Cobb and his crew's simple, colorful, and realistic stage design that, in the story, sprung from the fervent imagination of Charlie Kelly—worked together to make "The Nightman Cometh" the series' signature episode.

"In my mind, and I think this might have been [in the script], but Charlie [Kelly] built the sets. Charlie designed the set, because it takes place in Charlie's apartment," says Cobb, the original *Sunny* production designer. "So I built a little theater model, a little maquette, and then thought about what would work with this sort of ridiculous musical that they'd written. And piecing this thing together is kind of a little cartoony, but also kind of intentionally trying to be dramatic, and just kind of being very theater-light, but giving room for [it being] just sort of ostentatious and big. It wasn't supposed to be a serious little set. And also, it had to be something very interpretive, kind of abstract in a sense. It couldn't be anything like the real thing, because that actually was a set."

The *Nightman* set of Charlie's apartment even included a nod to the infamous German shepherd painting that had been removed in season 2 because RCG found it distracting. So did fans, but they loved it anyway, and so the creators gave it a proper *Sunny*-appropriate funeral later in the series.

Director Shakman's extensive theater experience was also a boon to "The Nightman Cometh." The episode was originally to be directed by Fred Savage, but when preparation for the installment went into overtime, it was transferred into Shakman's block of episodes, which made him very happy. Still most known for his plenteous output of television directing (including *Six Feet Under*, *Psych*, *House*, *Mad Men*, *Game of Thrones*, *Billions*, *Succession*, and *WandaVision*), Shakman directed the upcoming *Fantastic Four* movie, and also founded the now-defunct Black Dahlia Theatre in Los Angeles, in 2001, and was appointed as the artistic director of the Geffen Playhouse, also in LA, in 2017.

Shakman decided to make the musical part of the episode as realistic as possible. He even had the cast rehearsing the rehearsal of the musical within the episode. It was his idea to bring in one hundred extras to be seated on folding chairs in the auditorium as an audience for the live performance. That audience had no idea what they were about to watch, and most were unfamiliar with *It's Always Sunny in Philadelphia*. Shakman directed the cast to go through the entire musical anyway, and he captured the audience's befuddled reactions. He also included The Gang's friend (and Frank's sometime lover) Artemis in the production, acting as sort of Charlie's stage manager. These were the kinds of details that ensured the episode's humor would shine through.

Image Credit: Bluebush Productions/3 Arts Entertainment/Rch/Kobal/Shutterstock

FX's marketing department didn't always have the biggest budgets to help *It's Always Sunny in Philadelphia* grow, but efforts like this season 7 promotional photo made up for it with sheer ingenuity. The best touch in this department store family portrait spoof: even Charlie's cat is color coordinated with The Gang thanks to a pair of (Charlie-invented) Kitten Mittens.

The friendship between Charlie Day, Rob McElhenney, and Glenn Howerton led to the creation of *It's Always Sunny in Philadelphia*; and the friendship between FX executive John Landgraf and Danny DeVito led to a casting suggestion that would help push the series to unparalleled success and a spot in television history. It was now–FX chairman Landgraf's suggestion that the producers add DeVito to the cast in season 2, bringing an endless well of debauchery and hilarity for sixteen seasons and counting.

Image Credit: WENN Rights Ltd/Alamy Stock Photo

Image Credit: Patrick McElhenney/© FX Networks/Courtesy Everett Collection

Trash Man. Mantis Toboggan, M.D. Seamus. Man-Spider. Man-cheetah. Ongo Gablogian, art collector. They're all alter egos of Danny DeVito's Frank Reynolds. But the fascinatingly coifed Ongo, who liked to dismiss most art as "derivative," is the Frank character who has inspired the most *It's Always Sunny* fan tattoos.

Image Credit: Patrick McElhenney/© FX/Courtesy Everett Collection

The Gang never misses a chance to don a costume or create an alter ego. In "The Gang Wrestles for the Troops," Mac, Dennis, and Charlie fashioned themselves as the "Birds of War" to compete in an ill-conceived but (sorta) well-intentioned event to honor American soldiers.

Image Credit: Abaca Press/Alamy Stock Photo

Charlie Day, Danny DeVito, Glenn Howerton, and series crew greet *It's Always Sunny* fans while filming scenes for the season 3 episode "Bums: Making a Mess All Over the City" on the streets of Philadelphia in 2007.

The live *Nightman Cometh* show is performed at the Moore Theatre in Seattle on September 22, 2009.

Image Credit: *Courtesy of Wesley Rosenblum*

The live *Nightman Cometh* show is performed at the Beacon Theatre in New York City on September 16, 2009.

Image Credit: *Courtesy of Brandon Rosenblum*

Image Credit: Courtesy of Cormac Bluestone

DeVito had the bus wrapped with the promotional photos and graphics from *Sunny*'s fifth season, which premiered while the cast was on the road, living the rock star life with the live performances. To that end, DeVito made sure the bus had a well-stocked bar and refreshments, and planned nice dinners and hotel stays so he and his castmates and the *Nightman Cometh* crew would feel like rock stars.

Image Credit: Courtesy of John Muraro

The author's tickets and afterparty passes from the live *Nightman Cometh* performance at the Beacon Theatre in NYC on September 16, 2009. Still waiting on that oft-discussed *Nightman Cometh* live revival on Broadway.

Charlie Day and Kaitlin Olson combine vulnerability and pure comedic talent to make one of *Sunny*'s most reliably great character pairings, as in this season 8 episode, "Charlie and Dee Find Love." Spoiler alert: they didn't, though Charlie made a romantic decision that shocked even the rest of The Gang.

Image Credit: Bluebush Productions/3 Arts Entertainment/Rch/Kobal/Shutterstock

Image Credit: Bluebush Productions/3 Arts Entertainment/Rch/Kobal/Shutterstock

They've been roommates, they once considered a platonic marriage for the legal benefits, and they even thought they might be father and son for a time. *Sunny*'s strangest friendship is also its best, as Danny DeVito and Charlie Day's Frank and Charlie rank right up there with classic TV comedy duos like Oscar and Felix, Ralph and Norton, and Joey and Chandler. Except more demented, of course.

Image Credit: Bluebush Productions/3 Arts Entertainment/Rch/Kobal/Shutterstock

What had driven Sweet Dee to accompany her booze and cigarettes with a dive into a month-old cake procured from the garbage? Her Paddy's Pub cohorts, of course, who then unfolded an elaborate scheme to "help" her feel better in the season 9 premiere, "The Gang Broke Dee," one of the many *IASIP* episodes that showcase the perpetual Emmy-worthiness of Kaitlin Olson.

Image Credit: Bluebush Productions/3 Arts Entertainment/Rch/Kobal/Shutterstock

And then there's this relationship between Rob McElhenney's Mac and Glenn Howerton's Dennis. They're roommates, and what probably qualifies as best friends within the dynamics of The Gang. But in some of their most infamous exploits, they might also more accurately be described as coconspirators?

Image Credit: Patrick McElhenney/© FX Networks/ Courtesy Everett Collection

Nate Mooney and Jimmi Simpson are The Gang's milk-loving, robe-wearing, unibrowed enemies, but *It's Always Sunny* fans can't get enough of them and all of their similarly ornery, monobrowed kin.

Image Credit: Patrick McElhenney/© FX Networks/ Courtesy Everett Collection

Undeniably, some of *Sunny*'s most hilarious moments have come courtesy of these two, and the genius performances of their portrayers: theater veteran Sandy Martin as the chain-smoking, grunting Mrs. Mac and the late *Pee-wee's Playhouse* and the Groundlings legend Lynne Marie Stewart as Bonnie Kelly, Charlie's sweet, bad boy–loving mom.

The Gang waves at fans in Philadelphia while filming the controversial season 12 premiere musical episode "The Gang Turns Black."

Image Credit: WENN Rights Ltd/Alamy Stock Photo

Image Credit: Patrick McElhenney/© FX Networks/Courtesy Everett Collection

Sports and beer frequently factor into *Sunny* episodes, but they never combined as cleverly as they did in the season 10 premiere "The Gang Beats Boggs," in which The Gang took a plane ride and tried to break Baseball Hall of Famer Wade Boggs's storied record of drinking seventy beers during one cross-country plane trip. Boggs himself, who addresses the real story of his libation exploits in chapter 11, guest-starred in the episode.

Image Credit: *Bluebush Productions/3 Arts Entertainment/Rch/Kobal/Shutterstock*

On "Mac Day" in season 9, The Gang had to do whatever Mac wanted them to do, so that meant Dennis, Dee, Charlie, and Frank had to make their shirts sleeveless.

Image Credit: *Patrick McElhenney/© FX Networks/Courtesy Everett Collection*

Season 11's "McPoyle vs. Ponderosa: The Trial of the Century" not only featured director Guillermo del Toro (a *Sunny* fan who had cast Charlie Day in his film *Pacific Rim*), but also several fan favorite recurring characters. Among them: Andrew Friedman (far left) as Charlie's hapless attorney uncle Jack Kelly, and Brian Unger (far right) as the Lawyer, who has been on the losing end of repeated devilries by The Gang.

Image Credit: WENN

There are few things (or people) Dennis loves more than he loves his Range Rover. This behind-the-scenes shot taken during production in Philadelphia in 2011 shows a complicated and unglamorous view of capturing Dennis in his sweet ride.

Image Credit: Gilbert Carrasquillo/Getty Images

Charlie Day is suited up to play everyone's favorite unofficial sports mascot, Green Man. Former Philadelphia Eagles Pro Bowl offensive lineman Jon Runyan and *Sunny* guest star is off to the right as they filmed scenes from season 4's "America's Next Top Paddy's Billboard Model Contest" in Philadelphia in 2008.

Image Credit: Alamy Stock Photo

Frank Reynolds... Feminist AF? Discuss, prompted by this iconic shirt sported by the iconic Danny DeVito in season 13's "The Gang Beats Boggs: Ladies Reboot."

Image Credit: Allison Dinner/EPA-EFE/Shutterstock

Their efforts, collectively and individually, have yet to be acknowledged by the Television Academy (inexplicably, the series' only Emmy nominations have come for Outstanding Stunt Coordination). But The Gang was finally invited to the party, literally, when Day, Howerton, McElhenney, Olson, and DeVito (previously an Emmy winner for *Taxi*) were asked to be presenters at the 75th annual Emmy Awards in January 2024.

Image Credit: MediaPunch/Alamy Stock Photo

It may look like Glenn Howerton standing with his *Sunny* castmates at the season 14 premiere in 2019, but it's actually Mac's infamous Dennis sex doll. Mac purchased the toy during season 13 when Dennis was off in North Dakota playing house with his son and the woman he'd impregnated during an unplanned layover in season 10's "The Gang Beats Boggs" plane trip.

Image Credit: AJ Pics/Alamy Stock Photo

At times, they may be each other's worst enemy, but twins Dee and Dennis Reynolds are also formidable adversaries for others, especially when they decide to team up together. In the season 6 holiday episode, "A Very Sunny Christmas," they plotted against Frank, who continued his lifelong tradition of gifting himself the things he knew they most coveted.

Image Credit: Alamy Stock Photo

From the season 11 finale "The Gang Goes to Hell: Part Two," in which The Gang nearly drowned after being locked in jail during a cruise, and the actors had been trained by (Emmy-nominated) *Sunny* stunt coordinator Marc Scizak to be able to hold their breath underwater for two minutes. But when they prepared to swim to the top of the eighteen-foot underwater tank, Danny DeVito got stuck halfway up and had to be rescued by the safety divers. Charlie Day later told Conan O'Brien DeVito was so frustrated by the experience he went straight home after getting out of the tank.

Image Credit: Alamy Stock Photo

Rob McElhenney's overall plan for *It's Always Sunny* was to deconstruct the network sitcom. But for season 7, he wanted to get specific, focusing on how the casts of particularly successful comedies would grow more and more attractive as the seasons progressed, thanks to the luxuries of becoming wealthier. His deconstruction of that idea: he gained fifty pounds in three months to introduce viewers to "Fat Mac."

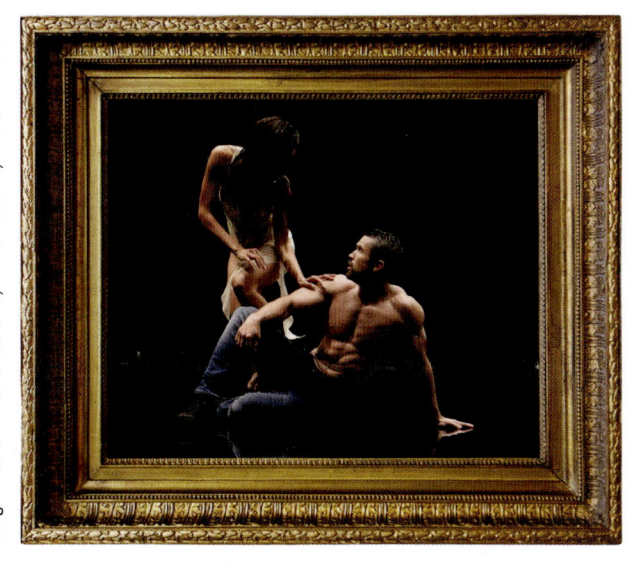

Image Credit: Patrick McElhenney/©FXX/Courtesy Everett Collection

In the unusually sincere and serious episode "Mac Finds His Pride," Rob McElhenney and dancer Kylie Shea performed a beautiful, intense dance, for which McElhenney spent months preparing. The season 13 gem was universally praised by fans and critics, who had watched Mac's long journey to accepting his sexuality and telling his father he is gay.

Image Credit: Patrick McElhenney/© FX/Courtesy Everett Collection

Breaking Bad star and longtime *IASIP* fan Aaron Paul had been on the *Sunny* cast's guest star wish list for years. In season 16's "Celebrity Booze: The Ultimate Cash Grab," Paul and *Breaking Bad* costar Bryan Cranston appeared as themselves in a storyline that saw the Emmy-winning actors promote their Dos Hombres mezcal brand. Rob McElhenney, Glenn Howerton, and Charlie Day's Irish whiskey brand, Four Walls, was not mentioned during the cheeky episode.

After all, it's no small thing to make a great episode of television comedy out of a story that, it seems obvious to (almost) everyone, is about a young person's experience with a pedophile.

It's that "almost," though, where the laugh-out-loud humor resided.

"Any time we deal with that kind of subject matter, I like to think it's coming from a more intelligent place," Charlie Day said. "A rape joke is not remotely a funny thing; a man writing a musical that he *thinks* is about self-empowerment, and not realizing that all his lyrics sound like they're about a child being molested, is a funny thing. The joke is coming from confusion and misunderstanding, which are classic tropes of all comedy."

"Classic" and "comedy" are most definitely the way fans immediately thought of "The Nightman Cometh" when it premiered on November 20, 2008. And though the number of viewers totaled 1.3 million—a Saturday morning episode of *SpongeBob SquarePants* and a Saturday evening syndicated episode of *NCIS* each earned three times that number—neither the folks at Nielsen nor the folks at FX had any idea of just how influential The Gang at Paddy's Pub was becoming among television comedy fans.

☀ ☀ ☀

Like the *IASIP* crew back in season 3, when the Dayman first came "ah-ah-ing" his way into the *Sunny* universe, fans really couldn't stop singing his praises, and his anthem about being a master of karate and friendship for everyone. They also loved those costumes.

Who wouldn't want to dress as a coffeepot-totin' pink princess, or a sunshine-yellow-tuxedoed suitor, or a silver-jumpsuited devil with a black stretchy codpiece (the series' costumers could have found no more appropriate piece of clothing for a character who is the self-proclaimed "golden god")?

The fans' love for this crazy show had grown immensely with the "Nightman Cometh" season finale, but social media wasn't yet the instantaneous review it has grown to be, and unless the *Sunny* stars ran into individual viewers here and there, they didn't know how zealous their fan base had grown.

Which is why they radically underestimated the popularity of Dayman, Nightman, and their story's music. They could all feel the momentum of the show begin to shift, though, and it was somewhat frustrating to end another great season on such a high note, then have to wait for almost a year to get back on the air and hopefully see that trajectory continue upward.

Then, in April 2009, they got an auspicious invitation.

Don McCloskey, a McElhenney musician friend from Philly, was going to be performing at the Troubadour in Los Angeles. The singer-songwriter thought the West Hollywood venue, legendary for so many performances—Elton John's first concert in America; comedian Lenny Bruce's arrest on obscenity charges for saying the word "schmuck" onstage; Richard Pryor's recording of his eponymous live debut album; Guns N' Roses' first show with their "classic" lineup in 1985—provided a perfect opportunity to invite McElhenney and his *It's Always Sunny* cohorts to join him onstage, sit in for a song, and share some of their many musical talents with him and his audience.

McCloskey had been a huge fan of "The Nightman Cometh," texting McElhenney to tell him it was his favorite *Sunny* episode. McElhenney and Olson said they were excited about the offer to perform with McCloskey, especially since they had already planned to be in the audience for his show. The singer was so happy his friends were joining him that he called Troubadour management and told them a few of his pals from the cast of *It's Always Sunny in Philadelphia* were joining him onstage for a couple of songs. The guy on the other end of the phone was unimpressed; he had never heard of *Sunny*. McCloskey told him he thought it would help sell tickets.

The Gang, or some members, anyway, were in. The Troubadour asked McCloskey how he would like to bill the events. His response: "Don McCloskey with special guests: *Some* of the cast members of *It's Always Sunny* singing songs from 'The Nightman Cometh.'"

Simple enough. Except what ensued was like a version of the telephone game, where every time information is shared it's changed a little bit. *LA Weekly* reported that the cast of *It's Always Sunny* would be performing *The Nightman Cometh*, implying the entire cast would be there. Fans responded so quickly that the Troubadour rep called McCloskey back and asked if he and his *Sunny* friends would like to do a second show. McElhenney said yes; it was just a cameo, a couple of songs, right?

But then the Troubadour website advertised the shows thusly: "The Cast of *It's Always Sunny in Philadelphia* Performing 'The Nightman Cometh' Live." Then, in smaller letters beneath that headline, the musician who had invited The Gang to perform with him was listed like a footnote to his own concert: "With Don McCloskey."

And before anyone could say anything different, could even make any corrections, two nights of this live performance sold out in seven minutes, the fastest sellout in the club's then fifty-two-year history. Hundreds of fans had rushed to buy tickets for the chance to see a TV episode performed live on a nightclub stage. So no matter how nervous some of The Gang might have been—and some (okay, all) of them were a bit nervous—they decided to embrace the adventure and give the fans what had been promised, though definitely not planned, anyway.

Bluestone also helped arrange the performances, and Shakman was requested to return as director for the Friday and Saturday night shows, on April 17 and 18. The sets from the television episode, the ones that Scott Cobb and his crew had fashioned to represent Charlie's apartment, were trucked off to the Troubadour. The show would include The Gang rehearsing the musical, then performing it, just like on TV. The entire main cast had committed to performing the live show in costume. Joining them: Artemis Pebdani and Mary Elizabeth Ellis, as Artemis and the Waitress, and a very special guest star standing in for Mae Laborde as Gladys: Rhea Perlman. Joining the fans in the audience: FX executives, including Landgraf, as well as *Sunny* director Fred Savage. McCloskey performed before the *Sunny*-related jollity, later joking that he had opened his own concert.

Oh, and that audience: they knew every word of "Dayman" and were not at all shy about singing along with the cast, as loudly as they could. The fans knew the dialogue, too, and some annoyed others by trying to repeat the words along with the cast. For an encore, the cast, including Perlman, returned to the stage and led a sing-along of "Dayman" with the audience. Ditto the second night, and Landgraf noted that the *Sunny* cast stood for nearly an hour on the stage after the show, signing the programs that had been designed for the special event. Collector's items, those.

"The Troubadour was stunning to us," Bluestone says. "I remember going to the [*Sunny*] office . . . and it was me, Rob, Glenn, Charlie, and Matt Shakman. And Rob is like, 'Okay, we have to do something at the Troubadour. We've kind of gotten involved, and apparently the show sold out faster than any show has, and they added a second night, and then that sold out. What are we gonna *do*?' So I think there were all these signs about the popularity of the show, but I think it's just a credit to everyone involved that none of us really were thinking about that. We just kept thinking 'How do we make people feel like they got their money's worth if they grace us by coming and seeing our show?'"

The serendipitous live performances were such a success that some people wanted more. Representatives at concert promoter company Live Nation took note of all the excitement surrounding the Troubadour shows—and all the tickets sold—and had a proposal for the *Sunny* cast: take that one live performance and turn it into a twenty-two-city tour.

With season 5 imminent, the timing was perfect to help promote the new episodes. But there was also some editing left to do and other preparations to finalize twelve new episodes. Besides, as fun and exhilarating as those Troubadour shows had turned out to be, they were also exhausting. Having to pull such a production together with so little time and planning was a feat; the genuine thrill of witnessing for the first time just how much their fans, en masse, appreciated everything they'd worked so hard to create provided an adrenaline rush that carried The Gang through those two wild nights. But to do it twenty-two more times, and take the whole shebang out on the road, across the country? That seemed daunting, overwhelming, even for the guys who had worked as writers/producers/actors on their series for four seasons.

Besides, Howerton had another big live event to coproduce: he was marrying his longtime girlfriend, actress Jill Latiano, in early September, and having time for a honeymoon would be nice, too.

No, twenty-two shows was not doable. But the cast was game for a shorter tour, a chance to share the experience of the live performance with even more fans, a chance to gain a little more widespread attention for the series heading into season 5, and, yeah, a chance to live like a rock star for a minute!

So they came to a compromise with Live Nation: from September 15 through September 25, a six-city tour—Boston (House of Blues), New York (Beacon Theatre), Philadelphia (two shows for the hometown crowd in the series' namesake city, at the Tower Theater in Upper Darby), San Francisco (Masonic Auditorium), Seattle (Moore Theatre), and Los Angeles (Hollywood Palladium)—with the season 5 premiere airing the night after the NYC show.

Howerton's honeymoon would have to wait; he and Latiano, who guest-starred in season 5's "The D.E.N.N.I.S. System" as the object of Dennis's creepy pursuit, did marry on September 5, in Silverado,

California, with their *It's Always Sunny* castmates in attendance. (A quick Google search will turn up photographic evidence of The Gang with the new marrieds at a photo backdrop, complete with silly props.)

Glenn and Jill would get to enjoy a working vacation of sorts. DeVito, who had enjoyed his time on the Troubadour stage immensely, decided he and his costars were truly going to live like rock stars for those ten days. He rented a tricked-out tour bus and had the whole thing wrapped with the marketing materials for the new *Sunny* season. So when the *Nightman Cometh* live production rolled into those cities, it was with the mobile announcement of their arrival, featuring giant heads of the cast members atop the diapered bodies of infants on the side of the bus. The FX marketing department worked on a shoestring for *Sunny* promotion in those early years, but the cleverness of their themes and visuals was always presented like it had been done on a bigger budget.

DeVito also planned fancy dinners along the way for everyone, and made sure there were libations on hand all the time: there was a bar on the bus.

"It was definitely his vision," says former RCG assistant Sean Clifford, who had just been hired before the tour and got to join The Gang and company on the bus to take care of the live show's props. "When we were rolling down the road, Danny wanted people to know that it was *Always Sunny*. Then when that bus showed up at the venues, the fans would be like, 'Oh, my goodness. This is amazing!'

"I was definitely as drunk as I could be almost the entire time, which was apparently perfectly acceptable as long as I didn't include the six props that were my responsibility," says Clifford, now an executive producer of Bravo's hit reality series *Summer House* and spin-off *Winter House*. "It definitely felt like we were [rock stars on tour]. There was an energy to it. You're getting out of a show. There's a party afterwards. You're going to bed really late, sometimes driving through the night. Then you're waking up and staying in hotels, and everybody already knew each other, so there was a comfort level there."

Once they were in town, the main cast and their small entourage—which included spouses Latiano, Mary Elizabeth Ellis, and Rhea Perlman; recurring star Artemis Pebdani as *Nightman* supporting cast; Cormac Bluestone, Matt Shakman, and the band; and the guy who helped start this whirlwind portion of the *It's Always Sunny in Philadelphia* history, Don McCloskey—made their mark on the venues.

Tickets for every performance sold out almost as quickly as they had for the Troubadour shows. The *Sunny* devoted turned out ready to party with the Dayman, the Nightman, the troll ready to pay the toll to get into the boy's soul (or hole, depending on how you chose to hear it), the coffee shop princess, Gladys, stage manager Artemis, and the lovesick adult version of the "tiny boy, baby boy, little boy" who adorned himself in a yellow tuxedo.

Some came dressed in *The Nightman Cometh* costumes. Some came dressed as Green Man. Some came having already enjoyed a few party lubricating beverages. McElhenney said he had done the same thing before each tour stop, which helped foster the spirit of the show, and made him, he felt, funnier. Fans would, as expected, sing along with "Dayman," and were giddy about the debut of new songs Bluestone and Day had written to flesh out the story and the performance even more for the live rock opera (songs like "I've Got a Troll in My Hole" and "It's Nature, Shit Happens").

Some overly enthusiastic (and perhaps overserved) fans ran around the aisles at the Masonic in San Francisco and had to be stopped by security from climbing onto the stage with the cast. At the Beacon in New York, when Charlie demanded Frank spit out his gum during the musical rehearsal, Day tossed the gum into the crowd; waiting fans were delighted to get their hands on a piece of the ABC ("already been chewed") refreshment from their beloved DeVito.

And when, at the end of *The Nightman Cometh*, Charlie descends from the "sky" as the grown-up little boy who fought the Nightman, his fancy sunny suit (with a cardboard sun attached—the man is deep, but also literal) forecasts he has an important message to deliver. The Gang was right; he didn't just write a musical for no reason. The real reason was that he wanted to propose to the Waitress.

Spoiler alert for no one still reading this book: She says no. Harshly, and with no equivocation.

Booing ensued in this finale moment. Charlie Kelly, more than any of the unlikely beloved *It's Always Sunny* characters, is the most beloved, the most endearing. He is the one viewers most root for. And he was shot down, live, in front of thousands of people each night.

When such sweet moments that are hard to come by in this "inherently profane" series, as McElhenney describes it, are soured, it stings, and the audience let it be known that they were upset with the Waitress's response.

That hasn't, of course, prevented them from watching the "Nightman Cometh" television episode again and again, hoping, perhaps—like we all secretly do when something bad befalls our favorite characters, the ones we invite into our homes every week—that the ending will be different this time.

The biggest takeaway of the "Nightman Cometh" chronicle on *It's Always Sunny in Philadelphia*: it is not just the humor but also that hope, even for these inevitably hapless characters, that keeps us watching The Gang at Paddy's Pub.

Chapter Six

THE HOUSE OF THE RISING *SUNNY*

After the pure rush of fandom love the cast received during the *Nightman Cometh* live tour in the fall of 2009, they understandably took a little break when the tour wrapped at the Hollywood Palladium. Season 5 had premiered right after their New York tour stop on September 17, and during their monthlong post–*The Nightman Cometh* vacation, the aftereffects of living out their rock star fantasies on a tour bus plastered with their bigger-than-life faces were still rattling around in their minds.

Had they dreamed it all? Did thousands of people at each of the six tour stops really buy up all the tickets in less than two hours, then actually show up—sometimes in Dayman and Nightman and Troll costumes—to scream for and sing along with the cast in person?

They really had, and the *It's Always Sunny* stars were still a bit stunned by that reality.

"It really gave us our first insight into just how many fans we had," Olson said. "Because we were basically being told: 'Nobody's watching the show, but FX likes it, so that's why you're still on the air.' We weren't having huge ratings, but we had a big fan base. And those people traveled and packed those theaters."

What followed, and how quickly the series advanced after the "Nightman Cometh" era, was a bonanza.

Sunny's upward trajectory began, of course, with the addition of DeVito in season 2. The show had delivered on all the promises of a great comedy in its short debut season, but as director Jerry Levine put it, "I think Danny DeVito came into [*Sunny*] and just exploded that ensemble."

DeVito's addition to the cast was followed by ancillary events that led to the swift increase of *It's Always Sunny in Philadelphia*'s profile. To boost revenue and cover some of DeVito's salary, Landgraf and his FX staff pitched Fox Home Entertainment (FHE) on releasing *Sunny* on the then-thriving DVD market. FHE was skeptical the series could make enough profit to justify the effort; fast-forward to September 2007 and the *It's Always Sunny in Philadelphia* seasons 1 and 2 DVD box set, which sold so well that it was one of FHE's bestsellers of the year, only behind *The Simpsons* and *Family Guy*. That same year, a move by Nielsen—the TV ratings folks—to sample the viewing habits of college students had another significant benefit to FX and *IASIP*. Given that *Sunny*'s target audience was men eighteen to thirty-four, FX expected the new measure would increase viewer numbers. Just to make sure, the network began a marketing campaign that fall aimed at college campuses. The series' ratings rose 24 percent.

Not everything worked. Hulu launched in 2008, with Fox owning a stake in the streaming service. Season 3's episodes of *It's Always Sunny* were offered to subscribers, and the comedy immediately became one of Hulu's most popular shows. Great . . . except when the next season of *Sunny* showed just a small increase in viewers *on* FX, executives theorized that the show's popularity was a blessing to Hulu but might actually be detracting viewers from watching The Gang on television. They then forced Hulu to remove *Sunny* from the service, which elicited a ruckus from viewers who had grown accustomed to having the laughs so readily available. Select episodes were returned to Hulu, but the experience left a bad taste in viewers' and TV execs' mouths.

But then cameth the Nightman to save the day. From the character's—and the song's—debut in season 3 to the full storyline and episode in season 4 and the iconic live performances and full soundtrack leading up to the premiere of season 5, the "Nightman Cometh" of it all shot *It's Always Sunny* into a whole new stratosphere, one in which it shed its "cult" status in television and pop culture and became simply a hit.

The season 5 premiere that aired during the *Nightman Cometh* live tour—"The Gang Exploits the Mortgage Crisis," in which Charlie squared off with the Lawyer again, Sweet Dee schemed to become a surrogate mom for some easy money, and Mac and Dennis busted out their Vic Vinegar and Hugh Honey personas to help

Frank sell a foreclosed home—increased viewership 23 percent on the season 4 premiere. The episode, written by Becky Mann and Audra Sielaff, led to the highest-rated season overall up to that time, topping season 4 in total average viewers by 36 percent. The Gang's weird, wild, wicked, wacky, witty show had caught on with people in a much bigger way than they'd understood before playing live in front of huge crowds.

Soon after the tour ended, FX and *It's Always Sunny* celebrated another big—and historic—win. Comedy Central paid FX $33 million for the exclusive syndication rights to air the series. Beginning in 2010, Comedy Central began airing two-hour blocks of *Sunny* reruns every Monday night, available to them three months after the installments debuted on FX. It was the first time one basic cable network aired the reruns of another basic cable network's ongoing series, and the agreement included a piece of the ad revenue pie for FX. It ultimately meant even more dollars, of course, as Comedy Central served as another venue to help draw more hilarity-seeking eyeballs back to the *Sunny* mothership.

Much of that windfall went back into the show. By season 6, the budget for the series was increased to $1.5 million per episode (roughly the same as the budget for a network comedy at that time). The whole cast got paycheck increases, and each member had his or her own dressing room (and none of them, as was true of some dressing rooms of the past, reeked of urine). The writing staff tripled and had offices. And *IASIP*, renewed through season 6 with a thirty-nine-episode pickup in 2008, was given another two-season renewal in 2011, while RCG signed an exclusive, three-year overall deal with FX, just as *It's Always Sunny in Philadelphia* had finally become profitable.

As Landgraf had promised McElhenney, Day, and Howerton when they signed on to do the series via the low-cost/creative-freedom production model he proposed, profitability meant a real financial reward was due to RCG. Their ownership stake had earned them a payday that, according to *The Hollywood Reporter*, would see them sharing $60 million for the overall deal they had signed.

There was an additional smaller—but still significant—windfall for the three creators, one they didn't have to share with their corporate partners. One of the highlights of season 5 was another classic *Sunny* episode, "Paddy's Pub: Home of the Original Kitten Mittens," in which The Gang's get-rich-quick scheme du jour was creating branded merchandise they could sell at Paddy's. The titular merch was Charlie's idea: pairs of knitted mittens ("mittons" in Charlie spelling) made for cat paws, because Charlie felt the felines in his life were stomping around making too much noise, and he thought this was a problem for many cat owners. He even made a charming video advertisement showing a kitten walking around in mittens.

Meanwhile, Frank tried to sell hard-boiled eggs with "Paddy's Pub" handwritten on them. Dennis created—what else?—floaty pens with photos of naked women inside. And Dee, whose Paddy's contract says she's entitled to all the bar's merch profits, demanded a cut of everything the guys made. Until Mac ate her only copy of the contract, which sent her to the Lawyer to regain her digested rights.

Then Mac came up with an idea so bold and bawdy and... absorbent that FX refused McElhenney's request to sell it in the official FX store. That would be the infamous Dick Towel. Like Kitten Mittens and the Shot Gun (shoot a liquor shot out of a gun and into someone's mouth), the Dick Towel is a literal product: a beach towel with an erect penis drawn on one-third of it, a flaccid penis on another third, and a butt on the back. The towel is designed to be wrapped around the waist so the user can choose which state of affairs he'd like to display. There's a Girl Dick Towel, too (shaved lady junk with enormous breasts, unshaven lady junk with smaller breasts, and a lady butt with a tattoo above it that reads "Girl Dick Towel"). The Dick Towel comes in Brown Dick Towel and White Dick Towel options, $29.99 each, available at DickTowel.com, just as promoted in the ad within the episode.

Day said RCG sold an initial run of twenty thousand to thirty thousand Dick Towels, and the fellas pocketed some nice coin. All-Pro NFL alum Chad Ochocinco even posed wearing a Dick Towel on X (then Twitter), Day pointed out.

As for how the Dick Towel came to be, McElhenney confirmed Day's assertion that he deserves credit/blame for the product idea. While visiting their son in Los Angeles, McElhenney's mothers (plural intentional; after his mom, Helena, divorced his father, she wed Mary, and he has two moms) came home from Venice Beach one day wearing oversize novelty T-shirts sold on the boardwalk with bikinis drawn on them. McElhenney said he couldn't imagine who would actually find those T-shirts funny, and then his moms came home in them. That stuck in his head and resurfaced when the writers' room was breaking the details of "Paddy's Pub: Home of the Original Kitten Mittens."

"Of course, we were all on the floor laughing with his description of it," Day said, "and drawing up various versions of it on a dry-erase board."

That was, by the way, a typical writers' room session at that time in the series' run. The number of writers had tripled with the new budget, and it was an increasing challenge to keep up the story ideas, the quality of the writing, and the level of cavorting The Gang could get up to after having done forty-five episodes full of talebearing and mischief-making. It required a room full of beautiful minds to attempt to top Kitten Mittens and Dick Towels. But in season 5, Charlie's heart was broken in "The Waitress Is Getting Married," though when the groom turned out to be a dud, Charlie sweetly, cleverly, secretly, and violently got revenge for his beloved. And a trio of gems from the wonderfully wacky imagination of writing team Scott Marder and Rob Rosell included "The Gang Wrestles for the Troops," in which The Gang put on a wrestling exhibition for the troops and pro wrestling legend Rowdy Roddy Piper guest-starred; "Mac and Dennis Break Up," one of the top two Mac and Dennis storylines ever, in which they realized they were acting like an old married couple, but Dee reunited them when Dennis camped out at her apartment . . . where feline whisperer Charlie tried to get some cats out of Dee's bedroom wall; and, on everyone's all-time top-ten *Sunny* episodes list, "The D.E.N.N.I.S. System," in which Dennis revealed his never-fail seduction method (and just how truly sociopathic he may be) with a mnemonic device that uses the letters of his name: "D" for "demonstrate value," "E" for "engage physically," "N" for "nurturing dependence," "N" for "neglect emotionally," "I" for "inspire hope," and "S" for "separate entirely." The episode, cowritten with David Hornsby, was inspired by a Marder and Rosell roommate who was fanatical about the 2012 Neil Strauss book *The Game: Penetrating the Secret Society of Pickup Artists*.

It was boom times indeed for *It's Always Sunny in Philadelphia* and beyond. The show's increase in profits, viewers, and critical acclaim had also become a boon to FX's efforts in building its premium brand of comedy. Using the low-cost/creative-freedom production model that got and kept *Sunny* on the air, the network confidently plunged ahead with four new comedies: *Archer*, *The League*, *Louie*, and *Wilfred*.

The way they became hits, and the tone, style, and quality they became known for, solidified that *Sunny* hadn't been a fluke. Setting really smart, creative people loose with their ideas, while also helping them suss out and stick to their visions, held value.

As the network's first successful, and signature, comedy hit, the team at *It's Always Sunny in Philadelphia* had chauffeured this era of ascendancy for FX.

Which is why it was a no-brainer that when FX launched FXX, a companion channel that would focus on its comedy gold mine, it would be anchored by *It's Always Sunny*. The spin-off network, which replaced the Fox soccer channel, debuted on September 2, 2013, with fellow FX transfers *The League* and *Legit*. But when FX held a party to celebrate the launch at Lure nightclub in Los Angeles the night after FXX officially hit the airwaves, it was the cast of *Sunny*—RCG, Olson, DeVito, Ellis, and guest star Jill Latiano—who got the most high fives from their fellow partiers. Robin Thicke performed for the entertainers from FX and FXX with a set that included the second-biggest hit record on the *Billboard* charts that year, "Blurred Lines," which had even Landgraf standing on top of a bench to get a choice spot for Thicke's performance. After making stops at the beer bar and hot dog stand near the entrance, the stars of *The League* and *Archer*, and other invitees like Nick Swardson and *Bones* star Emily Deschanel (married to *Sunny* star/producer/writer David Hornsby), made their way to the gang from *Sunny* to congratulate them on their ninth season, which would premiere on FXX the next night. Season 9 would also include the series' landmark one hundredth episode.

The night, and their new place in the FX family, was another proud moment for the *Sunny* cast and crew. Introducing the show's panel at the 2013 Summer Television Critics Association press tour at the Beverly Hilton in August, FX executive vice president of publicity John Solberg said *IASIP* "is no longer the little show that could. It's the show that is launching a network." He then welcomed the cast to the stage as "the people responsible for one of the greatest success stories in television."

Sunny had already been renewed for its tenth season that March, so there was plenty more debauchery, good times, and celebrations to be had.

Chapter Seven

SUNNY DEE

Why, you might be asking yourself after a perusal of the contents, is there a whole chapter on "*Sunny* Dee," but no "*Sunny* Day" or "Frank-ly *Sunny*"? Why is the only chapter devoted to one character, one cast member, devoted to Sweet Dee Reynolds and the underrated brilliance of Kaitlin Olson?

Your answer: "The underrated brilliance of Kaitlin Olson."

In a world, or rather, a bar, full of degenerate characters, Sweet Dee is singular.

She's as selfish as the rest of The Gang, as neurotic as the rest of The Gang, and often more insecure, devious, and angry than the rest of The Gang, and without her, The Gang wouldn't be nearly as terrible, plotting, entertaining, and yes, as lovable as *It's Always Sunny* viewers find the whole group to be.

One of the funniest people in Hollywood, and on the A-list of television's most comedically talented stars, Olson has it all: from a natural ability to play with everyone around her to a commitment to fearlessly tackling the craziest, silliest, and most inventive stories her costars and their room full of talented writers can conceive.

Innately gifted, Olson worked hard to be successful, while staying upbeat every step of the way. During her journey to the top levels with the prestigious and highly competitive Groundlings, for instance, she worked the equivalent of a full-time job with the improv troupe, while also holding several part-time jobs on the side—hair salon receptionist, boutique salesperson, and recruiter for a biotech company, among them. They're the types of jobs many performers do to pay the bills while honing the skills that, in Olson's case, earned her a spot in the Groundlings rising-star Sunday Company and guest parts in television sitcoms before her breakout role on *Sunny*. That has since led to movie roles, parts on other TV series, and a trio of Emmy nominations, including 2022 and 2024 nods for playing the daughter of Jean Smart's legendary Vegas comedian on HBO's *Hacks*.

Olson has approached her career with a steady optimism, which is not necessarily the norm in an industry where constant rejection *is*. "I just decided that I wasn't going to be miserable," she said. "It's beautiful [in Los Angeles]. . . . I had great friends, I got right into the Groundlings, which was really, really fun, and I just decided not to be miserable like everyone else was. It took a while. I did a lot of auditions, but in the meantime I was doing what I loved, which was sketch comedy. I think that once you start beating yourself up about not booking jobs right away, and you're miserable, you're going to give up faster."

Most importantly, Olson forged ahead without fear—or at least by acting fearlessly. A self-proclaimed funny child growing up, the actress said she was shy outside of her home, a six-acre farm in Oregon. When she was twelve years old, she flipped over on a bicycle and landed on her face. She wasn't wearing her helmet, and the injuries resulted in a hole the size of a lime in her skull and reconstructive surgeries to repair wounds to her face. With a shaved head and swollen bruises, she was about to enter junior high, a scary, insecure time for many girls, but downright terrifying with such a trauma in her recent past.

"It was really, really bad," Olson said. "Honestly, it's probably the greatest thing that ever happened to me. That was a real serious source of adversity that took years to fight back from."

That experience, and fighting through the long recovery and the reactions from some of her less kind classmates (she has told a story about one little hellion who stood in line behind her, trying to toss jelly beans into the hole in her skull), is a source of her humor, and of her fearlessness in going for it in her work.

As Olson told her future husband, then just her showrunner during *Sunny*'s first season, she was not interested in playing a clichéd role: the girl who admonishes the male characters for their naughty behavior, the straight man to the characters who are having all the fun, getting all the great lines, being as bad as they want to be. And when RCG told her during season 1 that they would do better, that they just didn't have much experience writing for female characters, Olson gave them a simple solution: Don't write for a female character. Write for me the same way you write for your own characters, for all the male characters. I'll add touches that will make Sweet Dee female. But it won't be anything that makes her less than—less loud, less obnoxious, less crude, less ambitious, less selfish, less arrogant, less entitled . . . especially not having less fun. Write a great character for me, Olson told them, and then stand back and let me run amok.

The surest way to appreciate Olson's performance on *It's Always Sunny*, and what she means to the series, is to recall her best, most quintessential Sweet Dee moments:

"WHO POOPED THE BED?"—SEASON 4, EPISODE 7

If there is one single moment that encapsulates why and how Olson is the champion of the sun, like Dayman, but also of all things bold and brave and hilarious, it is the moment when she ran headfirst into the door of a parked car in this all-around berserk episode. And that she asked—no, *begged*—to be allowed to do it. And then begged to do it more than once, just to make sure the director had a choice take.

In Dee's half of the episode (the other half revolved around the rest of The Gang doing a *Law & Order*-level investigation on whether it was Charlie or Frank who had shat in their shared pullout bed), she was trying to get her *Sex and the City* on during a night on the town with her best frenemies, Artemis and the Waitress. While shopping for a pair of designer shoes for her generously sized tootsies, Dee told the salesperson she'd wear them out of the store. The employee informed her that her credit card had been declined. So Dee handed her another one, and then, with the ridiculously too-small heels on, took off stumbling toward the door with the boutique employee hot on her trail. Dee, as clumsy as she is shady, tripped on the way outside and crashed, hard, right into the passenger-side door of her car. It left a dent in the door. Splayed on the sidewalk when the clerk reached her, a dazed Dee looked up and asked about her credit card, "Did it not go through?" It was a masterpiece of practiced klutziness.

"It's just one of the funniest moments of physical comedy, I think, in the history of the show," Day said.

"They didn't want me to do it," Olson says of the *Sunny* producers (one of which, of course, is her husband). "They had a stunt double there. I was watching behind the monitors, and I was just like, 'Please just let me try it.' So they let me do one. They were like, 'We're literally going to let you do *one*.' They switched out the door to the car so it had a little bit of a give to it, but they were only going to let me have one . . . they only had a certain number of those special car doors, so there was only one left, and I was like, 'Please, just let me do it.' So they let me. . . . I think something to do with knowing I only had one shot to just go for it. I don't know, but I loved it. I love stuff like that. I'd rather do my own stunts when it's somewhat safe."

Fun it was, but like many of the stunts she has performed, it was not without consequence. "A lot of trips to the chiropractor, but at least it looked good," she says. "That was really all that mattered."

"Who Pooped the Bed?" is not just a watershed performance for Olson as a physical-comedy genius. The episode is also a highlight on the *Sunny* reels of Artemis Pebdani and Mary Elizabeth Ellis (whose drunken wipeout as the Waitress while responding to a condescending saleswoman made for a shoe store scene that would have done Carol Burnett and Vicki Lawrence proud on *The Carol Burnett Show*).

Pebdani says she always looks forward to Dee and Artemis storylines, and she was thrilled at the chance to play with her friend and former roomie, Ellis (the two actually met as students at Southern Methodist University in Dallas, then reconnected after each relocated to California to pursue acting). Pebdani and Ellis were also costars in Discount Cruise to Hell, a "theatrical trash band" Pebdani describes as "performance art vomit and funny and musical and all the things." (Yes, a sample of the band's work is googleable.)

"Who Pooped the Bed?"—with its *Sex and the City* nod and the "poop detective" story, both of which work in no small part because Artemis the actress makes sure Artemis the character comes to play—is *Sunny* at its best.

"It's also interesting to give Kaitlin the girl time," says Pebdani, whose eclectic résumé includes a stint performing as a stand-up comedian . . . while in a full-body cast. "I know that's the joke of it, but also that it's girl time, and what they do is just as awful as what the guys do."

"THE GANG SOLVES THE GAS CRISIS"—SEASON 4, EPISODE 2

Frank's faulty intel led him and Dee to stalk and systematically ruin the car and other possessions of an innocent young man they mistook for Bruce Mathis, Dennis and Dee's biological father. Since their late mother, Barbara, gave all the money she got from Frank in their divorce to Bruce, Dee and Frank wanted to find a way to get it back and prevent Bruce from spreading it around in acts of charity. But Frank and Dennis came to believe Dee was plotting to kill them both to clear a path for her to retrieve Barbara's cash for herself. When a nervous Dee was acting too shifty to convince Frank she wasn't planning his death, he tried to get her to admit she actually was by waterboarding her in the grossest place he had access to: the urinals in the men's bathroom at Paddy's. It worked; Frank insisted Bruce Mathis was a terrorist and that Dee was working for him. Not true, but she confessed to it anyway, because... waterboarding in the Paddy's bathroom.

It was another spot-on performance by Olson, as Dee *was* possibly plotting the deaths of her family members to get all her mother's cash, but that still left her as the sanest member of The Gang in this particular farce. Pure chaos ruled the day as Dennis, Charlie, and Mac stole Dee's life savings (hidden in her sock drawer) so they could buy gasoline to store in barrels at Paddy's and sell it later when the price went up. Olson is insanely funny when Dee is up to no good and trying to pretend she isn't, and when she's panicked and out of sorts because the rest of The Gang is making her life pure hell.

On top of the tomfoolery in the storyline, Olson pulled off the waterboarding scene while dealing with the aftermath of some tomfoolery in real life. During a July 4 celebration, her neighbor picked her up over his head and accidently dropped her onto the street. She landed on her hip, and her back broke. Season 4 of *Sunny* was in production, but the actress had more far-reaching concerns: she and McElhenney were scheduled to get married that September, and her doctors were telling her she might not be able to walk for eight weeks.

"And I just remember thinking, 'Am I going to be able to walk down the aisle at my own wedding?'" Olson says. "I found a really amazing acupuncturist . . . this magic man, [and he] was like, 'Well, your bone won't heal for eight weeks, but we can repair that tissue. I can get you walking.' So it was just a ton of acupuncture, and I started being able to put some weight on it after about three or four weeks."

She was able to walk down the aisle in September 2008, when she and McElhenney tied the knot at a Malibu vineyard with their *Sunny* costars in attendance.

On the set of *IASIP*, however, there was simply a lot of toughing it out: Olson recalled the waterboarding scene as one of her most painful on-set experiences. "There have been times on the show where I have been literally in so much pain I can't believe I stuck through with it," the actress said. "They put wetsuit material over my face thinking that would block it, but I got waterboarded! I was laying on a broken back, inverted, being waterboarded. I was like, 'I'm a team player, but I can only hang in there a few more minutes.'"

"HUNDRED DOLLAR BABY"—SEASON 2, EPISODE 5

Dee decided to enhance the boxing lessons former pugilist Frank was giving her, so she started taking (by the handful) pills that left her physically stronger but also loaded with rage for whoever might unknowingly flip her trigger switch. In a threat she dropped on the opponent she was supposed to meet in her debut bout, Dee got in the woman's face and promised, "I will eat your babies, bitch!"

Sweet Dee, not so much, but the intense viciousness with which Olson delivered the trash talk made it a fan favorite of the character's dialogue for the next nearly two decades. It's a phrase Olson said McElhenney came up with on the set, between takes, and it's one she still loves, too. "Somebody yelled it at me when I was with my kid once, and I thought it was hilarious," she said. "Luckily, he was young enough not to know what was going on."

"MAC'S MOM BURNS HER HOUSE DOWN"—SEASON 6, EPISODE 6, AND "THE GANG SAVES THE DAY"—SEASON 9, EPISODE 6

Another favorite mood to watch Olson play with Dee: excitement about something she really loves. It doesn't happen as often as it should, because the rest of The Gang simply won't stand for it. But in "Mac's Mom Burns Her House Down," Dee was readying herself for an evening with Josh Groban. She and Artemis acquired backstage passes to a Groban concert in the park, and Dee wanted to look her best: self-tanning lotion was going to make her skin pop against a pair of tiny white shorts. "Josh Groban likes his ladies to pop," Dee declared. Unfortunately, she was also getting sick at the time, and Frank's efforts to help her get well were self-serving and, of course, had the opposite effect. Dee was left tied up in Frank's apartment, covered with bedbug bites, next to a possibly dead dog, and unable to get to the park when Artemis left a message saying Groban was feeling frisky backstage, and suggested Dee should hurry down to "tap that ass."

But three seasons later, in the series' one hundredth episode, "The Gang Saves the Day," Dee finally got her moment with "Grobes" in a fantasy. The Gang was trapped inside a convenience store that was being robbed, and each one of them daydreamed a scenario in which he or she would save the day. Dee actually fantasized that she shot the rest of The Gang, turned the thief in to the police, and joined the witness protection program, where she became a huge TV and movie star and the fiancée of, yes, Josh Groban, himself an *It's Always Sunny* fan who made a cameo appearance and sang a song about how Dee is beautiful and blond and doesn't look like a bird at all (the rest of The Gang constantly insists that she does). The Reynolds-Grobes union was not meant to last, however; in her marvelous delusion, Dee divorced Groban after seventeen minutes of marriage to be with Brad Pitt.

The bottom line of this Olson performance: as much as she can work up a good fury, plot a devious stratagem, or wallow in insecurities, Olson makes watching Sweet Dee get everything she wants just as much fun.

"DENNIS REYNOLDS: AN EROTIC LIFE"—SEASON 4, EPISODE 9

It's a double serving of greatness in this simple Dee story, which found her and Charlie agreeing to walk a mile in each other's shoes to see who has the worst life. For Dee, that meant donning a pair of Charlie's thermal underwear, peeing in a can, eating cat food, huffing glue, and drinking a bedtime beer, so she would be sick enough to pass out and get to sleep before the fifty cats that hung around outside Charlie's apartment window started howling and kept her awake. (Why fifty cats? Because of the ten thousand rats in his building, Charlie explained.)

For Charlie, walking a mile in Dee's shoes meant accompanying wannabe actress and comedian Dee to her nightly humiliation at the Laff House, the comedy club where she attempted to tell jokes but couldn't get through them without violently dry heaving onstage. It was not only our introduction to one of Dee's signature moves, but another example of the way that anytime Olson and Day combine for a storyline, it's a showpiece. In this one, Charlie poked fun at Dee's dry heaves, but when he took the stage and tried to make the audience chuckle, he had caught the dry heaving himself.

As for the origins of Olson's dry heavery, she said she did it one day on set when she and Howerton were goofing around, and he couldn't stop laughing. She added it to her physical comedy repertoire then and there.

"MAC AND DENNIS: MANHUNTERS"—SEASON 4, EPISODE 1

To get Dee and Charlie to stop eating the deer meat he hunted, Frank told them they were feasting on human flesh. They didn't believe it . . . at first. But as their appetite for what they came to believe was man meat grew, and Frank's mind game rattled them even further, Charlie and Dee became convinced they were addicted to human meat. They considered getting some from the morgue, but ethics—and a cheeky discussion about race when they were trying to choose between a dead white guy and a dead Black guy—turned them off the dead meat.

While trying to come up with somewhere else to shop for man meat, the twisted duo walked around the streets of Los Angeles (subbing for the streets of Philadelphia), eating sandwiches, hoping to sate their hunger for fellow humans. Dee wanted to eat every person they passed on the sidewalk, while pecking at her lunch.

"I can't even remember why or what's going on in that episode," Olson laughed about the episode years later. "I just remember walking down the streets of [Los Angeles] pecking at a chicken hoagie, like a bird, and [Charlie and Dee thinking they were] eating human meat. [Charlie's] just so much fun to play with. Scenes with Charlie are great, because your goal ends up being just to try and make Charlie break while you're shooting.

"It's such a good energy, because I'm saying things that are scripted, but really I'm going to tweak stuff and just see how many times I can make Charlie laugh. And it's not like full scenes are rewritten, it's just a line that ends up being our favorite was something that somebody just came up with on the day."

"THE GANG BUYS A ROLLER RINK"—SEASON 15, EPISODE 3

This is one fans had been waiting on for years: a big chunk of The Gang's origin story. And for Dee, it turned out the "Sweet" in her name wasn't originally used sarcastically. In this flashback to 1998, Dee truly was a sweet, friendly, optimistic person, with a group of pals made up of supportive people who wished her well. She and her pre-Gang gang spent a lot of time at a roller rink, where Charlie worked, where Mac sorta worked but also hung out and sold drugs, and where Dennis visited them all while working for Frank (whom he called "Father"). All three of the guys complimented Dee on how she was "pure of heart," was funny, had natural charisma, and was sure to succeed as she prepared to move to Hollywood.

Then, it happened: while performing her goodbye skate routine with her friends, Sweet Dee crashed into a wall and hit her head pretty hard. Her skates—her size 11 men's skates, it was prominently noted, because even in flashbacks, there had to be some Gang gibe at Dee's physicality—were too loose, even though she had asked Charlie to tighten them earlier.

When Dee picked herself up after her fall, she had been transformed into Sour Dee. Everything was a nasty insult to her brother and Mac and Charlie. They were concerned about her, but she didn't care. She called her other friends "bitch" and wanted to be left alone. She called The Gang losers and declined their invitation to buy the roller rink with them. She was going to Hollywood to become rich and famous and marry Scott Wolf, she said. The rest is Gang history, and viewers got to watch the conversion of Sweet Jekyll into Rotten Hyde, courtesy of Charlie, a loose skate axle, and a multifaceted performance by Olson.

"DENNIS AND DEE GO ON WELFARE"—SEASON 2, EPISODE 3

Every TV comedy fan has at least one go-to scene, that moment from a favorite show that always elicits a laugh and perfectly epitomizes his or her favorite characters. This is one of those scenes for no small number of *Sunny* fans: Dee and Dennis, sitting on a stoop, drinking beer from cans in brown paper bags and singing along with Biz Markie's "Just a Friend," while enjoying the jewelry pieces they'd purchased with their recent unemployment checks. Is it the fact that they were bopping along with the tune, while singing? Or that they'd clearly been imbibing for a while (or, as Mac put it, it was one o'clock in the afternoon and they were already "piss-ass drunk")? Or is it that, even in this rare moment of bonding for the Reynolds twins, Dennis still had to make it a point to criticize Dee's singing skills?

It's all of that, actually, along with their excitement and pride when they shared with Mac that Dennis was going to become a veterinarian and Dee was going to New York to be on Broadway. Then, when they were bored of Mac lecturing them about their plan to go on welfare when unemployment ran out, they simply turned up the volume on their boom box in the middle of his reprimand. It is a pure joy to watch the siblings take so much pleasure in being so unabashedly self-absorbed, lazy, and greedy.

"WHO GOT DEE PREGNANT?"—SEASON 6, EPISODE 7

It's known for being *Sunny*'s great Halloween episode, and for the beloved Liam McPoyle quote, in which, while trying to make Mac agree to call his sister after Mac had sex with her in the men's room at Paddy's, Liam bellowed at Mac, "You will call *HER*!" But this treasure is a mix of seasonal slapstick, mistaken identity, and a night in which Dee forced the rest of The Gang to show genuine interest in her life.

The evening began with The Gang piling on Dee for her recent ravenous appetite for sandwiches. They assumed she was getting fat, and told her so, despite the fact that she had repeatedly told them she was pregnant. They were more interested in attending a sleepover at a local museum, where they believed things were going to come alive at night, like in those *Night at the Museum* movies. Dee, annoyed by their fat jokes and that they kept ignoring her pregnancy news, decided to mess with them. She said one of them was the father of her baby, and that she had gotten pregnant during the Paddy's costume party on Halloween. She knew they all had fuzzy memories of that night. She knew they would stew in the alcohol-soaked memories they did have. She knew any conclusions they could come to would set them off in a terror and, at least, ruin their night at the museum.

Tickled at that promise, she had no idea just how crazy their notions would get. Costume changes (Dee swapped her angel costume, which the guys said made her look like a bird, because of the wings), fistfights, and the involvement of the McPoyle siblings led to a shocking paternity reveal: Dennis was the father of his sister's baby!

The guys rushed to Dee's apartment and confronted her with the news; Dennis stood in her hallway, unable to move. Then Dee confirmed the truth, like a bad episode of *Maury*: Dennis was not the father! Nor was Mac, nor Charlie, nor Frank. None of them had impregnated her on Halloween, and just to torment them a little further, she wasn't going to tell them who the father truly was.

But it didn't matter. Since the pregnancy no longer impacted any of them, they didn't care. They still had time to make it to the museum sleepover. But Dee, for one evening, had them right where she wanted them.

The full details of Dee's pregnancy would not be revealed until the end of the season, but Olson was pleased RCG and the writers came up with an ingenious way to write her personal pregnancy—she was soon to give birth to her first son, Axel—into season 6. No hiding behind furniture, or sticking Dee behind the bar for twelve episodes. Her baby bump was on full display, and she was in full Kaitlin Olson comedy mode. "Dee Gives Birth," the twelfth episode of season 6, continued the mystery of the father of Dee's baby, but it wasn't just a question of the baby's paternity—it was about who the baby's mother was, too. Mac, Charlie, Dennis, and Frank had gathered all of Sweet Dee's former romantic dalliances at the hospital so she could reveal the father after giving birth.

But when Dee was brought into the waiting room holding a newborn in her arms, there were two surprise guests standing beside her wheelchair, thrilled to take *their* new bundle of joy home: Mac's ex Carmen (Brittany Daniel) and her husband, Nick (Windell Middlebrooks). Sweet Dee was a surrogate for Carmen and Nick, and the offbeat sincerity (for *Sunny*) of the storyline not only allowed Olson to play out her pregnancy with Axel McElhenney on-screen but also allowed the writers to give an update, and a happy one at that, on Carmen.

"I really like how they handled it," Olson says about Dee's pregnancy. "I think it's unique, and that's always what we're going for."

Olson also reveals the writers had alternative notions to work her real-life pregnancy into the season. "One of [the other ideas] was having me get fat, which I thought would be funny, and having me wear a fat suit the entire season [with] a bigger and bigger butt. That was going to be difficult, I think, with continuity, because we shoot out of order. But I thought that would have been pretty funny."

"PTSDEE"—SEASON 12, EPISODE 7

Even Dennis—Dennis!—thought Dee was going too far, that she had just done the worst thing she had ever done—and this is a character who once held a (fake) funeral for her (fake) dead baby, just to get out of a (real) IRS audit. In "PTSDee," Ms. Reynolds was brutally rejected, in front of Dennis and Charlie, when the male stripper she had a one-night stand with the previous evening showed up at Paddy's to retrieve the watch she had stolen. He was unhappy about his life path—his daughter wasn't even speaking to him, he shared—but hooking up with Dee was his new "rock bottom," he told her, in front of Dennis and Charlie. Dee was so livid she couldn't speak coherently and stormed out of the bar.

But she had a plan. Pretending to want to help her stripper crush, she convinced him there was nothing wrong with his stripper life. She got him a gig stripping at Paddy's for a sorority gathering. She even offered to help reunite him with his daughter.

And her word was good: when the music started blaring, stripper Mike (Carter MacIntyre) pulled his cap down over his eyes and stripped to a thong. As he danced off the stage and down into the dark audience, he jumped up onto a chair and repeatedly thrust his crotch into the face of one of the excited young women. Then the lights went up. He was thrusting into the face of his daughter. She immediately recognized her dad and screamed. He jumped off her chair and covered his thong area with his cap. Disgusted and horrified, his daughter ran out of the bar, telling him to never talk to her again.

Enter Dee, laughing, pointing at Mike, telling him this was his rock bottom: "You sticking your dick in your daughter's face!" Dee kicked him out of Paddy's and joined her friends at the bar, where she continued to laugh about her victory until Dennis pointed out that was *her* rock bottom. But there's no denying: a pridefully traumatizing Dee is a Kaitlin Olson spectacle to behold.

"THE GANG BROKE DEE"—SEASON 9, EPISODE 1

They had finally done it. Years of calling Dee a bird, saying she looked like a bird, telling her she wasn't funny, and not pretty, not talented, not going to be a success, not going to find love—a girl could only take so much, and Dee had taken enough. So she got herself a cake from the trash, lit some cigarettes, stopped showering and brushing her hair, and, with a forkful of dirty cake in one hand and a bottle of hooch in the other, drowned her sorrows. So down and dejected she couldn't even stir up enough energy to fire off some zingers back at the guys, Dee told them her life was hopeless and she was going home to be miserable.

They followed her—her door was unlocked, so they barged in without knocking and yelled out to ask her if she'd killed herself yet. They found her slung on her couch, cigarette still in hand, eyes barely open, talking just above a whisper.

"We realize we may be, in some ways, responsible for the state you're in," Frank confessed.

So they came up with a plan to help her out. Charlie, Mac, and Frank were going to sign her up for an open mic night at a comedy club and actually support her pursuit of a comedy career.

"Yeah, you know, you're right in that sweet spot between suicidal and actually dead . . . most comedians, they thrive there," Charlie reasoned.

Since Dee was no longer trying, maybe she wouldn't even dry heave when she tried to tell a joke.

Dennis, meanwhile, had a plan of his own. He thought Dee was right to give up. Instead, he would find her a man. Not a good one, he told her. He wouldn't find a smart man or a handsome man, but likely a below-average man, who would take Dee off The Gang's hands forever.

Dee's spiritless attitude worked. Her lack of self-care provided joke fodder. The audience loved her self-deprecation, her sound effects, her frequent use of the word "vagina." She got a manager, Snyder (Ken Davitian, *Borat*)—who she was sleeping with—and began to gain a following. Charlie, Mac, and Frank, as they promised, supported her by launching a Sweet Dee fan club, complete with her face on T-shirts. She even had a catchphrase: "I'm Sweet Dee, and the joke's on me!"

Dennis, who continued to photograph below-average men to pair up with Dee, was incensed about her refusal to accept any of the potential mates he chose and exasperated about the appetite for her broad, crass comedy stylings.

But Dee powered on, her star rising quickly and sky-high. One night after a performance, a more powerful Hollywood manager, Michael Rotenberg (Peter Jacobson, *House*), approached her. He offered to represent her and fly her to Los Angeles to appear on *Conan* the next day. She dumped Snyder—and her friends—and agreed to sleep with Rotenberg, too.

But with even the hint of major success, Dee's insecurities returned. So did the dry heaves.

She was shepherded onto Rotenberg's plane the next day. Dennis tried to board with her, claiming to support her success, pleading to be at her side. She, literally, booted him off the boarding ramp. On the flight to *Conan*, Dee's nerves continued to fray. She tried to calm them with many, many drinks. The dry heaves turned into full heaves.

At the airport, Michael covered her head with his jacket to shield her from waiting paparazzi and put her into a limo. When they arrived at the studio to tape *Conan*, Michael again covered her head to shield her from more paparazzi. Inside the studio, the dry heaves returned. But as Dee was about to step on the *Conan* stage, Michael told her she was going to be a star.

Instead, she stepped from behind the curtain and into Paddy's Pub, where Charlie, Mac, and Frank showered her with confetti, and explained she'd been tricked. Thanks to a lot of Frank's cash and the help of a bar full of people (all wearing "Joke's on Dee" T-shirts), they had planned an elaborate deception that built Dee, only in her mind, into a famous comedy star. The managers, the comedy club audience members, the staff at *Conan*—all were paid by Frank to play a role in the scheme. Even Dee's fellow comedian Landslide (played by *Breaking Bad* breakout Lavell Crawford) was really a garbageman paid to be the headliner at the comedy club where Dee performed. And Michael's private plane? Frank chartered it and scheduled a six-hour flight around Philly, which Dee never actually left. She did actually sleep with Snyder and Michael.

Only Dennis was not part of the official Gang plan. All his actions were real. He, too, had been duped by Frank and the fellas. He pretended to laugh it off.

Dee did not. Mac and Charlie told her they plotted this travesty because she was "all mopey and annoying," because she'd gone too far with talking about suicide. Incredulous that they accused her of going too far, Dee screamed and tore down the fake stage curtains. She ranted and raved and threw things around the bar. Glasses and bottles were shattered. She was on a rampage. She was back!

The Gang without an indignant Dee was just not The Gang. When she was sitting in the bar, at her lowest and eating the trash cake, her friends were lobbing insults at her, and she just didn't care.

"Fight back at us," Dennis prodded.

It was a hint at what the rest of The Gang really thinks of Dee, and how, in their own sweet, sick way, they do respect her, just as she is.

Dee's role is to keep The Gang on their toes. For her, Dennis and the other guys keep her striving to achieve her dreams, find true love, gain their respect and approval. Oh, she's never going to do any of those things, and they're going to keep telling her so. She knows that. But she will continue to strive, and they will continue to tear her down. It's what works for them, the most dysfunctional of self-created television families.

It was a cruel trick on Dee, but it provided Olson an opportunity to display a kaleidoscope of patented emotions for Dee: freak-out, arrogance, rage, cruelty of her own, and her dry-heaving anxiety brought on by crippling insecurity. Her frantic rehearsal for what she thought was her *Conan* debut, unfolding during her plane ride around Philly, was Olson at her Carol Burnett–, Lucille Ball–, Will Ferrell–, Chevy Chase–, Melissa McCarthy–, *Danny DeVito*–level physical comedy best.

And she was a champion trash-cake eater.

"I ate a lot of cake, quite a bit of cake," Olson said. "You see someone doing an eating scene, and I'm always paying attention to like, ugh, those poor people, because normally you're just moving food around on your plate and pretending to eat, because you can shoot it fifty times, that same scene. But I had to devour that cake. We probably shot that scene six or seven times. I believe I ate an entire cake."

"THE GANG BUYS A BOAT"—SEASON 6, EPISODE 3

Having come into a tidy little sum of cash from their Dick Towel venture, Dennis and Mac decided to use it to buy a boat. Imagine the kind of boat $2,500 will buy, and that is exactly the boat they got. Dee, who had contributed no money to the purchase of the watercraft, was therefore tasked with cleaning it and getting rid of the many old gewgaws filling it. But first, she wanted to show The Gang her dance moves, because they were planning to host some celebrity-style parties onboard.

Mac was unimpressed with Dee's party dance. He told her she looked like "those inflatable dancing things at the used car lot," and said he was going to bring one of them onto the houseboat to show her. Dee was cool with that; she would have a dance-off with "the guy," she said.

And while Mac and Dennis were off partying on a real boat, Dee did perform her moves beside Inflatable Dancing Guy, which proved Mac's assertion: side by side, Dee and Inflatable Dancing Guy were in sync. "I'm learning some amazing moves from this guy," Dee said, as she and IDG swayed along to Steve Winwood.

The idea for Dee's wild dance came, like her dry-heaving gag, while trying to amuse her costars when hanging out on the *Sunny* set.

"I was dancing, and Glenn was like, 'How long are your arms in relation to your body? I don't think this is normal. You have an abnormally large wingspan. You look like one of those inflatable guys at the car dealership,'" Olson says.

Nailing a specific imitation of an inflatable dancing guy, matching its moves, required a lot of serious physical work. Olson was six months pregnant while filming those iconic scenes, on a boat, in the middle of the night, frustrated that her body wouldn't bend backward as far as she wanted it to because it was housing little Axel McElhenney. "I'm pretty sure I ripped my stomach muscle moving like that," she said. "I worked so, so hard on that dance, and I think it ended up looking fantastic."

Olson's commitment to wringing every possible laugh out of the situations Dee is put in has contributed greatly to the success and longevity of *It's Always Sunny*.

But she has spent a fair share of time in chiropractors' offices because of those stunts she loves to do. And once, in the worst injury she's ever suffered on the *Sunny* set, the actress landed in the emergency room, with a worried husband accompanying her.

The cast was shooting season 9's "The Gang Makes *Lethal Weapon 6*," and among the multiple roles Olson played in The Gang's second installment of their self-made, Frank-financed unofficial *Lethal Weapon* sequels was that of a cop. On this particular day of filming, the action took place in an abandoned warehouse.

Olson tells the story: "My only job was to run in and stop and pull a gun on them . . . I ran in and slid to a stop. But suddenly there was no ground underneath me. The ground was like a metal grate, and my leg went down, and the metal grate went into my leg.

"That was horrible. But the best part about that story is that I just calmly sat down. I get super calm when I am very hurt, and Rob [McElhenney] was like, 'Uh-oh.' And he came over and lifted up my pant leg . . . and he just put the pant leg down and was like, 'Okay, could someone call the medic and also could someone else call 911?' My leg was just wide open. . . . We [got] to the hospital, and at the hospital they said, 'We know it's your leg, but is there anything else that's bothering you? Is there anything else?' And they just kept asking me, and I was like, 'No. Are you kidding? My leg's wide open.'

"And then [a nurse] said, 'Well, what is going on with your stomach?' And I looked down, and I forgot that I was wearing a blood pack, because in that scene I was supposed to get shot. My blood pack had exploded, and it looked like I'd been shot in the stomach. [Rob and I] were laughing, we were like, 'No, no, no, that's not real.'"

One other thing that wasn't real during that trip to the ER: McElhenney's skin color. The Gang infamously used blackface to portray LAPD police detective Roger Murtaugh (played by Danny Glover in the real *Lethal Weapon* movie franchise), partner of detective Martin Riggs (played by Mel Gibson in those movies). In The Gang's version of the story (which has so far spanned three *Sunny* episodes), Mac originally played Riggs and Dennis played Murtaugh; eventually, Mac wanted to switch roles with Dennis, and when they did, Mac insisted on portraying Murtaugh in blackface, to prove his belief that it was not racist or in poor taste.

So McElhenney was wearing blackface while shooting the scene in which Olson injured herself. He was still wearing the blackface when they arrived at the hospital.

Which neither *Sunny* star noticed until they'd just finished explaining that Olson hadn't been shot in the stomach. "Then I look up at Rob and realize he's fully dressed as a Black man," Olson says. "And I was just like, 'Oh my god, we are bad, this looks bad; we are in the middle of an emergency room and . . .' It was an interesting trip to the ER."

Olson's turn as a cop had to be written out of the scene after the brutal injury, which did enough damage to the inside of her leg that it required plastic surgery to fully repair. But she did still portray Rianne, daughter of Murtaugh, in blackface. Rianne was about to marry Riggs, played by Howerton's Dennis at the beginning of The Gang's movie, then by Mac in the final scene.

As Olson told them back in season 1: Just write for me like you write for yourselves. Let me rack up dozens of iconic Dee moments—beloved, wacky moments of slapstick, of dry heaves and dances with inflatable partners, of faked baby funerals and ruining father-daughter relationships, of being so controversial certain episodes would be censored from DVD releases and streaming services. Just let Dee free to be *Sunny*.

Chapter Eight

PHILADELPHIA FREEDOM... TO GET REAL WEIRD WITH IT

"I don't know how many years on this earth I got left. I'm going to get real weird with it."
—Frank Reynolds ("The Gang Gives Frank an Intervention")

Let us count the ways Frank has followed through on his pledge to get real weird with it since that season 5 installment, which saw him getting drunk and taking The Gang not to the barbecue he had led them to believe they were attending but to the funeral of his recently deceased brother-in-law, who he hated... so he could try to sleep with his widowed sister-in-law, Donna (Nora Dunn), who didn't get along with her sister, Frank's dead ex-wife, Barbara.

After repeatedly striking out with Donna in his quest for a revenge "plow," Frank eventually engaged in sexual activity with Donna's daughter, his niece-in-law, Gail (Mary Lynn Rajskub). Nicknamed

"Gail the Snail" by her cousins Dee and Dennis, Gail is clingy, obviously indiscriminate and randy with her affections, and given to the repulsive habit of snorting her own mucus, loudly, far up into her nose. Dennis and Dee would torture her as a child, putting her into a clothes dryer and throwing salt at her, like she was an actual snail.

By the end of the episode, Mac had broken into Donna's house with the intention of sleeping with her, Gail had given Frank a hand job under the kitchen counter (in front of her mother), The Gang had refused to pay the counselor they'd hired to run Frank's intervention, and Charlie had chased Gail out of the bar with a saltshaker. Mac also inadvertently let it slip to Frank that he once slept with Barbara.

To repeat, this is just one episode. It's a quintessential one, in terms of getting an accurate peek at the characters and their level of degeneracy in just twenty minutes and thirty-three seconds (including opening credits). As of the end of season 16, *It's Always Sunny in Philadelphia* had aired 170 episodes (163 since Danny DeVito joined). If we assume The Gang engaged in three crude, narcissistic, or downright sociopathic behaviors in each of those episodes (and that estimate depends on what qualifies as crude, narcissistic, or downright sociopathic behaviors to you), that means we could list at least five hundred incidents of bodaciously bad (but almost always hilarious) Gang behavior.

We could compile those behaviors in alphabetical order. We could break them down into lists of bad behaviors by episode, by each character, by each type of scheme The Gang was perpetrating. We could organize them by who the victim or victims were in each instance (or, in Mac-speak, by who The Gang was "versus-ing" at the time).

But this chapter will instead focus not just on The Gang's *worst* behaviors, but on The Gang's most *controversial* behaviors and episodes. Because one of the most popular questions people ask about *It's Always Sunny in Philadelphia* (after "Is that show still on?!") is "How *do* they get away with [fill in the blank]?!"

As in, how do they get away with the cast performing in blackface? How do they get away with the characters using the N-word, the T-word, and the R-word? How do they get away with selling alcohol to minors, kidnapping a local newspaper critic who slagged Paddy's Pub, faking cancer (multiple times, with multiple characters)? And: How has the show never been visited by the cancellation fairy?

Before answering the "how," a deeper dive into *Sunny*'s most controversial episodes is in order. Those are less subjective than rounding up The Gang's naughtiest moments, because the *most* controversial episodes are the ones that have been "canceled," in effect, by streaming services.

June 2020 was pandemic times, and Black Lives Matter protests were happening across the country. During this global health crisis and monumental cultural shift, people were watching TV—a *lot* of TV. Everything was a binge, and viewers were embracing their favorite, most comforting shows. They were especially relying on favorite comedies and recommendations of new ones from their trusted fellow binge-watchers. But that backfired a bit when viewers began to notice some beloved series had problematic storylines in their histories. *Scrubs, 30 Rock, Community*, and even *The*

Golden Girls were among critically acclaimed, viewer-loved comedies that had selected episodes removed from streaming services, syndication, or digital rental services, all because of the use of blackface. In the case of *The Golden Girls*, there was no actual blackface; Blanche (Rue McClanahan) and Rose (Betty White) entered the living room wearing mud masks while Dorothy (Bea Arthur) met the Black family of her son's fiancée, and so it appeared they were wearing blackface. Still, the episode was packed with various other tension-filled moments revolving around race, and it was pulled from Hulu. As of fall 2023, the episode has been added back to the Hulu lineup.

As for *It's Always Sunny in Philadelphia*, The Gang's infamous use of blackface (and yellowface and brownface) led to Hulu yanking five episodes from the service's *Sunny* library. Season 4's "America's Next Top Paddy's Billboard Model Contest," season 8's "The Gang Recycles Their Trash," and season 14's "Dee Day" all included Dee-created characters. Among them: Martina Martinez, a "streetwise Puerto Rican girl who's always quick with a sassy comeback," as Dee describes her; and Taiwan Tammy, an East Asian woman with large fake teeth. They're characters she thinks are hilarious. She created them to star in YouTube videos she hoped would go viral and that she was certain would attract the attention of *Saturday Night Live* producers. Charlie tried to convince her the characters were not funny; that they were very, very racist. But as can be said for most of The Gang, most of the time, Dee is completely un-self-aware when it comes to her comedic talents (as ironic as that is given how supremely gifted her portrayer is). Dee isn't stingy with her offenses as Martina and Tammy, either.

In "Dee Day," it was Sweet Dee's turn to run The Gang for a whole day; the rest of them had to do anything she asked, without complaining about it. If they displayed one second of dissatisfaction with what they were doing on Dee Day, they'd have to repeat another twenty-four hours under her leadership. One of the things on her agenda was making the guys perform a show—purely for her amusement—in costume. Dennis donned a red wig and green suspenders to play Crazy Paddy, Dee's ode to Irish stereotypes, while Charlie dressed as Mr. Covington, Dee's silver-haired portrayal of a British butler and nanny. Mac took over the Taiwan Tammy persona (complete with those obnoxiously large fake teeth), and Frank went full-on Martina Martinez, with darkened skin, super-enhanced chest, and high heels. For the performance, Dee also scripted a passionate kiss between Paddy and Mr. Covington, while Martina was to receive a full-body massage from Tammy (with a happy ending specified). It was a rare chance for Dee to have all the hand with the guys who love to torment her, with their intense discomfort as a bonus.

The other two episodes of *Sunny* Hulu removed that summer were season 6's "Dee Reynolds: Shaping America's Youth" and the season 9 installment "The Gang Makes *Lethal Weapon 6*." The season 6 episode revolved around Dee and Charlie going back to school, her as a substitute teacher at her old high school and Charlie as the school's janitor. The episode also featured a pair of outstanding guest appearances: Emmy-nominated *The Kids in the Hall* star Dave Foley as Principal MacIntyre; and future *Black Bird* Golden Globe winner Paul Walter Hauser as Richie, an outcast student befriended by Charlie when he's bullied for being a Juggalo, i.e., a face-painting fan of the horror hip-hop duo Insane Clown Posse.

All of that, delicious storyline that it was, took a back seat to what Dennis, Mac, and Frank did to deal with their boredom in Dee and Charlie's absence: reshoots for the DIY *Lethal Weapon 5* movie The Gang was producing. That, too, was one of their most brilliant ideas . . . until Mac insisted that he, as Mel Gibson's LAPD detective Riggs, swap roles—mid-movie—with Dennis, as Danny Glover's detective Murtaugh. And for his interpretation of Glover's character, Mac would perform in blackface.

This was not an instance of The Gang's tendency to be completely clueless to cultural awareness and sensitivities. Dennis tried to convince Mac that blackface was a bad idea. In fact, the *Lethal Weapon 5* reshoots were not so that Mac could perform in blackface; he had already filmed that performance. Dennis thought Mac should reshoot his role without the blackface.

Mac, often the voice of least reason but most volume, refused. He asserted a lot of great actors have performed in blackface. Dennis brought up, sarcastically, "the great C. Thomas Howell in *Soul Man*." But then, with Frank's help, Mac pointed out Laurence Olivier in *Othello*. Dennis acknowledged Olivier was a great actor and then employed a racist voice in noting that any Black people working on the movie would have issues with him. Even the moments of seeming lucidity are tainted. One step forward, two steps back...

Besides, Mac wasn't letting go of his claim there was a certain nobility in blackface. Even after Frank tried to help Mac make his point by showing a photo of Al Jolson in blackface from *The Jazz Singer*—which even Mac denounced as offensive—Mac thought there were times when blackface was okay, because it was about actors trying to create an illusion. Dennis said no, it was never acceptable. Mac's counter: Ian McKellen plays a wizard in the *Lord of the Rings* movies, but that does not mean "he goes home at night and shoots laser beams into his boyfriend's asshole." And because Mac couldn't prove he wasn't offensive without being offensive, he continued, "Tom Cruise is a midget, but he plays guys that are normal size in movies." There was further discussion about Olivier's light shade of blackface in *Othello* being close to James Earl Jones's skin color, and Frank thinking James Earl Jones was in blackface (Dennis had to inform him that James Earl Jones has a black face, because he is a Black man).

There can be value in the idea that discussing the topic might provide some awareness of blackface and its history, particularly since it was defended by arguably the least informed (Mac) and most immoral (Frank) members of The Gang. And a large part of *It's Always Sunny*'s younger audience might not have been exposed to discussion of any kind about blackface (or yellowface or brownface) and why it is offensive and has become more problematic during recent cultural shifts.

The discussion is typical of The Gang's logic and reasoning abilities (or lack thereof), and it probably would have been effective, as such, if they had just let Mac explain why he wanted to portray Murtaugh in blackface, instead of actually showing him playing Murtaugh in blackface as well.

Other shows responded differently. During the summer of 2020, *30 Rock* creators Tina Fey and Robert Carlock addressed the blackface episodes (which spanned multiple storylines and characters) of their Emmy-winning NBC comedy by writing a letter to streaming and rental services and asking them to remove the offending installments.

"As we strive to do the work and do better in regards to race in America, we believe that these episodes featuring actors in race-changing makeup are best taken out of circulation," Fey wrote. "I understand now that 'intent' is not a free pass for white people to use these images. I apologize for pain they have caused. Going forward, no comedy-loving kid needs to stumble on these tropes and be stung by their ugliness."

Again, while executive producer Fey doesn't make excuses or defend any lack of ill intent in using blackface in her show, she does specify the "use" of "these images" as a regrettable decision.

The *Sunny* producers, meanwhile, largely allowed the show to do the talking for them, expressing their thoughts on the controversial episodes pulled from Hulu with a season 15 meta episode titled "The Gang Makes *Lethal Weapon 7*." Written by Keyonna Taylor, who is Black, and Katie McElhenney (Rob McElhenney's sister), the episode opened with Frank outraged at the censorship he discovered at the local library. The Gang's *Lethal Weapon 5* and *Lethal Weapon 6* had been pulled from the library's shelves because of "insensitivity."

The rest of The Gang isn't as offended by the library being offended by their movies. Dennis said he wasn't sure how they talked the library into displaying the *Lethal Weapon*s in the first place. Frank said they were works of art. Dennis agreed they would have been, if Mac hadn't insisted on the blackface.

Mac didn't deny his mistake. He said his heart was in the right place, but he had done a lot of learning and a lot of growing in the previous year. The rest of The Gang said they had, too. It was time to put *Lethal Weapon 5* and *Lethal Weapon 6* behind them and look to their future.

"Now we have the path forward and the knowledge to do the right thing," Mac said. "And I think it's obvious what that right thing is."

Charlie answered for everyone. "Make *Lethal Weapon 7* . . . the show must go on!"

That wasn't it for the group mea culpa, though. During The Gang's production meeting for their next sequel, Dennis said it was important that the new movie "can be seen and enjoyed by audiences of today's moral and ethical standards."

Not like the previous films, and that one mistake they made, Mac said.

Two mistakes, since he did blackface in *Lethal Weapon 5* and *6*, Dennis reminded him.

Well, but Dee did blackface, too, Charlie pointed out, so three mistakes.

Plus multiple insensitive characters in the past, Charlie remembered, so four mistakes.

And Frank did redface as the villainous Chief Lazarus in the *Lethal Weapon* movies, Dennis added. So...

The bottom line: The Gang has made a lot of questionable decisions, "insensitivity"-wise. But they were declaring themselves accountable, and ready to do better. To start, they pledged to make different casting choices. Namely, no Mac playing Roger Murtaugh, and no one at all in blackface.

First, they cast their old pal Pepper Jack (Marcuis W. Harris), the pimp who took Dennis's *Fraggle Rock* thermos way back in season 3 ("Mac Is a Serial Killer"). Pepper Jack proved to be too intimidating to them, so they recast the role of Murtaugh with Geoffrey Owens, now standing in as Fake Don Cheadle after his stints as Fake Tiger Woods and Fake Donovan McNabb. Fake Cheadle made such an impression on The Gang that, no longer interested in doing the right thing, they handed over complete creative control of *Lethal Weapon 7* to him. The result was a movie renamed *White Saviors*, which mocked The Gang and their "quasi-wokeness." As they sat in the movie theater, watching the screening and listening to Fake Cheadle's remarks afterward, The Gang said they felt ignored, misunderstood, and used.

So, of course, seeing themselves as victims of an exploitation, and without an ounce of irony, The Gang decided to do the only thing they could: make *Lethal Weapon 8*. Mac immediately volunteered to play Murtaugh.

The Gang, as was always the plan for how *It's Always Sunny* evolved, learned nothing. But a key to the show's success, and to how and why *Sunny* "gets away" with its more outrageous and controversial moments, is that the gang who creates the series has learned plenty throughout the twenty years the comedy has been on the air.

There is a trust between the *Sunny* fandom and the creators: no matter how low the show goes, the intentions of McElhenney, Day, and Howerton are considered righteous by their loyal viewers. They mock, satirize, and ridicule that which is mockable, satirizable, and ridiculous, but they don't set out to offend.

Self-mocking, of which "The Gang Makes *Lethal Weapon 7*" is a great example, is one of their favorite kinds of mocking to do. The whole plot of making yet another homespun *Lethal Weapon* movie proved that, but Dennis got in an extra dig at The Gang after their attempt to make Pepper Jack their movie star failed. "Guys, there's a larger issue at play here, and that is that all the people of color that we know are people of the bridges and the streets," Dennis said. "They're pimps and prostitutes, which, I tell you, says a lot more about us than it does about them."

"It's not a great look," Charlie added, in a winking nod by RCG that *Sunny*'s casting choices, including guest and recurring actors, have not always been a grand show of diversity.

In a virtual press conference before the December 1, 2021, season 15 premiere—which included back-to-back episodes "2020: A Year in Review" and "The Gang Makes *Lethal Weapon 7*"—McElhenney talked about when RCG and the other writers decided to address Hulu's 2020 decision to remove five *Sunny* episodes.

"We tend to not talk about seasons of the show until we are in the writers' room, because otherwise, we'll just go crazy," he said. "When we sat down that first day, we realized that we should address this in some way. And, obviously, we wanted to tackle it the same way we tackle everything, which is through the prism of this very specific situation and these very specific people.

"We knew that we wanted to do it in a responsible fashion... and that's what we did."

During the same Zoom conference, McElhenney expanded on his explanation for how and why he and the other writers and producers make certain storyline decisions, and why they may later view some of those storylines in a different light.

"I find that my barometer is off for what's appropriate sometimes in situations, because we've spent fifteen years making a show about the worst people on the planet, and because it's satire, we lean so heavily into this idea," he said. "We are always right on the razor's edge, but that's the only way that satire works. And then I go and do something else, and I may be pitching something, and then I realize, 'Oh, that's wholly inappropriate for the show that I'm doing, because these are supposed to be real human beings.' Whereas on *Sunny*, they are cartoon characters, and we can, kind of, get away with a whole lot more."

The Gang on-screen, and the gang behind the scenes, do get away with quite a bit. More, obviously, than some people can believe, hence the oft-repeated "How do they get away with that?" questions about so many of The Gang's most atrocious deeds. Consider this: the series' first episode, "The Gang Gets Racist," debuted with a cast unknown to most television viewers. And the characters' introduction to TV land included the use of the N-word uttered by one of the main characters, Charlie. Charlie was quoting a guest character, Terrell, a Black friend of Dee's played by Malcolm Barrett, but even going back to 2005 when the episode premiered, it was a shocking word to hear on a random Thursday night during a basic cable comedy.

Yet, as an example of TV censorship's inconsistency, "The Gang Gets Racist" has never been pulled from any major streaming service, nor has it been withheld from syndication. Even during that tumultuous summer of 2020, the use of the N-word wasn't mentioned as an offense worthy of ridding Hulu, Amazon Prime Video, or Apple TV+ of "The Gang Gets Racist." The episode remains available on all those streamers.

There's even inconsistency among the services that pulled the aforementioned five episodes in 2020. "America's Next Top Paddy's Billboard Model Contest" returned to Hulu in August 2021, but was once again MIA from Hulu in September 2024. All five episodes remain unavailable to rent or purchase on Apple; yet "The Gang Makes *Lethal Weapon 6*" is available for purchase on Amazon Video, as of fall 2024. Also, all five *Sunny* episodes banned in 2020 can be purchased via YouTube—but only as part of purchasing the whole season each episode aired in.

It's important to note that it's certainly not a unanimous vote by *Sunny* fans, comedy viewers in general, or culture critics that the controversial episodes should have been removed from the internet. Not because they necessarily defend the content, but as *New York Times* culture editor (and now cohost of NPR's *Pop Culture Happy Hour* podcast) Aisha Harris wrote in 2020, "It's a disservice when creators and streaming services try to erase the evidence of their use of blackface from the internet, when what we should really be doing is trying to understand it: why it persists, and what, if anything, it's trying to say." Wiping the content also clears the creators and the streaming services from having to remain accountable for their ideas and how they work them out with their TV series and movies.

RCG and the rest of the cast and writers have always had the support of FX leadership, even when The Gang's schemes have gotten irredeemable to the nth degree (Exhibit A: the continuous ruination of one Matthew "Rickety Cricket" Mara).

"I realize we discuss subjects that don't normally get discussed, but I'm never concerned that anything's not going to make it to air," Olson said. "FX has always supported the voice and encourages us to push things even further."

Howerton added about the creators' relationship with the network, "They're fans. We don't have a lot of trouble with them ... we were so under the radar [at the beginning], and we were able to get away with pretty much whatever we wanted. If anything, they were always pushing us to go further." FX produces the series, so there's no outside studio to answer to. And as that push to go further became the precedent for the series, *Sunny*, like other edgy comedies— Howerton pointed to *Family Guy* as an example—became known, and appreciated, for that kind of humor.

"I can tell you the standards are a little bit different for newer shows that have a little bit more [attention] on them from the very beginning," he said.

With that freedom to swing for the fences comes great responsibility, however. And when a series has made a misstep, either by their critics' estimation or their own, no one wins when the episodes are tucked away. No one learns anything from an episode they can't reference or discuss in an informed way.

Sunny producers and cast have held themselves accountable for their storyline regrets, and have not taken steps to edit or remove the offenses. A common grumble from fans on the popular *IASIP* Reddit is the difficulty of watching those banned episodes via legal means. (The *Sunny* season 14 DVD box set was released without "Dee Day"; appropriately, it is not titled as a "complete season" set, as previous season collections are.)

RCG's biggest regrets of the series are summed up in two words: the R-word and the T-word. As discussed in chapter 5, "Dee's Dating a Retarded Person" is forever a reminder of the use of the R-word in an otherwise classic *Sunny* episode, one that introduced a storyline that would expand into their game-changing success with "The Nightman Cometh."

As Charlie Day suggested on the *Always Sunny Podcast* episode "Sweet Dee's Dating a [Redacted] Person" about that television episode, RCG would still do the show, with the same concept, but the execution would be different.

"It's super fucking funny, and I think it's okay, like, if we had to do it now, we, the characters, would dance around the usage of the word, and it would be just as funny," Day said. "Those are the adjustments you make . . . the characters would be not wanting to say the R-word . . . you can make a joke out of that."

Larry David famously did something much like that when he wrote the Emmy-winning *Seinfeld* classic "The Contest," in which none of the characters said the word "masturbation," even though that was the episode's "A" story. Instead, they used euphemisms like "master of my domain," "lord of the manor," and "queen of the castle." "The Contest" topped *TV Guide*'s 2009 list of "TV's Top 100 Episodes of All Time."

Then there was the T-word, the deplorable slur The Gang used to refer to Carmen (*Sweet Valley High* star Brittany Daniel), the transgender woman Mac dated in seasons 1 and 3. Initially planning to set her up with Charlie, Mac became attracted to Carmen, especially after she complimented his physique. The two began publicly dating, though Mac was embarrassed about this with his friends. He explained to Dennis he was biding his time so he would be first in line to date her after her gender transition surgery (many jokes were made about Mac's discomfort with the very visible protuberance in Carmen's jeans).

On one of their dates, not only did he pull back from her when they embraced (so their waists wouldn't touch), but he turned around and punched her in the face when she playfully approached him from behind and tapped him on the shoulder. It was established this was a reflexive reaction for Mac—he had done this before. In a flashback to the Paddy's Christmas party, Dee approached Mac from behind with a sprig of mistletoe and tapped him on the shoulder, but instead of a kiss, she got socked in the kisser.

But when he hit Carmen, two guys saw what they thought was Mac beating up a woman. He told them he wasn't, that Carmen was a man. Then they decided they had witnessed a hate crime, and chased Mac all the way back to Paddy's, where he told his friends he had accidentally punched Carmen. He demanded, twice, that Dee fetch him a drink after all the excitement. She got her revenge for the mistletoe slug and dished up some much deserved comeuppance to Mac as she—not at all accidentally—slugged him in the face.

Carmen returned in season 3's "Mac Is a Serial Killer," inexplicably still willing to date Mac, even though he continued to be uncomfortable with dating her before her planned surgery. He acted so evasive about who he was spending his nights with that, as the title hints, Frank had the rest of The Gang suspecting Mac might be the local serial killer he read about in the newspaper. Mac tried to break up with Carmen—which she prevented by commenting on his (allegedly) swole body once again. But when Mac refused to let anyone (especially the rest of The Gang) see them on a date in public, he told Carmen, "Look, it's not like I'm ashamed of you. I'm ashamed of myself."

That was, finally, the last straw for Carmen. She dumped Mac, and the two didn't see each other again until the season 6 premiere, "Mac Fights Gay Marriage." His stance on gay marriage was sparked when he ran into Carmen, who had gotten the transition surgery. Instead of immediately calling him, as he delusionally expected she would,

Carmen had gotten married to a supportive man named Nick (the late *Body of Proof* and *The Suite Life on Deck* star Windell Middlebrooks). The matrimony constituted a gay marriage in Mac's ill-informed, insanely jealous mind; Nick being with Carmen means he must be gay, Mac said. But The Gang pointed out that Mac slept with Carmen, too, and before her surgery, so what did that add up to for him?

Frank broke down all the gay marriage mathematics with one of his most famous, and quotable, philosophies: "Who gives a shit if gays want to be miserable like everybody else and get married? Let 'em do it. It's no skin off my ass."

But Frank's pithily perfect, if pessimistic, slogan for equal opportunities in marriage aside, the episode closed out another unfortunately repellent treatment of Carmen, who was referred to with the T-word five times.

Carmen eventually got a satisfying ending when she and Nick picked up their baby at the hospital from surrogate Dee in season 6, a storyline that meshed perfectly with Olson's real-life pregnancy. It was designed as a way to treat Carmen with more respect and sensitivity. But McElhenney himself has admitted on several occasions the show would have treated the Carmen character differently, and certainly would have referred to her differently, if they could arrange a do-over on those early episodes.

"[The characters] were calling her a slur during the first few years, which was most definitely out of ignorance. It was never supposed to be inflammatory or hurtful, but nevertheless, it was," McElhenney said. "We can't go back and re-edit those episodes, but what we can do is make sure that as we're moving forward, we're making those adjustments and doing our due diligence."

Daniel, who had costarred with Howerton on the short-lived Fox sitcom *That '80s Show* (playing his character's bisexual ex-girlfriend), was among the friends RCG invited to see the original pilot. She remembers thinking the show was hilarious, and she especially loved the Carmen character.

When she found out FX gave the creators money to reshoot the pilot, she asked her agent to let it be known she'd love to play Carmen if they were interested. They were, and she did. That reshot pilot later became season 1's fourth episode, "Charlie Has Cancer."

"After each take, we'd talk about it, like, 'Oh, let's try this, let's try that.' I always loved that collaborative process," says the actress, who had already starred with comic actors like David Spade, the Wayans brothers, and comedy troupe Broken Lizard, and had come to appreciate that style of working. "We were working, and everybody [on *Sunny*] was just throwing out really great ideas. It was fun."

Daniel said she didn't know initially Carmen was going to be a recurring character, but she was ready any time the call came asking her to return.

"The only thing that I knew after the pilot was that she was a love interest to Mac, and that she is transgender. And I felt like you'd never seen anybody like me playing a character like that before," Daniel says. "So I thought, oh, this could be really funny and different.... I just made it like, okay, she really sees something in Mac and really likes him. There's some kind of chemistry between the two of them, so she did whatever it took to win him over. And because [she had been] a man, she knows what men like and need, and men like to be complimented. So I was just thinking about what would win over this guy, and thinking about [his] character."

Daniel also offers a great explanation for why Carmen, a sweet woman who was obviously savvier than her boyfriend, was willing to put up with his often casually harsh behavior. It's an intriguing theory that suggests Carmen was in charge of the relationship all along. "Off the top of my head now, the only thing I can think of is that she was getting exactly what she wanted. So she was fine with [the situation]."

Since Daniel's last appearance on the show in 2010, her professional and personal lives have been packed. She went on to star on The CW football-themed dramedy *The Game,* and reunited with her *Sweet Valley High* costar and identical twin sister, Cynthia, in a *Cheaper by the Dozen* movie remake. And after a successful battle with stage IV non-Hodgkin's lymphoma, she met her husband, Adam Toumi, and welcomed a daughter, Hope, via a surrogate, using an egg donated by her sister.

Like every other recurring actor who's talked about the series, Daniel said she would love to return.

"I always left the set going, 'Okay, they'll call me the next season, or the season after that, but nothing yet,'" she said. "But I have to say . . . I've worked on more than eighty episodes of another show, and people come up to me over this small recurring character all the time. I guess people love Carmen. It's just so funny to me. I'm surprised people even remember me on this show!

"I love the character. I love working with all of them . . . I know that they would be probably a bit more sensitive with certain things [now], but in terms of my approach, it would be the same. I can't think of anything I would do differently. Because I would serve any character."

As much as the show's creators have thought about the things they might approach differently and the words they wouldn't repeat on the series, *It's Always Sunny* fans, and even critics, have largely given a thumbs-up to even The Gang's most misanthropic adventures and deeds.

Sometimes the creators hope to get fans more riled, however.

"We were disappointed that there wasn't more negative feedback," Howerton said. "In the first season, we were doing all of this stuff about molestation and abortion. And we didn't do it to get a rise out of people. We did it because we thought that's what's going on in the world, and this is the kind of shit we think is funny. These were issues that people tend to get a little stirred by."

Ultimately, each of the three *Sunny* creators has a pretty good handle on the reasons the comedy has steered clear of series-threatening controversy across the nearly two decades they've remained on the air.

Day, for one, thinks *Sunny* humor isn't as shocking as some people may believe. "I'm more surprised by what people get away with on dramas. People get their face shot off and cut in half. That's why none of this stuff in a comedy seems shocking to me. It's always social commentary and tongue-in-cheek. We showed Danny DeVito's butt. So what? I saw a little kid get poisoned with ricin and nobody seems to care. I don't find what we do shocking. Edgy, sure, but I think it's just satire."

Howerton suggested people haven't gotten more upset by The Gang's antics because The Gang always loses. "It's like *South Park*. I think we also get away with [outrageous stories] because the characters are never rewarded," he said. "They're always losing. They always wind up in the same place they started in."

But even after the saying of the N-word, the R-word, and the T-word, after the blackface, the yellowface, and the redface, and after destroying Cricket, painting a baby with shoe polish to tan him, selling alcohol to minors, planning to dig up their dead mother and then actually doing it, making a terrorist video to intimidate a rival, multiple kidnappings, planning to eat a corpse and a homeless person, attacking Santa, torturing Dee on multiple occasions for sport, and trapping a host of their rivals in a burning apartment (just to name a fraction of their greatest hit jobs), McElhenney has the simplest, and likely the most spot-on, reason cancel culture hasn't come for *It's Always Sunny in Philadelphia* and its brand of satire.

"I think everybody kind of gets it."

Chapter Nine

SUNNY STANS

"*Sunny* is not just a signature show for FX, but the cornerstone of success for FX comedy and one of the all-time great comedies on television. It has generated billions, literally billions, of viewings across its airings on FX, FXX, syndication on Comedy Central, and its availability on streaming platforms."
—John Landgraf addressing members of the media before the premiere of *It's Always Sunny in Philadelphia*'s fifteenth season

Billions of viewings; *billions*, with a *"b."* When Landgraf shared that incredibly impressive statistic, 154 episodes of *IASIP* had been available for fans to watch on various platforms at various times. That means, obviously, there have been a lot of repeat viewings. That's really no surprise, as no series earns a "cult hit" status label without its devotees committing to viewing it over and over again. A friend once told me he had watched "The Nightman Cometh" at least once a day since it was released on DVD in September 2009... and he emphasized the words "at least."

How many times have other *Sunny* fans, across streaming, DVDs, and linear TV, watched and rewatched "The Nightman Cometh"? For many, enough times to memorize every single word, song lyric, and movement Mac makes as he karate chops his way across the stage; enough that they remember how Dee mimes writing when she offers her phone number to perspective suitors, how Dee frustrates Charlie so much that he refers to himself repeatedly in the third person when she objects to the "Little Boy" song; enough times they're still tickled by the exact moment Dennis becomes a total lickspittle when he points out to Frank that Charlie told everyone "no gum" during rehearsal, and the exact way Gladys says "What is happening?" And enough times that it's still a pleasant little surprise when Charlie, in his sunshine-yellow tux, descends from the school gymnasium heavens to reveal the true purpose of the musical.

And that is just one episode. Among those billions (*billions*, with an "s") of viewings are also the many rewatches of "A Very Sunny Christmas" (at least) once a year. The straight-to-DVD holiday special is a double-length, standalone gem of merry malevolence and mischief-making as The Gang blasts back to the past to discover their true meaning of Christmas: little boy Charlie (in his signature long underwear) getting the gift that led him to his huffing hobby and eventually realizing why his mom had a revolving door of Santas visiting her in her bedroom every year; Mac putting two and two together to understand that for every present he unwrapped, another kid in his neighborhood was missing one; and Frank Scrooge-ing Dennis and Dee's gifts from them every year (continuing to the present day—pun intended—when he bought Dennis's dream Lamborghini and Dee's dream designer bag... for himself).

There's also an industrial snowblower, Charlie going all zombie on a mall St. Nick, a delightfully twisted Rankin/Bass–esque clay animation segment, tiny Mac squealing with joy when he ripped the wrapping paper off his (stolen) Cabbage Patch Kid, and Charlie getting confounded by a Simon game.

And the pièce de résistance of the special, and for many fans, the whole series: Frank, naked as a newborn baby, at a company Christmas party, crawling out from inside a leather couch, which he was sewn into so he could eavesdrop on the revelers. DeVito loved every minute of the gag. In fact, when RCG asked if he would be willing to pop out of a leather couch, naked and sweaty and in front of a roomful of extras, he didn't hesitate to say yes, and couldn't wait to share tales of how he'd performed the scene as a totally denuded DeVito, save a ball sack—it's just what it sounds like—to keep his family jewels snug and tidy and pouched. Part of what inspired the idea for the scene—shot in one take because it was quite toasty inside the couch—was a nature video McElhenney had watched of an animal being birthed (presumably sans ball sack).

"You stick everything in a sack, and then they tie it up like a little change purse. Just so you're not dangling. Or trolling," DeVito said, in a sly reference to his *Nightman Cometh* character, another slice of *Sunny* he loved playing.

He also loved the response he provoked from Olson, who was so distracted by DeVito tumbling naked out of the couch before her that she forgot her line. An easily found Reddit video clip captures her reaction.

She later told a journalist, "He fires out of that couch and somersaults to the ground in a way that allowed me to see every single part of his body. Parts I wasn't anticipating. . . . The moral of the story is that Danny DeVito has a mesmerizing b-hole."

There is very little DeVito doesn't love about playing Frank Reynolds. At eighty years old (he was sixty-two when he joined the *Sunny* cast), he's physically spry, and mentally, emotionally, and spiritually young at heart. Stick him inside a McPoyle RV bathroom, or have him slime across the floor covered in hand sanitizer, fall out a window, or get stuck inside a playground coil in his underwear, and he'll have as much fun doing it as the rest of us will have watching him.

"At this moment, I'm really like Frank. I've been infected by the youth I work with," DeVito said. "They've taken Danny and usurped him as a gentle human being. I'm now crude and rough around the edges. More importantly, like Frank, I don't give a shit."

And that's why, more than fifty years into his illustrious Hollywood career, DeVito is at his most popular, most beloved, among fans of all ages, including ones who have never even heard of *Taxi*.

John Landgraf, DeVito's former producing partner at Jersey Television and longtime personal friend, said his idea of pairing DeVito with the *Sunny* gang in the first place wasn't just about bringing an A-list star into the mix with four incredibly talented but then-unknown aspiring stars. "They're just creative soulmates," he said. "That guy is just brave and up for anything; he's just a kamikaze artist and comedian. He'll not only do anything if he thinks it's good and funny—he'll push you harder. So it was just kind of that way from the beginning."

DeVito has earned the love of *It's Always Sunny* fans, and sometimes their disgust, in myriad ways: By dressing Frank up like a man-cheetah, a Man-Spider, and the Trash Man. By pooping in the sofa bed he shares with Charlie, cleaning his toenail gunk with a knife, and pretending to be Dee's husband to get at his dead ex-wife's money. By having sex with Charlie's dream girl, the Waitress. By creating and operating multiple sweatshops. By waterboarding Dee and setting her on fire . . . in separate incidents.

DeVito has even carried one of his characters-within-the-character—the troll from "The Nightman Cometh"—into his personal Twitter account. There, he provides a trove of Trollfoot posts, a sometimes daily photo travelogue of his foot . . . Trollfoot vacations in Italy! Trollfoot goes to Moscow! Trollfoot visits Anderson Cooper at work! Trollfoot being licked by a kitten! Trollfoot trying on a Lorax wig! Trollfoot on strike in Los Angeles during the 2023 SAG-AFTRA strike!

Sometimes eccentric, sometimes uncivilized, very often pickled on Paddy's potables, and always hilarious: Frank Reynolds has indeed gotten real weird with it on a regular basis across his sixteen seasons of *Sunny* so far. And that, along with the way DeVito embraces every minute of being Frank, is the crux of why Frank has become a multigenerational fan favorite, and why DeVito has come to a point in his career where he is a universally adored personality as a TV and movie star. He has built a long, critically acclaimed body of work, and there's an ever-growing audience that loves him the naughtier, and even grosser, he gets.

"Frank is in a pantheon of delicious vulgarians," *New York Times* columnist Maureen Dowd wrote in a profile of DeVito. "Characters who compress the seven deadly sins into one compact package, yet somehow still charm."

As an homage to the character, *How I Met Your Mother* star Cristin Milioti dressed up like Frank Reynolds—bald cap; thick, oversize specs; spitting up a foamy quaff from a can—for a 2021 *W Magazine* article, in which she shared she had watched *IASIP* for years, then binge-watched the whole series again during the COVID-19 pandemic.

"I [think] that Danny DeVito's performance in *It's Always Sunny* is one of the most demented performances I've ever seen," Milioti said. "The things he's doing are so almost avant-garde in their rancidness . . . [The couch scene in "A Very Sunny Christmas" is] one of the funniest pieces of physical comedy I've ever seen."

Take the Boston *Sunny* fan who bought a '90s van, named it Vanny DeVito, put that moniker and the actor's face on it, and drove it cross-country, handing out bumper sticker mementos along the way. But he wasn't the only one. The idea, and the pun, has proven so popular that dozens of others have joined in, including a Florida couple who sold their house and most of their possessions to fix up their own Vanny and drive him (with their cat and dog) all the way to California and into British Columbia. A Vanny DeVito has even gone international, with a mom, dad, and their two daughters "ditching 4 walls for 4 wheels" and "road schooling" around Europe. There are enough Vannys on Instagram to create a . . . caravanny.

Another fan decided to honor DeVito and Frank Reynolds's Trash Man character by creating a secret trash altar in a random men's bathroom inside a building at his university. Sadly, the publicity the shrine generated meant it didn't remain covert very long, and the administration at SUNY Purchase in New York ordered the display—accessible via a secret door that only opened by tugging down on a paper towel dispenser—removed. The strange hidden room that contained the sanctum was literally filled with garbage; underneath a poster of DeVito and a tiny cardboard cutout of him were pleas for others to make offerings to "our lord and savior Danny DeVito, patron saint of trash men." They did, compiling a heap that included mini DeVito cardboard figures, water bottles, condoms, tampons, empty cigarette packs, and messages for DeVito. DeVito was touched, tweeting of the peculiar adoration, "Your shrine honors me. My heart is filled with love and garbage."

The cardboard cutouts of DeVito in the college bathroom shrine are not the only instance of a substantially weighted paper product used to celebrate the actor. In 2022, a DeVito fan tweeted a photo of his Christmas tree . . . which was a life-size cardboard cutout of DeVito wrapped in a string of white lights. The man, the myth, the Christmas tree proxy himself responded by tweeting, "Love being your Christmas Danny." The original post and the reply sparked the sharing of pics from many other fans who brought DeVito into the holidays as Christmas ornaments, Christmas tree toppers, and another DeVito cardboard cutout tree the celebrant called "Danny DeTreeto."

But the queen of all things cardboardy and DeVito is an aspiring comedy director who went viral in 2018 when she took a cardboard cutout of Danny DeVito to her high school prom.

Allison Closs was about to finish her high school career in Carlisle, Pennsylvania, a small town outside Harrisburg, and wanted her senior prom to be memorable. The prom would also be her goodbye to school dances, events she had eschewed since her sophomore year when she asked a friend to a dance and he behaved badly. Dances, then, were off her list for the rest of high school, until her prom loomed.

Closs considered going with a date of the human variety, but there was no one she wanted to go with, and, she says, no one who wanted to go with her. Closs is a smart, charming, enthusiastic young woman. She refers to herself as a "really quirky and unique person" who was bullied a lot.

"I always believed I was a 'good weird,'" she said, "but lots of people growing up were making me feel like I was a 'bad weird.'"

But if taking a cardboard-cutout Danny DeVito to your prom is bad weird, who wants to be good weird?

Closs chose a DeVito from Amazon that was dressed casually, but with a sport coat, and attached him to an indoor scooter board (like the ones from gym class) with a leash, so she could maneuver him around all evening (this also seems like something Frank would enjoy). To get him properly gussied up for the prom, she outfitted him with a tie from her brother's closet and a boutonnière she stuck onto his jacket.

Closs's classmates were tickled about their prom's celebrity guest, and Allison and cardboard-cutout prom-date Danny DeVito (CCPDDD) had a smashing time. She says her fellow promgoers were lined up all night to take photos with CCPDDD; even a paper version of DeVito brings the fun wherever he goes.

It was no surprise, then, when the whole night went viral. The very savvy Closs let a local reporter in on her plans, and that reporter shared the details with a contact at the Associated Press. The story went national, and then before Closs went off to college that fall, she found out DeVito and the *Sunny* crew heard about his cardboard doppelgänger. McElhenney used a viral photo of Closs in her prom dress to have the *IASIP* props department make an Allison cardboard cutout, and surprised her with an Instagram post of actual live Danny DeVito taking cardboard-cutout Allison to the set of Paddy's Pub. "Hey Allison—I heard you took cardboard Danny to Prom. What a coincidence. He took cardboard Allison to Paddy's . . ." McElhenney wrote. Closs's written response to seeing herself, cardboard version, at Paddy's: "I AM SHOOKETH."

With outlets from *Time* magazine and Yahoo to Jimmy Kimmel's late-night talk show sharing the most famous prom night since Sissy Spacek's in *Carrie*—the BBC even covered it—all that was left after the two cardboard cutouts became *Sunny* memes was for the two living, breathing humans to meet.

In September 2018, Closs got a call from a producer of CBS daytime chat show *The Talk*, inviting her to talk about being the subject of a story that went viral. She had suspicions that there might be more to the appearance—could they possibly be planning to have DeVito on the show, too? she wondered—but put that out of her mind as she did some very fast packing for the trip to Los Angeles. After she took a seat at the table with hosts Sharon Osbourne, Sara Gilbert, and Eve, Closs happily repeated her story. Gilbert then led her over to another part of the stage, where the hosts presented Closs with a collection of new DeVito cutouts: *Taxi* DeVito, *Twins* DeVito, Matilda's dad DeVito, the Penguin DeVito from *Batman Returns* . . . and then, live and in-person, she met real-life DeVito!

He was his usual charming self, and even made a PG-rated, Frank-appropriate joke about the cutouts going with her to her dorm. Closs says she was so nervous and starstruck that she worried her dry mouth would prevent her from being able to speak. She covered her mouth with her hands, as if she was still surprised; really, she was trying to secretly twist her tongue around to summon up enough saliva to be able to chat with the actor. She did, and though she says she wishes she could have been less shy, her meeting with DeVito was a lovely capper to an unforgettable, monthslong experience.

Closs still has the original cardboard cutout DeVito, which has accompanied her to college and now to her home in Los Angeles. "He's taken a lot of damage over the years," Closs says. "He cannot stand upright on his own. He has to be put in a corner." Sounds just like Frank . . .

Closs is already earning experience toward her ultimate goal of directing. She connected with DeVito's agent when they met at *The Talk* and has worked as a production assistant and written her first movie script, a family comedy called *A Tail's Tale: A Mermaid's Tale*, which she plans to produce. She also kept the bonus cardboard DeVitos *Talk* hosts presented to her.

She calls them her Council of Dannys.

DeVito has been a particular draw for *Sunny* merchandise sales, too—the weirder, the better.

Anyone fancy a Danny Pack, a fanny pack that looks like DeVito's face, complete with side tufts of hair? How about a pair of Danny DeFeetos slippers to match? Danny DeVito coloring book? Danny DeVito—as art dealer Ongo Gablogian—stained glass suncatcher? Danny Dorito sticker or T-shirt (DeVito's head on a Dorito) or Danny DeCheeto fridge magnet (Devito's head on the "body" of a Cheeto)? Or perhaps, in these trying times, you could be offered a Danny DeVito prayer candle and matching lighter?

There are DeVito sequined pillows in a variety of characters he has portrayed; DeVito refrigerator magnet dolls, with multiple outfit changes; and a 3D printed figurine of Frank stuck in a playground coil.

You can buy Frank Reynolds air fresheners, Frank Reynolds head-shaped planters, Danny DeVito glow-in-the-dark gnomes, hanging

Frank Reynolds earrings, and an Operation game board with Frank's body and Frank-specific body parts (donkey brains, itchy trigger finger, rum hamstring) as a magnet.

It's maybe a tough premise to understand for the *It's Always Sunny* uninitiated. But for longtime fans, the people who populate the *IASIP* Reddit to confab with their fellow devotees, the ones who tattoo their love of the series and the characters all over their bodies—and get *real* specific with those tats—the ones who show up at Comic-Con and live *Always Sunny Podcast* events in *Sunny* costumes . . . for those fans, The Gang and the recurring characters and guest stars are beloved. Even the most amoral, disgraceful, irredeemable action by Frank and the rest of the Paddy's crew hasn't seemed to diminish the affection fans have for them and their associates.

Among their reasons: as cast members have pointed out many times, The Gang never wins. Sometimes they lose to lesser degrees than at other times, but they never win. They usually look like buffoons at the end of their chicanery. Because of that, viewers often see them as underdogs, and who doesn't love an underdog?

They're often seen as sympathetic figures because they're so vulnerable. Sweet Dee, for instance, wants nothing more in life—not money, not fame, not the baubles her dismissive mother took to her grave instead of bequeathing them to Dee—than the respect of her equally dismissive twin and the rest of her friends. How can you not root for Dee to actually receive some respect, at least sometimes? Or ever?

And what about her friends? The Gang are her only friends. She is one of their only friends. They are one another's only friends. If it weren't so utterly sad and pathetic, it would be kind of sweet that they can rely on one another. Except they can't rely on one another for anything positive, unless it benefits them in some selfish way. But even that's sweet sometimes, too.

Their loyalties aren't born out of affection for one another (well, maybe Mac's feelings for Dennis, which could also be summed up as more lust than love, or even like, much of the time), and they rarely even display any loyalties. They're usually up for bonding together in an opportunity to "versus" another group or person, but that's more about their inherent antisocial tendencies than any pro-friendship designs.

Yet, even in this regard, their group activity motivated by bad intentions is . . . charming? It's not the kind of comradeship that would be everyone's cup of tea, but given the milieu in which they operate (always scheming, usually while drunk, frequently while fighting), their relationships with one another are as close as any of them are likely to get to genuine friendship or love, and that is a vulnerability, something that can earn our empathy.

Other times, The Gang earns our affinity simply by making us laugh so much, and with the pure joy they all find in being as bad as they want to be. Quickly enough, we come to love them not only in spite of what they did but *because of* what they did. It's like why viewers never turned their backs on another all-time favorite FX character, Michael Chiklis's dirty cop Vic Mackey on *The Shield*, or on another could-have-been FX antihero, Bryan Cranston's Walter White on *Breaking Bad* (which Landgraf passed on for FX before it landed at AMC). Once those characters won over viewers, they had us; we were loyal to them no matter what they did, and we couldn't wait to see exactly what those next moves would be. Ditto Tony Soprano, Dexter Morgan, Omar Little, and Daenerys Targaryen, though it should be noted that their misdeeds caught up with all those dramatic series antiheroes and antiheroines, and not just with a deadly end. One of the greatest series finales of all time found Vic Mackey losing everything and everyone he cared about—and stuck at a desk job.

Most comedies don't end in such a hopeless manner, and the point could be made that The Gang gets their ultimate comeuppance in every episode, just by having to lead the same kind of life over and over again, with no forward movement. But when it does come time for the series to wrap, will RCG decide to give the characters a more definitive, and perhaps punitive, finale? A *Seinfeld*ian ending?

Or, will The Gang go on wreaking havoc, tormenting one another, just living their lives, together, the way they always have?

※ ※ ※

The *It's Always Sunny* fan base, of course, encapsulates love for the whole Gang, not just the senior Reynolds. Whatever you're looking for in a television comedy character, there's a Gang member for that.

Want a bar-owning, mostly illiterate musical savant who likes to eat stickers, chalk, and cat food, is obsessed with a woman who is skeeved by him but has slept with every other male member of The

Gang (and, finally, even the skeeve-er), is an expert in bird law and the nocturnal behavior patterns of cats, celebrates Philly sports as Green Man, has a flawless work ethic for janitorial duties, is annoyed by but takes care of his mother, writes musicals and patriotic anthems, likes ghouls and magnets, is capable of working himself into a tizzy, and is the sweetest member of his friend group (this is obviously a relative assessment)? Charlie Kelly is your guy.

In the market for a psychopathic (sociopathic? both?) bar owner who loves his classic Range Rover more than he loves humans, is prone to intense and hilarious rages, secretly wears makeup, has created an elaborate personal system for manipulating women, slept with the Waitress, frequently proclaims himself to be the brains and the looks of The Gang, is perfectly coiffed, likes expensive clothes and other pricey goods but does not like working to pay for them, collects videotapes of his own sexual exploits, refers to himself as a golden god, tried to have sex with Charlie's mom and Mrs. Mac but was rejected by both, was married briefly and regrettably to his cat-obsessed high school girlfriend, admits to not feeling emotions, is the twin of Dee, whom he likes to torment and taunt, fathered a son who lives in North Dakota, is narcissistic and lives for insinuating "the implication," and loves the music of Rick Astley? Dennis Reynolds is your dude.

If you're looking for a bartender / aspiring actress / aspiring comedian who is the subject of ridicule about her looks and lack of talent from the only people she can consider friends, who pretends to be self-assured but is the most insecure among The Gang, who held a fake funeral for the (fake) dead baby she pretended to have to avoid a government audit, who pretended to marry Frank in a ceremony performed by her biological father, who is constantly told she looks like a bird, who just wants her brother to like and respect her, who was once called the Aluminum Monster because she wore a back brace, who dry heaves when she gets nervous, who was a surrogate mom for Carmen and Nick, who trained to be a boxer and tried out for the Philadelphia Eagles, and who teamed up with her brother to become a crack addict so she could receive welfare? Sweet Deandra Reynolds is your gal.

For the fan whose laugh tank would be full with a character who is another co-owner of Paddy's, who considers himself the bar's bouncer, who most aggressively insults Dee, whose Christmas tradition was receiving stolen goods courtesy of his parents and throwing rocks at trains with Charlie, who denied he was gay and then came out of the closet and went right back in and then finally did a beautiful and emotional dance at his dad's prison to confirm he is gay, who gained fifty pounds and then lost it and got really swole, who wants to be BFFs with Chase Utley, who just wants to play a game of catch with his dad, who had sex with Dennis and Dee's mom, who loves and hates Dennis, who may be in love with Dennis, who thinks he is a master of karate, who likes to cut the sleeves off all his shirts, and who loves his parents deeply even though they seem to have no affection for him ever, and who dearly loves his wandering scruffy old dog, Poppins, then Ronald "Mac" McDonald is your fella.

And we already know who the licentious elder statesman of The Gang is... it's Frank Reynolds, the man who never met a vulgarity he didn't indulge, a hornswoggling he didn't perpetrate, or an offense he wouldn't commit toward someone, be it operating a sweatshop in the Paddy's basement, turning Dennis into a prostitute and acting as his pimp, or tricking Dee and Dennis into digging up the skeletal corpse of their mother. And still, we laugh, hard and often, and we wear Danny fanny packs.

DeVito and Frank are certainly not the only *IASIP* characters (DeVito, as much as Frank, is most definitely a character) who've inspired a deluge of *Sunny*-themed merch throughout the last two decades. Most recently, the show is featured in its own edition of Monopoly, with the Paddy's Pub Basement and Paddy's Main Room as the Boardwalk and Park Place of the *IASIP*-themed board; Dennis's face on the Paddy's Dollars; and the Chance and Community Chest cards renamed Dayman and Nightman. For game tokens, you can be Rum Ham, kitten with mittens, Charlie's rat stick, Poppins, the Birds of War hat, or Mac's duster coat.

There's also an official *It's Always Sunny* Trivial Pursuit game, an official *Paddy's Pub: The Worst Bar in Philadelphia* cookbook, and a set of *Sunny* Funko Pop! figurines that feature The Gang in their *The Nightman Cometh* costumes (with two versions of Charlie, one in his yellow tuxedo Dayman costume and one as the musical's director).

In addition, the official FX store has featured *Sunny* goodies since the early days of the comedy, including mugs, pint glasses, phone cases, *The Nightman Cometh* Christmas stockings, and button-down shirts with patterned fabric featuring Charlie Kelly: King of the Rats, Frank as the Trash Man, and Charlie and Frank as the Gruesome Twosome, as well as Nightman and Dayman, Pepe Silvia, and Rum Ham versions.

When iPods were still a thing, there was an *It's Always Sunny in Philadelphia* one.

And for *Sunny* fans looking for more unique and homemade goodies, entrepreneurs have gotten real weird with it: Fight Milk candles, a handmade CharDee MacDennis game, and the cutest little handmade plush Rum Ham . . . my, what pineappley eyes you have, Rum Ham!

What may come as a pleasant surprise is the number of celebrity fans who get their guffaws, chortles, and titters from watching The Gang.

Lin-Manuel Miranda, author of the music, lyrics, and book for *Hamilton*, revealed his *Sunny* fandom to Day and Ellis . . . in the middle of a performance of his classic Tony and Pulitzer Prize–winning musical. Day and Ellis were in the audience for a 2016 Broadway show when Miranda, starring as the titular politician of his musical, pointed out to the audience and exclaimed, "Holy shit, Charlie and the Waitress!" Later, Miranda told Day he was a huge fan of *IASIP* and had "Dayman" stuck in his head onstage. Day was so inspired that he later proposed making the *Sunny* season 12 premiere, "The

Gang Turns Black," into a musical episode. Meanwhile, Miranda has talked with RCG about someday taking *The Nightman Cometh* to Broadway, and the playwright guested on the November 2022 "The Nightman Cometh" episode of *The Always Sunny Podcast* to geek out about *their* classic musical.

Day, by the way, is often how the cast finds out about their famous fans. While working on and promoting his movie projects, and sometimes just while out in the wild meeting his fellow stars, Day learned Samuel L. Jackson, former *Saturday Night Live* star Pete Davidson, the late, great Robin Williams, and Sean Penn were all *It's Always Sunny* fans. Day recalled that Davidson, because of his *Sunny* love, was nervous about meeting him when Davidson had a small role in Day's Prime Video romantic comedy *I Want You Back*; Davidson later asked Day to make a guest appearance in his autobiographical Peacock comedy series *Bupkis*. Day was also told Williams and Penn liked to watch *Sunny* together. The two Oscar winners had both guest-starred on another one of their mutually favorite comedies, *Friends* . . . oh, to think about the delicious chaos Williams could have created if he'd had a chance to guest-star with The Gang.

Among the other famous *Sunny* devoted:

- *Lost* cocreator Damon Lindelof loves *Sunny* so much he moderated The Gang's first trip to San Diego Comic-Con in 2008, and invited McElhenney for a multi-episode guest appearance as Aldo, a member of the Others who did not have a happy ending on the island.

- The Kings of Leon, the alternative rockers from Nashville—brothers Nathan, Caleb, and Jared Followill and their cousin Matthew Followill—are huge fans of The Gang, and as is often the case, the feeling is mutual. So much so that the three Followill sibs were invited to guest-star in the two-part season 7 finale, "The High School Reunion," in which we learned Mac's real, full name (Ronald McDonald) and the Followills stopped playing rock stars for a night to pour beverages at The Gang's titular return to their high school. The Paddy's crew was just as popular as could have been predicted . . . even the bartenders were annoyed by them.

- *Harry Potter* star Daniel Radcliffe told his fans during a Reddit "Ask Me Anything," "I love that show," prompting *Sunny* fans to suggest he should guest-star, playing Charlie's British cousin "who does even dirtier work for even less money" than Charlie.

- Director Guillermo del Toro is such a fan of Charlie Day that he cast him in his 2013 sci-fi monster movie *Pacific Rim*, playing Dr. Newt Geiszler. RCG then invited del Toro to perform a very special guest role on *Sunny*: Pappy McPoyle, the patriarch of the McPoyle clan. Pappy has a bird, Royal, who pecked out the eyes of Liam McPoyle and the Lawyer.

- Rapper and music producer Mike Posner called *IASIP* his favorite show.

- Portugal. The Man, the rockers from Alaska and now Portland, are such *Sunny* fans that they worked out a very cool, soothing arrangement of "Dayman" that they often play in concert.

- Taylor Swift, and her brother, Austin, are fans of the show and of Ellis, whom T. Swift cast in the music video for her song "Anti-Hero." Ellis plays Kimber, Taylor's daughter in the clip, which Swift also directed.

- *Game of Thrones* showrunners David Benioff and D. B. Weiss are additional creatives with a mutual admiration relationship with RCG. Benioff and Weiss love *Sunny* so much they wrote an episode of the series—season 9's outstanding *Flowers for Algernon* spoof "Flowers for Charlie"—and they guest-starred as Bored Lifeguard #1 and Bored Lifeguard #2 in season 12's "The Gang Goes to a Water Park." Meanwhile, in "Winterfell," the season 8 premiere of *Game of Thrones*, McElhenney made a cameo appearance during which his character's left eye was removed with an arrow.

- Another TV creator on the *Sunny* bandwagon: multiple-Emmy-winner Matthew Weiner. The *Mad Men* creator and showrunner as well as writer and executive producer on *The Sopranos* was so steeped in the deep drama of his jobs that *IASIP* was not initially on his radar. But during a ski trip with his kids, he had to wait around for a business call, and started watching an *It's Always Sunny* marathon his kids were glued to.

Cut to five hours later, when he and his sons had digested ten episodes, and Weiner had become a newbie fan. "I frequently watch them on an airplane, because I can watch five of them, and I'm just happy," he says.

He and his children would later visit the Paddy's Pub set, and RCG put three of the kids in an episode as extras. Weiner also went on to moderate a Paley Center discussion with the *Sunny* cast in Beverly Hills in 2016, and he and RCG talked about him writing a *Sunny* episode.

As for why the collaboration never happened, Weiner says it was probably up to him to get it started. He probably flaked, he says. "Out of fear."

"I don't know, because they are so smart, so clever. There is always a plot, but I am constantly surprised by where they go with [the storylines]. And that's hard to do. Also, I can't not like all the characters. They can do a lot of terrible things. They've done terrible things to each other, to strangers. They've stolen, they've made fun of the wrong people in every political stripe. It's got a real conversive tone to it. I know it sounds like an exaggeration, but I always still believe that they care about each other. That's hard to do, to pull off."

- Day met sixteen-year-old Malia Obama, who told him she was a huge fan of *Sunny*.

- Day and *The Kids in the Hall* star Dave Foley met when both participated in a charity event and when Foley told Day he was a fan, RCG invited Foley to play Principal MacIntyre, a high school administrator whose career takes a bad turn when Dee and Charlie are in his employ.

- Vegas-based rockers Imagine Dragons are *Sunny* fans and fans of real-life *Sunny* marrieds McElhenney and Olson, whom the band chose to star in their 2021 "Follow You" video. The video's storyline: Kaitlin surprises her husband with a private performance by his favorite band . . . which is the Killers. *Her* favorite band is Imagine Dragons, and as they start performing, Olson starts fantasizing about the band members. McElhenney begins fantasizing about himself, taking over for each of the musicians. The story ends with the frisky couple fleeing the Venetian concert hall to go celebrate McElhenney's birthday alone, while Dragons lead singer Dan Reynolds is left chuckling that they're skipping out after just one tune.

- Matchbox Twenty lead singer Rob Thomas randomly ended up in the season 4 episode "Dennis Reynolds: An Erotic Life," playing a deranged version of himself in a rehab facility, teaming up with comedian Sinbad to intimidate fellow patient Dennis. The out-there scenario—definitely among the series' more absurdist comedy episodes—began when Matchbox Twenty was playing the Staples Center in Los Angeles. The band loves The Gang, so they called the cast's reps and invited them to the concert. The Gang said yes, showed up early, and spent the whole day. Thomas said they got drunk together after the concert, and RCG insisted he was going to be in a future *Sunny* episode.

As batty as TV Rob Thomas was in the storyline, and the character was quite out of control, there was an aggressively shocking alternative ending that might have proven too traumatic had it aired, even by the most extreme *It's Always Sunny* standards. When Dennis realized he needed to leave rehab, TV Rob Thomas advised him to make a break for it while Sinbad wasn't looking. Dennis worried about leaving TV Rob Thomas behind on his own, but TV Rob told him, "Don't worry about me, man. I'll be just fine." Then, once Dennis was safely out of the building, TV Rob Thomas removed a gun from his robe, put it to his forehead, and with the camera trained on a photo of Sinbad, pulled the trigger. The graphic scene ended with splatter covering Sinbad's photo, and a feeling of, "Did I really just see that?!" For those who haven't, it's another video easily found on YouTube.

☼ ☼ ☼

The cast is clearly appreciative for a viewership, celebrity and otherwise, that has continued to show up for seventeen seasons and counting.

DeVito, for one, is especially grateful for the fans, and is that rare A-lister who genuinely enjoys talking with them. If you ever encounter him in the wild, don't be nervous about approaching him for a selfie.

"Listen, [seventeen seasons] *Sunny* has been on because of that," said the man who was honored with a Danny DeVito Day holiday every November 17 (his birthday) in his hometown, Asbury Park, New Jersey. "Do you know when you got to worry? When you're walking down the street and nobody wants a selfie. So bring on the selfies, baby."

Chapter Ten

THE GANG'S ALL HERE...
INCLUDING THE MAYOR
OF TELEVISION

It's Always Sunny in Philadelphia started with three friends trying to create comedy success with a project—about a group of friends—that would be, among other things, a deconstruction of a series like *Friends*.

The theme of friendship, and family, was baked into the goodness of the series from the get-go.

The friendship among McElhenney, Day, and Howerton is the heart of *Sunny*, and they each also brought other friends into the mix early on. Day's girlfriend and soon-to-be wife, Mary Elizabeth Ellis, played Charlie's on-screen obsession, the Waitress, in the series premiere. And Ellis's real-life roommate, Artemis Pebdani, played Sweet Dee's friend Artemis in season 1. Day's longtime friend Cormac Bluestone guest-starred in season 1 and eventually became a composer on the show. And, of course, Jimmi Simpson and Nate Mooney, Day's pals from the Williamstown Theatre Festival, have played twisted, incestuous brothers Liam and Ryan McPoyle since the first season.

One of the most special guest stars of the series came from Day's family: his ninety-four-year-old grandmother, Anna Scapin, who appeared in "The Gang Gets Stranded in the Woods," in season 6. She's in a quick shot, sitting at a piano with Charlie, during a montage of Dennis and Charlie's drunken hangout with Philadelphia Phillies stars Chase Utley and Ryan Howard.

"It's her finest work, though," Charlie says about his grandma, who passed away in 2012. "She called me to say how excited she was to actually get a check in the mail, and she said she hadn't . . . [She was] ninety-four years old. She said she hadn't received a paycheck in something like twenty years."

Howerton's friend and Juilliard classmate Morena Baccarin (*Deadpool*) played Carmen in the original $200 *IASIP* pilot (but was unavailable when RCG began filming the first season for FX), and another friend and Juilliard alum, Sam Witwer (*Being Human*), guest-starred in season 3's "Dennis and Dee's Mom Is Dead," playing the muscular guy in the store when Mac, Dennis, and Charlie are looking for party guests for Dennis's mansion. Witwer is also the lead singer of the band the Crashtones, who Howerton has performed with (including on the *Flash Gordon* theme song that inspired a favorite element of "The Nightman Cometh").

The rest of The Gang have also brought friends and family into their on-screen madness. Olson's longtime friend and fellow alum of the Groundlings, Dax Shepard (*Punk'd*), guest-starred in season 10's "Ass Kickers United: Mac and Charlie Join a Cult," as a member of said cult, and another Olson pal, Tricia O'Kelley (*Gilmore Girls*), guested in season 13's "The Gang Gets New Wheels," playing Dee's (temporary) new friend.

DeVito has made the *Sunny* set a family affair on several occasions. His late father-in-law, Philip Perlman, guest-starred as "I.V. Man," seeking divine medical intervention in the second-season episode "The Gang Exploits a Miracle." And Philip's daughter, DeVito's wife, Rhea Perlman, finally guest-starred in season 16's "The Gang Gets Cursed," playing Dee's neighbor Bertha Fussy, who Dee thought had put a curse on her after they had beef about a noise complaint. Rhea Perlman's performance also completed one of the coolest casting accomplishments on *Sunny*: every member of the main cast has now seen his or her spouse appear on the series.

DeVito's oldest daughter, Lucy, was his first family member to guest on *Sunny*, and it was quite a memorable appearance. Lucy played a waitress at Guigino's, The Gang's favorite fine dining eatery, in season 2's "Mac Bangs Dennis' Mom." Frank, anxious to get back to his wilder, premarriage ways, met up with his ex-girlfriend Angie, who had been his partner in those old days of having sex on a gravesite and driving a stolen motorcycle into a river. However, when Frank learned Angie was no longer chasing fun but instead was a widow with seven kids and wanted to talk about nothing else, he tuned her out and began leering at the waitress and her legs—the waitress played by DeVito's daughter Lucy.

"It was kind of creepy, like Frank ogled her a little bit," DeVito said. "But listen, it's always sunny in Philadelphia!"

※ ※ ※

McElhenney, too, has infused *Sunny* with his friends and family. His dad, Bob, played the "tweaker" who pulled a gun on Mac and Dee in season 3's "Bums: Making a Mess All Over the City." His sister, Katie, is a *Sunny* writer. His brother, Patrick, is the series' still photographer. His youngest son with Olson, Leo, played "Water Fountain Kid" in the season 16 episode "Risk E. Rat's Pizza and Amusement Center."

McElhenney has also mentioned real-life personal connections in the show. He's referred to, and filmed at, his high school alma mater, St. Joe's Prep. And as clichéd as it may sound, he has practically made his beloved hometown a series character.

Then there's the real-life friend who has been part of the series in various ways since the beginning, who has been a key player in some of the most classic *Sunny* episodes, and who credits the show and the opportunities his friend has given him with helping him build his whole career.

Todd Biermann has known McElhenney since they were fourteen years old. They were the two smallest kids in their freshman class at St. Joe's Prep, both a little over five feet tall, both weighing under ninety pounds. That commonality didn't initially lead to friendship. "It actually made us a little antagonistic towards one another, early on, because we were both kind of the small, scrappy smartasses," Biermann says.

Eventually, the two bonded, and formed a friendship that has lasted through their St. Joe's days, through college time at Temple (though McElhenney's time at the Philadelphia university was brief), through the beginnings of their professional careers, through marriages and kids, and through joint Father's Day celebrations. Both have homes on the West Coast while still maintaining strong Philly ties.

It took a while—more to come on that—but *It's Always Sunny* bonded them once again, with both finding the biggest creative successes in a project that pays homage to their hometown and, in its own absurd way, their friendship.

When McElhenney, Day, and Howerton made the deal with FX to create a seven-episode first season of *Sunny*, Biermann was still living in Philly. McElhenney had already ended his seven-year stint in New York and headed west to Los Angeles. Biermann had started getting his first major television experience, working as a production assistant on the TLC breakout series *Trading Spaces*. Based on a British series called *Changing Rooms*, *Trading Spaces* followed two sets of neighbors who were given $1,000, forty-eight hours, and the expertise of an interior designer and a carpenter to perform makeover magic on a room in each other's houses.

Biermann was doing well with the reality series—so well that he would eventually get a contract with the show and start the process of buying his first home in Philly, where the *Spaces* production company was based.

Biermann even tried to get some free home remodeling for his buddy Rob, who was by then living in the West Hollywood garage apartment he rented when he wrote the first script for the original *Sunny* pilot while waiting tables and trying to make something solid happen in the entertainment industry.

"So I tried to put him on the show," Biermann says. "I could at least get him a couch or a bed or something to set up, because it was a fairly new apartment, and he didn't have much . . . he had a mattress on the ground. But it didn't work out, sadly, to put him on *Trading Spaces*; we couldn't pull it off logistically, but that's when he showed me what was then called *It's Always Sunny on TV*."

RCG started working on "Charlie Has Cancer," the second DIY episode of *Sunny*, and Biermann, on hiatus with *Trading Spaces* and with a ton of frequent-flier miles burning a hole in his wallet, headed to Los Angeles and volunteered his assistance with their production. He acted as a director of photography, location scout, assistant director, background actor—whatever was needed.

"It was a bunch of twenty-five-year-old kids with, like, pizza money and a couple of cameras," he said. "It was nothing, except it was those guys: Rob, Charlie, and Glenn."

When FX bought *Sunny*, Biermann was still working on his reality gig in Philly, and RCG hired him as the production manager when FX paid for them to reshoot the pilot in their series' title city. Then FX picked up six more episodes for a debut season, and RCG offered him a paid job on the show.

He turned it down.

Biermann loved working with his friend, and he had quickly made new friends in Day and Howerton. But he had also just gotten his first mortgage and signed a new two-year contract with *Trading Spaces*. *Sunny* was only guaranteed to run for those initial seven episodes, and Biermann just didn't think that was a good risk. So he thanked Rob, Charlie, and Glenn, appreciating the scripted television experience he'd gotten, and continued on his reality TV journey.

And then, as was always his goal, he started working in more scripted programming, and took a job as Denis Leary's assistant on his favorite show, *Rescue Me*. He thought he might turn the experience of that job into an opportunity to write scripts, then turn writing personal stories into the chance to direct them. Plus, his dad was a firefighter in Philly, and he knew that world of banter and brotherhood. Leary and company got the tone of that world just right, he felt. But then he started dating Andrea Roth, the actress who played the ex-wife of Leary's Tommy Gavin, and at the same time realized he didn't have the discipline or patience for writing. The *Rescue Me* gig ended—but he ended up marrying Roth, and they share a beautiful daughter, Ava. He also redoubled his commitment to directing, which was what he most wanted to do moving forward.

He laid this situation out in a conversation with his friend McElhenney and told him he was sorry he hadn't taken better advantage of the opportunity RCG presented him with all those years ago. McElhenney said little, but the next day called Biermann and offered him the chance to shadow *Sunny*'s main director at the time, Matt

Shakman, the former child star turned Emmy-nominated director of *WandaVision*. McElhenney also offered Biermann the chance to direct a season 8 episode of *Sunny*.

"It changed my life," Biermann says. "I directed one episode. It took maybe two or three more years of banging down doors and trying to get an agent and get established as a director. [*Sunny*] gave me a couple of episodes the following season. And then the network liked my episodes, so they gave me two more the following season. It took three years to get a few more credits and get established. And now, I've directed over a hundred episodes of twenty-five different TV shows."

Biermann says RCG also really set him up for success by pairing him with Shakman, "an incredibly talented, brilliant, lovely human being." And his first episode, "The Gang Gets Analyzed," was a cheap-and-easy "bottle episode," where the only guest was *Reno 911!* and *The State* star Kerri Kenney-Silver and all the action took place in two rooms on one set. He had no stunts or locations to scout. It was all about The Gang revealing themselves and what makes them tick to Kenney-Silver's overwhelmed therapist.

"They gave me something that was very, very manageable," he said. "It was like a stage play kind of episode. It was awesome. I mean, it was all very interesting. Yes, because Rob and I had been friends for a long time, Kaitlin as well. I was at their wedding. We spent Father's Day together this year. They're very close friends. So Rob definitely very much set me up for success, and I was familiar (with the rest of the cast). I had already met Danny at their wedding, and I knew Charlie from when we were younger. And I knew Glenn when I helped them on the pilot. So it was all familiar. Everybody was very supportive. Also, everybody knew that I was Rob's friend, so all the departments couldn't have been nicer to me."

He had a particularly memorable experience directing DeVito in "The Gang Gets Analyzed." The two had a lot of friendly chats when Biermann learned New Jersey native DeVito had spent a lot of time in Philly when he was a kid. But on the first day of filming with him, Biermann gave DeVito a note on his performance.

"He goes, 'No, I'm not doing that. That's the worst note I've ever heard.' And how do you respond to that? You stand up, and you walk away and say, 'Okay, we're going again'? I came back with my heart in my throat, and I heard Charlie ask him if everything was all right. He said, 'Yeah, I'm just busting balls.'

"But he made me earn it. It was definitely tough love, and then he went exceedingly out of his way to give me wonderful praise to the network and to the executives and could not have been a more wonderful collaborator over the years. He's a special guy."

Biermann went on to direct gems like the season 9 finale "The Gang Squashes Their Beefs" (in which they most definitely did not); "The Gang Beats Boggs," as in Baseball Hall of Famer and episode guest star Wade Boggs; "The Gang Does a Clip Show," i.e., the *Seinfeld* spoof episode; and "Mac Finds His Pride," the seminal season 13 finale for which McElhenney trained for months to perform a beautiful modern dance as a way for Mac to tell his imprisoned father he's gay.

"I think and [hope] that he gave me the opportunity to direct that episode because he probably can be maybe a little more vulnerable with me than he can be with other people, just because we have such personal history," Biermann says. "But I think he was also probably like, 'This can really help Todd, because it's going to be a special episode.'"

Biermann, who's developing an anthology series with McElhenney that will live in the universe of the McElhenney / Day / Megan Ganz–created Apple TV hit comedy *Mythic Quest*, has also directed episodes of *Mythic Quest*, *Younger*, *Broad City* (a job he says McElhenney helped him land with a call to series star Ilana Glazer), *The Mick*, and *Black-ish*, and is a producer and director on *Sunny* and *The Other Black Girl*.

That whole impressive résumé establishing him as a go-to television comedy director, Biermann says, was made possible by that one phone call from McElhenney, and the offer to join the *Sunny* crew as a director in season 8. "It's all of it. I have no comedy directing career without it."

Biermann says there was one more *Sunny* collaboration between him and RCG: the opening credits that have taken viewers on a tour through Philadelphia hotspots for seventeen seasons. "That was originally all shot out of my parents' old, beat-up 1990s Cadillac; it's all shot out of the sunroof."

The friendship between McElhenney, Day, and Howerton hasn't survived and thrived across the past twenty years without a hitch or two, however. They're smart, opinionated creative people, and sometimes those opinions aren't always in sync.

What they've relied on 100 percent of the time as the key to making sure their friendship, and *IASIP*, continue to run smoothly in those times of dissent is a simple but effective two-out-of-three rule.

If McElhenney thinks his opinion on a line of dialogue, how to play a scene, or a storyline idea is correct, but Day and Howerton disagree, their opinion wins. If Day is the one whose opinion is opposite Howerton and McElhenney's, they win. Ditto if Howerton's riding solo with his take on things versus the other two; in that case, McElhenney and Day would have their way. And because three people can almost always find a way to one idea that two of them can agree on, or at least lean toward more than another, it's a pretty fail-safe way to make decisions, especially since part of the agreed-upon process is that the odd man out will accept the opinion of the other two, no further arguments necessary.

Still, the intense effort it took to keep the show on the air as it slowly built its first round of loyal viewers never let up. Once *Sunny* had earned its more mainstream-level status and accolades, a concentrated dedication was still required to maintain the quality of the storylines and, always, the humor. But merely "maintaining" wasn't achievement enough for RCG, the cast, or the network. And all that pressure, most of it self-imposed, led to burnout.

It's Always Sunny in Philadelphia premiered on August 4, 2005; by December 20, 2012, a little more than seven years later, the cast and crew had completed eight regular seasons, including a musical episode and a Christmas special—ninety-four episodes in total. That time period also included creating and integrating the Frank Reynolds character; prepping, producing, and touring for the live *Nightman Cometh* shows; weddings for regular cast members McElhenney and Olson, Day and recurring star Ellis, and Howerton and guest actress Latiano; and the births of four children for the original cast.

The cast members were also moonlighting with film and TV guest roles during this time frame, and McElhenney was famously gaining fifty pounds to portray a major weight gain for Mac, all in the name of humor and a very specific deconstruction of sitcoms from the past. He noted that a lot of comedy casts would begin their shows looking one way, but with great success (and really great salaries) would show up on-screen seasons later with major zhuzhing done to their bodies, hair, teeth. He never name-checked a specific series or cast, but it was assumed he was referring to the multimillionaire cast of *Friends*.

The bottom line about this litany of packed schedules for the *Sunny* gang during those first eight seasons: it was a nonstop era of work and creativity and growth and building a thriving, massively popular television comedy—FX's first hit comedy, which helped build the network's reputation in the genre. By the time RCG and company got to season 10, they were a pop culture phenomenon—and they were all nursing a serious case of burnout.

All three *Sunny* EPs have talked often about the writing of the series as being the most taxing aspect of making it. They've had high hopes and high standards from the beginning. They didn't want it to be any old sitcom, even if that's all it would have taken to make *Sunny* a hit. They wanted it to be legitimately good—no, *great*. They wanted the series to be smart, to say something about a lot of different things. By season 2, because of the effort RCG put into the scripts, every joke, every character turn, every laugh they could honestly wring out of a situation—*Sunny* had already started to convince a good number of viewers that the series was good, on its way to becoming great. Those viewers included more experienced fellow TV writers and showrunners like *Lost* cocreator Damon Lindelof; *Game of Thrones* creators David Benioff and D. B. Weiss; and *Mad Men* creator/showrunner, as well as writer and executive producer on *The Sopranos*, Matthew Weiner.

But as the seasons wore on, RCG experienced mental and physical exhaustion, even with a whole writers' room full of fellow scribes. Just the thought of opening another writers' room season became fatiguing when there was such little downtime between seasons.

The *Sunny* writers' room runs via a simple, organized method. Brainstorming sessions (where the whole writing staff "breaks stories," i.e., comes up with an initial list of story ideas for the season) open the writers' work for the season. Individual writers are then assigned draft scripts and go off and write, and rounds of edits and rewrites go back and forth until the script is in finalish shape.

Then there is "the RCG pass," which Howerton has called the final step. That's when he, McElhenney, and Day go through the script to ensure everything makes sense, get the story as tight as possible, and punch up and add jokes when necessary. The *Sunny* writing staff has a deep bench of talent, but the RCG pass is the creators' stamp of approval on a script, and Howerton calls it the most fun part of the writing process.

But those breaking-stories sessions can be fun, too. There are desk toys and snacks of all varieties inside the writers' room, though there were definitely times when the candy and junkier fare gave way to protein bars and less sugary, fat-laden goodies. Like during season 13, when McElhenney was in peak physical form to play a completely jacked version of Mac. Or like his weight gain to play "Fat Mac" for season 7, when McElhenney wanted to poke a little fun at all the actors who were suddenly getting swole to win major movie roles. In a *Sunny*-specific spin on the idea, Mac would randomly take off his shirt to reveal his ridiculously sculpted abs, and the rest of The Gang would tell him to put his shirt back on. After all the work of getting into that shape, and then to have his friends so brutally and repeatedly dismiss him . . . well, it was harsh. And it did nothing (nothing good, anyway) for Mac's body dysmorphia, an ongoing issue that was introduced all the way back in the first season, when the slightest mention of his muscles from Carmen would send him over the moon and make him forget his concern that she still had a penis.

But Slinkys and snacks aside, breaking stories is tough, and is the writing process at its most stressful. Coming up with eight, ten, twelve, fifteen (for season 3) episode ideas at a time is incredibly pressure-filled, particularly with the block-shooting method. As the show gets older, the pressure only intensifies, because the series has already covered so many topics and put the characters into so many absurd situations. It's tough to match those finely tuned installments, let alone top them with fresh takes for the characters and new misadventures that follow The Gang to different places when you know they'll always end up back at square one: on a stool at Paddy's Pub, no richer (except for that Dick Towel money they blew on the boat), no more socially advanced, and certainly no wiser. When you've done that at least one hundred times (with multiple storylines in most episodes), as they had by season 10, with the self-imposed mantra to avoid repetition and push the boundaries of what a cable comedy can do, that is the recipe for burnout. And all the writing work doesn't include the time RCG spends in the editing room, or on promotion and general producer duties.

Which is what led Howerton to tell a *Rolling Stone* writer in a July 2013 interview that the tenth season of *It's Always Sunny in Philadelphia* would be the series' final one. The season hadn't been written yet—season 9 wouldn't even premiere until a couple of months after the interview was printed—but Howerton told the magazine the *Sunny* team didn't want to overstay their welcome, so they'd decided to call a wrap on the series at the end of the tenth year.

"We want to leave them wanting more," Howerton said. "We spend a lot of time trying to find new lines to cross . . . we're looking to surprise [the audience]. I think we're proud of what we've done so far, so it's time to stop. I'm sure there are already a few people who are like 'Jesus Christ is that show still on? Go away.'"

Fortunately for everything that has come, so far, after season 10—including high points like "Mac & Dennis Move to the Suburbs" (a go-to favorite for Dennis rage and Mac's suburban ennui); "Being Frank" (the title tells it all); and one of the series' universally praised standards, "Mac Finds His Pride"—Howerton's *Sunny* death notice was premature.

But he was not the only member of The Gang who needed some downtime, or at the least, some time away from the Paddy's set and a chance to go off and work on other projects. So, though the series obviously, and thankfully, did not end after season 10, the *IASIP* production took a longer break between seasons: the season 9 finale aired on November 6, 2013, and season 10 didn't premiere until January 14, 2015, more than a full year later.

During that yearlong break (though RCG and the writers' room had to report back to work before the whole year passed to prepare scripts for season 10), The Gang scattered to work on other projects and spend time with their families. Howerton was an executive producer on the drama film *All the Wilderness*, starring DeVito as a therapist trying to help a teen deal with the death of his father. Day spent the time watching the fruits of his big-screen moonlighting continue to pay off with the release of his films *The Lego Movie* and *Horrible Bosses 2*, a sequel to his first major buddy comedy hit with Jason Sudeikis, Jason Bateman, and Jennifer Aniston.

McElhenney did some memorable TV guest-star work on Mindy Kaling's Fox and Hulu comedy *The Mindy Project*, beginning a recurring role as Lou Tookers, a multi-tattooed former convict and substitute English teacher, now an IT guy and the cousin of Ike Barinholtz's nurse Morgan. Howerton also had a more extensive recurring role on *Mindy*, playing attorney Cliff Gilbert, Mindy's will-they-or-won't-they crush and future ex-boyfriend who Mindy dumped at his grandmother's funeral.

Olson's *Sunny* break included a high-profile guest spot on *New Girl*, playing Ashley, the high school nemesis of lead character Jess (Zooey Deschanel) and her best friend Cece (Hannah Simone). When Jess's dad, Bob (Rob Reiner), showed up for a visit, he brought Ashley back into Jess and Cece's lives... as his new girlfriend, who he planned to marry, much to Jess's chagrin. Olson had fun horrifying Jess by laying out Ashley's past: she was a sex addict until her fourth stint in rehab, and one of her high school conquests was a D.A.R.E. counselor, to whom she definitely did not just say no.

As is almost always the case, DeVito had more fun than people decades younger than him. His extended break included starring in a music video for boy band One Direction's song "Steal My Girl." It was a *Sunny*-worthy absurd story: DeVito played the director of the group's video-within-the-video, set in a desert, with the pop stars dancing and singing to their song while surrounded by a chimpanzee, a ballet dancer, sumo wrestlers, a lion, a marching band, mimes, and a guy riding around on a penny-farthing. Meanwhile, DeVito ran around and danced with the band until all of them, inexplicably, were drenched with a rain special effect. DeVito was paid well for his very special guest appearance, and it's easy to imagine this as a scenario for which Frank Reynolds would pay *them* to participate in.

And add Harry Styles and his former bandmates to the list of celebrity fans of *IASIP* and Frank; they even posed in a group photo with Trollfoot for DeVito's Twitter account.

The upshot of this lengthier break between seasons was that the cast and crew returned to the production refreshed and with a renewed enthusiasm for *Sunny*. There was no longer talk of ending the show. Going out into the larger world of Hollywood not only gave the cast the opportunity to act with other funny people and see how other productions were run, but it also allowed them to appreciate how smoothly their show operated and to cherish the familial vibe that enveloped it.

McElhenney has repeatedly referenced a conversation he once had with Larry David in which the *Curb Your Enthusiasm* and *Seinfeld* creator told him to never quit *Sunny*, never voluntarily walk away from the great situation they have created with FX, and, most importantly, appreciate one another. Whenever the cast is off doing other things and satisfying other career goals, playing different characters and expanding the types of projects they work on, they do so knowing *Sunny* is their home base. That provides a certain kind of confidence and security as they go forth and work with other people, new productions, and then return to that home base with friends and family and one another, refreshed and excited to continue creating this thing they started.

David is probably one of the only people in the television industry who can appreciate firsthand what a good thing the *IASIP* creators and cast have going. David debuted *Curb* on HBO in 2000, and produced twelve seasons, with the show ending in 2024. He has taken plenty of breaks; his eighth season aired in 2011, his ninth in 2017. His most recent season debuted after more than a two-year break. David has the freedom with his network to do a season when the creative inspiration strikes him, an incredibly rare, open-ended scenario. His point to RCG remains the same: recognize what you've got and don't let temporary frustrations color the bigger picture. Don't ever formally end the series; there's no good reason to ever intentionally choose to end this TV world you've created.

Unlike David's unique situation with execs at HBO, who have confirmed in the past there were periods when they were unaware of when—or *if*—David would return with new *Curb Your Enthusiasm* seasons, RCG works very closely with FX on such decisions regarding *Sunny*. Fortunately for them, their biggest champion from the beginning, then newly installed network president Landgraf, remains the head of FX and continues to support the show, which was renewed in 2020 through at least an eighteenth season.

Even with all his belief in the talent of the cast and the abilities of RCG as writers and producers, Landgraf said when *Sunny* launched, "I could never have predicted that it would be the longest-running live-action sitcom in television history.... That's just crazy."

He called *It's Always Sunny* the first successful deconstruction and reconstruction of a sitcom, and explained that taking a chance on

Sunny was sparked by his team's commitment to crafting a TV hub that would sincerely attempt to contribute something to television in the form of unique, quality programming.

"We started with the notion of, if we're channel 248 on DirecTV, why would anybody watch the same thing? Why would they go to Channel 248 to watch what they could get on Channel 2, 4, or 7? They just wouldn't, right? Therefore, we have to give people a unique reason to come to a place that was, at least at that time, less familiar to them on their dial," Landgraf told a gathering of the Television Critics Association in 2019.

"But the thing that's amazing about [*It's Always Sunny*] is that those five really hilarious degenerates at the center of it are the most active schemers you have ever seen. They care so deeply about stuff that no one should care about; they go so far out of their way to achieve nothing that they drive the story."

Landgraf has earned his status as a much-respected executive—perhaps TV's most respected executive—among television critics for his willingness to answer questions, even the tough ones, with candor. Unlike many TV executives who seem to view their jobs the same way they would if they were selling cars or soda or any other product, Landgraf has always made it clear he sincerely loves television and the business of television. He especially loves quality programming, both watching it and helping creatives tell compelling, provocative stories. He considers it his job, and the job of the writers and directors and actors and crews he works with, to not just make great TV programs, but to add something significant to the industry, to the medium. Interacting with the reporters and critics who cover television in a mutually respectful manner is one way that Landgraf has built his sterling reputation.

It was during his state-of-the-network address at the August 2015 summer press tour, at the Beverly Hilton in Los Angeles, that Landgraf came up with the term "peak TV." He called it a state in which the TV landscape had become so overstuffed that even he could no longer keep track of every scripted series. According to FX research, there were 280 scripted series in 2010; by 2014, that number swelled to 371, with Landgraf predicting the total would blow past 400 by the end of the year. He believed that was close to the maximum number of shows the medium could handle, adding that too much good TV made it difficult for networks and streamers to help viewers separate the outstanding wheat from the good-enough chaff. The audience "is overwhelmed by the sheer volume of TV shows," he said.

Yet by 2022, the number of scripted original series ballooned to a record-setting 599. Landgraf once again thinks this will be the peak. We shall see.

In the meantime, one good turn of phrase deserves another, and the risk-taking executive who coined "peak TV," which encompasses the era that includes most of his major FX successes, has earned a phrase that sums up what the people who watch television for a living think of him.

After Landgraf jokingly said in one of his speeches during a TCA press tour that he would do certain things differently if he were the "mayor of television," *Rolling Stone* magazine's chief TV critic Alan

Sepinwall (then a writer at Uproxx) said he and several other people in the room agreed they would now think of the chairman of FX Networks as the Mayor of Television.

It's an unofficial gig, of course, but when Sepinwall wrote an article that referred to Landgraf with the honorary title, it stuck. Many journalists have since repeated the nickname in their own missives—votes for Landgraf as the Mayor of Television.

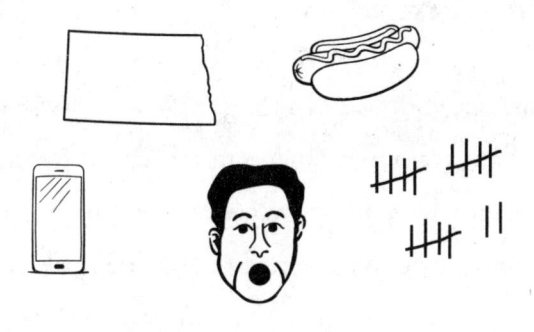

Chapter Eleven

STILL *SUNNY* AFTER ALL THESE YEARS

When McElhenney learned that DeVito, the beloved comedy actor he'd grown up watching on *Taxi*, was interested in joining the cast of *It's Always Sunny in Philadelphia*, he was shocked.

Not that McElhenney lacked confidence or pride in the work he and costars Day, Howerton, and Olson had turned out for their audience during the first season. But this was Danny DeVito... Emmy winner, Golden Globe winner, Oscar nominee, Hollywood legend as an actor, director, and producer. Why would someone with his experience and stature within their industry want to become a cast member on a fledgling comedy on a network with no real comedy presence, one that was mostly known at that point for the gritty cop drama starring the guy from *The Commish*? Sure, FX, *The Shield*, and Michael Chiklis would soon make their marks as prime cable talent.

But when the network was planning *It's Always Sunny*'s sophomore season, and Landgraf was trying to match up his friend and former colleague DeVito with his largely unknown, badly-in-need-of-an-injection-of-star-power *Sunny* cast, the FX we've all come to know and addictively watch was still in its budding phase. Hence McElhenney's surprise at DeVito's interest in *Sunny* as his future workplace.

Once DeVito signed on to join The Gang and started working with his new cohorts, McElhenney was in for an even bigger shock. While directing the season 2 premiere, "Charlie Gets Crippled"—the episode that introduced Frank Reynolds to Paddy's Pub—McElhenney said DeVito asked how McElhenney wanted him to play a certain scene.

"Is *he* asking *me* how he should play this scene, this character?!" McElhenney wondered. He and the rest of the cast, when initially pitched by Landgraf the idea of DeVito joining the show, had some concerns that the veteran actor might turn out to be a diva, or someone who might come in and disturb the very strong and easy rapport they'd developed while making season 1. Yet, here was DeVito, having already made an effort to get to know his new coworkers by inviting them to a barbecue at this home, as humble as could be, not acting like a diva, soliciting opinions from an actor thirty-three years his junior and with three fewer decades of experience.

McElhenney later approached DeVito about why he had wanted his acting opinion. What could he possibly offer to someone with DeVito's experience, especially in giving renowned comedic performances? DeVito's explanation was one that McElhenney took in and remembered as *Sunny*'s seasons unfolded.

DeVito told McElhenney a big part of the reason he joined the series is that he liked the cast, and he respected their talents, humor, work ethics, and what they were trying to accomplish with *Sunny*'s deconstructionist viewpoint. Also, more specifically, he wanted to work with a group of young people who would expose him to fresh ideas, new ways of thinking about their creative pursuits. He was certain that being around their energy would be invaluable to him continuing to learn and grow and feel enthusiastic about his work, which is a very important part of his life.

He didn't want to become comfortable and afraid to try new things; complacency is the enemy of innovation. And he made it very clear that he wasn't threatened by those around him, no matter their age or experience level; he welcomed, in fact sought out, that which would allow him to stay on top of his game and most engaged in the industry and the world in general.

It was a confidence booster for McElhenney to hear how highly DeVito had already assessed RCG's talents and their likeliness to create a genuine success with *It's Always Sunny*. But the philosophy DeVito shared about how he was approaching his future as a still-hungry veteran actor was one of his most important contributions to *IASIP*, especially to the show's longevity.

Those insights about being unafraid to look to new talent and fresh voices, and to be in the best position to maintain your goals, really stuck with McElhenney. As *Sunny* continued to thrive and the seasons wore on, RCG, like any writers/producers that committed to quality storytelling, became more and more exhausted by the writing process. Breaking episodes—and multiple story ideas within many of those episodes—is an often-daunting task. RCG had put together many stellar writing rooms, but before the end of season 9, *IASIP* had already aired one hundred episodes. Even with the colorful collection of brilliant recurring actors and guest stars, that's a lot of stories to revolve around just five main characters.

The show's writing team mainstays have included Scott Marder and Rob Rosell, the scribes behind so many classic *Sunny* episodes; brothers Dave and John Chernin ("The Gang Beats Boggs"); Becky Mann and Audra Sielaff ("Dee Gives Birth"); Lee Sung Jin (then credited as Sonny Lee) and Patrick Walsh ("Paddy's Pub: Home of the Original Kitten Mittens"); and Dannah Phirman and Danielle Schneider ("Old Lady House: A Situation Comedy"). Among other writers who've made huge contributions: the particularly prolific David Hornsby (forty-three episodes, including "The Gang Runs for Office"), Luvh Rakhe ("The Gang Gets Analyzed"), Conor Galvin ("Making Dennis Reynolds a Murderer"), and Ross Maloney, who is also a producer on *The Always Sunny Podcast* and a writer of the official *IASIP* cookbook. Maloney wrote one of the best episodes of the past few seasons, the season 16 finale, "Dennis Takes a Mental Health Day," which, in a nod to *The Usual Suspects*, cleverly gives us the most realistic, and relatable, understanding of Dennis's rage and how his mind works. Also relatable: the episode was inspired by Howerton's real-life experience with technology that's supposed to make life simpler and easier but, in his case, ended up ruining the better part of a weekend because of a glitch between his phone and a Tesla.

But while those rooms have been staffed with funny, gifted, accomplished writers, that doesn't mean those people are sticking around forever (or however long *Sunny* continues, which, as some cheeky memes with The Gang photoshopped into their geriatric days predict, may be forever). Many of the writers from the series' early and middle years have already moved on to other projects and development deals.

The Chernin siblings, for instance, created *The Mick* and continued to collaborate with Olson. McElhenney's sister, Katie, was a staff writer on *Sunny* and is now a staff writer on the Apple TV+ comedy *Mythic Quest*. Danielle Schneider was a writer for the 2022 Academy Awards telecast and is an actress who guest-starred on HBO's *Hacks*, one of Olson's moonlighting gigs. And Lee Sung Jin, who post-*Sunny* wrote for *Silicon Valley*, *Tuca & Bertie*, and *Dave*, also created the Emmy-winning Netflix dramedy series *Beef* and signed a multiyear overall deal with the streamer. (Like many a story from back in his *IASIP* days, Lee was inspired to write the series about a bitter road-rage war after "this dude in a white SUV honked and yelled at me.")

As writing talent has come and gone, then, the brunt of the extra work ultimately fell into the laps of McElhenney, Day, and Howerton; when one of them was off working on another project—like when Day was working on his streak of big-screen hit movies that included *Horrible Bosses* and *Pacific Rim*—the other two picked up the slack. It took a toll: Howerton quit *It's Always Sunny* in 2017 because of his frustration with, and sometimes downright hatred of, the grueling writing process and the time devoted to it, as well as his frustration with not having the chance to really sink his teeth into playing other characters. Though Howerton would have preferred the show end altogether and advised his costars that's what should happen, McElhenney and Day had followed Larry David's counsel about never turning up their noses at the chance to keep *Sunny* as their creative home base as long as FX continued to renew the show.

Howerton's decision to move on left a messy situation in his wake, one in which everyone was loath to confirm his *Sunny* status publicly, hoping his move wouldn't be a permanent one. In the season 12 finale, "Dennis' Double Life," it was revealed that during The Gang's trip to chase Wade Boggs's beer-drinking record in the season 10 opener, Dennis had a fling that resulted in the birth of a son. The only thing more shocking to his friends: he was going to leave them, and his beloved Range Rover, behind and move to North Dakota to raise his child.

Fans were confused: Had Howerton really left the show? It seemed impossible, but then he went on to star in the NBC sitcom *A.P. Bio*, playing an arrogant (and not altogether un-Dennis-like) Harvard philosophy professor who, after being fired, has to move back to his Toledo, Ohio, hometown and teach advanced-placement biology at his old high school, while living in his dead mother's house. And here comes the real Dennis similarity: bounced professor Jack decides to use his classroom full of gifted teens to help him exact revenge on the man who took his spot at Harvard.

Meanwhile, back in *Always Sunny* TV land, production took an extended break. Season 12 ended on March 8, 2017; season 13 didn't premiere until nearly eighteen months later, on September 5, 2018. That was a much-needed hiatus for everyone to pursue outside opportunities. So would a refreshed Howerton possibly find his way back to Paddy's?

Not immediately. In Dennis's absence, the rest of The Gang hooked up with a slick marketing whiz, Cindy, played by guest star (and *Sunny* fan) Mindy Kaling. Cindy scheduled Paddy's as host to political conversation events, selling "Conservative Whine" to liberals, while pushing the red "Make America Great Again" hats to conservatives. Paddy's was having one of its most successful scheming periods ever, but there was a pall over the bar. Mac missed Dennis so much that he ordered a custom Dennis sex doll that Dee, Charlie, and Frank suspected him of *interacting* with. The shockingly lookalike, life-size figure was created by the *Sunny* props department after they learned a national company that made such dolls would have the right to sell a Dennis look-alike to all their customers if the *IASIP* production commissioned one from them. The Dennis doll, with its prominent, wide-open mouth in the shape of an "O," even made an appearance on the red carpet, alongside Howerton, during the season 13 premiere in Los Angeles.

By the time Howerton walked the red carpet with his doppelgänger, what many had suspected was confirmed: though he would continue to star in *A.P. Bio* on NBC, the actor was also returning to *Sunny*. Not as a writer, not yet anyway; but Dennis would return from North Dakota and resume his life with The Gang. (There has been little acknowledgment since of his son, Brian Jr.—named such because Dennis told the little boy's mom his name was Brian—or Brian Jr.'s mom, other than Dennis's insistence that sometimes it's best to raise a family from a distance.)

Howerton appeared in more than half of the ten installments of season 13, and by season 15, he had resumed his role in the writers' room, too.

But that bump in the road with Howerton, and the writers' room drain on RCG's time and creative reserves, got McElhenney thinking about what DeVito had told him about the importance of surrounding yourself with fresh ideas and youthful energy. The *Sunny* creator also came to realize that despite hiring some female writers on staff in the past, the series lacked the diversity RCG felt it should have. Landgraf had begun his own diversity campaign well before the COVID pandemic, and during a virtual press conference in 2020, he reported that in 2021, 46 percent of television episodes on FX would be directed by people of color, and 35 percent would be directed by women.

McElhenney had known for a while, but was especially reminded when Howerton returned to *Sunny* after his brief sabbatical, that he needed to follow DeVito's philosophy. He needed to inject renewed energy and fresh insights into *IASIP* as it headed toward a record-breaking fifteenth season and the title of longest-running live-action comedy series in television history.

In 2017, McElhenney reached out via social media to Erin Ryan, a *Daily Beast* journalist whose Twitter account so entertained the *Always Sunny* creator that he assumed she was a comedian. When he found out she was a journalist, he read some of her work and was impressed enough to tell her he thought she had the skills to write for TV. He soon asked if she wanted to write for *Sunny*.

"It was literally that," she said. She became a staff writer on *Sunny* for season 13, then spent the debut season of *Mythic Quest* as a story editor. During her season on *Sunny*, Ryan wrote "The Gang Solves the Bathroom Problem," while also sharing a five-part series about the experience of being part of the writers' room for the *Sunny* website. She painted a picture of the writers' room as a fun place to be—snacks, gum, writing utensils, notebooks, and other stationery items galore—but there was pressure, too. "I'd written jokes for another TV show before, but *Sunny* was my first scripted TV writers' room," Ryan wrote. "I very badly wanted to not suck."

One of the biggest takeaways from her website missives involved her specific experience as a female in the writers' room of a comedy often cited for its crude humor. There were stories about the *Friends* writers' room, and the constant and detailed talk about those writers' sex lives and their conjectures about the intimate lives of the female *Friends* stars. In that regard, just as RCG aimed to deconstruct *Friends*, their writers' room was a deconstruction of the kind of workplace that would leave its female participants feeling less than respected.

"Before I worked for him, Rob was always anecdotally a cool and supportive mentor, but in the room it was clear that he, Charlie, and Glenn had established a norm of behavior that was refreshingly egalitarian," Ryan blogged. "I'm a woman who has worked in a lot of mostly male places that traffic in opinions and information.

I'm used to being interrupted or ignored.... At *Sunny*, people react to ideas rather than identity. I never felt like I was being talked to like a girl, not by my bosses, not by the producers or other writers, not by the assistants (later, when I'd visit the set, the rest of the cast and crew would continue talking to me like a person rather than a girl). It was wild. Who would have guessed that a show with an episode titled 'The Gang Finds a Dumpster Baby' would be the most woman-friendly place I've ever worked?"

One of RCG's most impactful hirings on the path to diversifying the writers' room and adding important new voices was Megan Ganz, a former *Modern Family* and *Community* writer.

"I can't begin to describe the degree to which she has added to the show," Howerton said. "I think we needed her. You start to lose a little bit of objectivity, potentially. Charlie had just starred in, written, and directed his first feature film.... Rob was still in postproduction on [*Mythic Quest*]. And I was coming off of *A.P. Bio* and working on *The Hunt*... so we really need somebody like Megan. I think with writing, the hardest thing to do is break a story. You know, to have an A-story, the B-story, the C-story, and find how they all weave together in a cohesive way. I don't know why, but that's the most difficult thing. And she is one of the best at that we've ever had. We can leave her in the room with the writers, and she can break a story. She's the rare writer we can send off on her own to do a draft that we don't have to rewrite the shit out of."

Ganz, also a director on *Sunny*, wrote one of the smartest and boldest recent episodes, the season 13 gem "Time's Up for the Gang."

The topic was ripe for a tie-in with The Gang, as they were forced to participate in an all-day seminar about sexual harassment if they wanted to get Paddy's off a circulating list of local bars that are not safe for women to patronize. Of course The Gang would be on such a list, if it were real; turns out Dennis made the list and included Paddy's so he could gather his fellow offenders together and tell them to clean up their acts, lest they get caught and take him down with them.

But while revealing this information to The Gang, he also called out Charlie's stalking of the Waitress; Frank's longtime history of sexually harassing the women who worked for him in his corporate days; Dee's assault of Charlie when the two had sex in season 10's "The Gang Misses the Boat" (Charlie said he didn't want to have sex with Dee, but she had her hand over his mouth and couldn't hear his protests); and Mac's objectification of lots of men, including Dennis, who told Mac he was tired of his blatant sexual advances. Finally, as both a boast and his own creepy public service announcement, Dennis detailed how he avoids retribution for his #MeToo behavior by getting receipts. It's been long established that he makes self-proclaimed "golden god" videotapes of all his sexual encounters, but we learned here that he also collects literal receipts in the form of text messages from his partners with a blunt confirmation that their encounters were consensual.

Dennis's presentation to the seminar attendees also included some general observations on the topic that are again tied to The Gang, like that both men and women can be harassers, and that whether or not someone is accused of harassment is sometimes based on how attractive they are (Dennis used himself as the example of a handsome man who gets away with victimizing people) or how much money and influence they have. Frank was the example for that one, though the episode was written not long after a string of charges of rape and other sexual abuses against Oscar-winning film producer Harvey Weinstein led to the #MeToo social movement.

For Ganz, the episode was an incredibly clever creative accomplishment, as well as a personal catharsis. As a longtime fan of *It's Always Sunny* before she joined the writing staff, Ganz used her sharp memory of The Gang's history to present a pointed primer on a subject that was especially prevalent in Hollywood-related headlines.

The episode also followed Ganz's allegations that *Community* creator Dan Harmon, during her time as a writer on the NBC comedy, had engaged in inappropriate, sexually harassing behavior against her—that he had feelings for her while he was the showrunner and had the power to make decisions about her position with the series.

Ganz made the incredibly brave decision to go public with her story in January 2018, six years after the harassment happened, as it continued to impact her and her confidence and trust in the industry. But Harmon is one of the most popular celebrity TV creators, and Ganz risked harsh treatment from his fan base when she shared her story on Twitter and asked for an apology. She received one, both privately and publicly, via his *Harmontown* podcast. Ganz called Harmon's apology, devoid of excuse-making and victim-blaming, "a masterclass in How to Apologize." It was as graceful a handling of the matter, on both sides, as could possibly be expected on social media.

As for tackling the topic in an *It's Always Sunny in Philadelphia* episode, Ganz said the key for her turning it into satire was making Dee as culpable as the rest of The Gang, which included going so far as to question whether the word "rape" was applicable to Dee's encounter with Charlie.

"Having her dance her way in at the top of the show, singing 'Time's up! Time's up!' while eating popcorn . . . it was so freeing to write a woman acting like that, because it's terrible, yes. But I sort of feel like that at times," Ganz said. "I've heard Charlie [Day] express this philosophy that 'If it's funny, it's not offensive, and if it's offensive, it's not funny.' And I really think that's true. I don't think there's any place you *can't* go in comedy. It's just a matter of whether you can land the joke or not."

Ganz's other best-known *Sunny* scripts are season 14's "Dee Day" and "The Janitor Always Mops Twice," a Charlie-centric, black-and-white nod to film noir mysteries, and the perfect example of how *Sunny* occasionally veers off into the more high-concept side of comedy, often with fun results.

The latter half of the series' sixteen seasons, in fact, is flush with episodes that are among *Sunny*'s best ever, even after so many years of RCG making groundbreaking, deep, silly, hilariously clever, brilliantly written, crude, progressive, impeccably well-intentioned television.

Season 9 began with the Olson showcase "The Gang Broke Dee" and ended with "The Gang Squashes Their Beefs." In the latter, Dennis and Mac's apartment burned down while The Gang was hosting Thanksgiving dinner for their enemies—the McPoyle brothers, Charlie and Frank's landlord and Frank's frequent nemesis Hwang (played memorably by Shelly Desai), Gail the Snail, Cricket, Maureen Ponderosa's brother Bill (played by Lance Barber)—to make amends for all the rotten things The Gang had done to them across the years. But when the fire started and Dennis locked his guests inside, well... they're gonna need another "I'm sorry" meal to make up for this one.

Season 9 also featured "Flowers for Charlie," written by *Sunny* fans and *Game of Thrones* creators David Benioff and D. B. Weiss. The episode spoofed Daniel Keyes's classic book *Flowers for Algernon* and the Bradley Cooper movie *Limitless* to tell the story of how Charlie became a test subject for an intelligence pill that made him super smart, while Frank just wanted the old Charlie back.

Another of the show's many excellent spoofs was featured in season 9's "The Gang Saves the Day." The series' one hundredth episode found the Paddy's Pub Five imagining how they could be heroes when they got caught up in an armed robbery at a convenience store. Mac, as he is wont to do, envisioned himself as a martial arts expert in a fantastic fight scene that director Dan Attias made look like a big-screen action sequence. Meanwhile, Charlie, sweet, sweet Charlie, had a daydream in animation, springing into action to save the Waitress when she walked into the convenience store just as the thief started shooting. Then their lives together unfolded, as inspired by the Pixar classic *Up*: the two tied the knot at the Marriage Store, with the Waitress dressed in her wedding gown made by cartoon rats; more rats built them a house; Charlie and the Waitress brought home a houseful of kids from the Baby Store; the kids grew up to become waitresses and janitors; and Charlie and their house finally floated up in the sky with helium balloons attached after his beloved Waitress died. In case anyone was feeling too sentimental after that, Frank dreamed about scarfing down convenience store hot dogs—the reason The Gang went there to begin with—while everyone else was caught in a shootout between the robber and the cops. *So* Frank!

Season 10 opened with the wonderfully wacky "The Gang Beats Boggs," in which The Gang flew from Philly to Los Angeles to see if they could drink more than seventy cans of beer during the trip, the number Major League Baseball Hall of Famer Wade Boggs drank, according to lore, on a cross-country flight during his playing days. It was an eventful journey: Frank and Dennis tried to have mile-high fun; Frank may have killed a college student with sleeping pills; Charlie dreamed he was talking to the ghost of Wade Boggs (who is still very much alive); and Charlie and Dee each drank seventy-one beers. But Charlie was declared the winner when he hit a line drive on a baseball field in Los Angeles, which Mac declared close enough to the rest of the urban legend: after drinking seventy beers, Boggs had two hits in a game the next day. Two seasons later, we'd learn Dennis had gotten off the same plane in North Dakota, where he got a woman pregnant, lied to her about his identity, and now has a son named Brian Jr.

And we'd learn during the week "The Gang Beats Boggs" premiered back in January 2015 that the Wade Boggs drinking record Charlie beat in the episode—drinking seventy-one cold ones to best Boggs's seventy—wasn't even the real number. Two nights before the episode premiered on FXX, Charlie Day was a guest on *The Tonight Show* with Jimmy Fallon and told the host Boggs had revealed to him on the *Sunny* set that the real number of cold ones he drank on the legendary flight was actually 107 beers. In one day.

Can that really be true?

"Oh yeah. Yeah, that's true," Boggs says. During a guest appearance on a 2011 episode of the USA Network dramedy *Psych* (titled "Dead Man's Curveball"), Boggs (playing himself) and fellow guest star Danny Glover discussed the beer binge, and Boggs told Glover's character the number was seventy-three. Before his chat with Charlie Day, seventy-three became the "official" number, at least according to Boggs and his clever plan to stretch the residuals from his television appearances.

"After that, when people would ask me what the real number was, I would say, 'Have you seen *Psych*?' And they'd go, 'No.' And I'd say, 'Well, rent it,'" Boggs says. "And every time [someone] would rent it, I get paid a residual. So I would never tell anybody. I would let *Psych* do my talking for me."

Was he trying to further the legend by boosting the *Psych* number by about a third when he claimed to have downed 107 brews to Day? Perhaps, but Boggs has definitely made a decision to have fun with the mythology around his past drinking habits, especially after suffering a tragic loss related to alcohol. He says his mother, Sue, was killed by a drunk driver in 1986. He originally turned down the request to appear in the *It's Always Sunny* episode that revolved around the stories of his ale consumption, but his wife and son, Brett, encouraged him to do the series. Brett (named after his godfather and Boggs's friend and fellow baseball Hall of Famer George Brett) is a huge *Sunny* fan, and when he accompanied his dad to the set, director Todd Biermann added him to the episode as an extra (he's the guy sitting next to Mac, the one Mac dumped a pile of Charlie's empties on).

Boggs, who has also guest-starred on episodes of *Family Guy*, *Arli$$*, and *The Simpsons*, and became an acquaintance of Danny DeVito nearly thirty years ago when he made his first-ever TV comedy guest appearance in a 1988 episode of *Cheers*, enjoyed his time on what he calls "one of the most hilarious sitcoms of the modern day" so much that he would happily return if asked.

"A lot of times when you have an athlete or nonactor people come to your set, it can be very awkward," Boggs says. "But [the *Sunny* cast and crew] couldn't have been more genuine or fun or gracious."

His only regret: he didn't get to film on the Paddy's set. "I'd love to walk into Paddy's, just hang out at the bar and chat with them," he said.

Season 10 also included an all-time fan and critics favorite, "Charlie Work," a chaotic masterpiece, directed by Matt Shakman, in which a determined Charlie kept a three-ring circus of meetings and scams and live chickens going to make sure the bar passed its annual health inspection—all while the rest of The Gang, in their usual fashion, made his job harder. One of the most talked-about scenes in *IASIP* history is a continuous ten-minute shot, made for just the kind of frenetic performance Day is beloved for, and inspired by a similar, six-minute tracking shot in "Who Goes There," a first-season episode of HBO's *True Detective*—and not, as so many fans have assumed, a shot in the movie *Birdman*.

In season 11, Todd Biermann directed the over-the-top premiere, "McPoyle vs. Ponderosa: The Trial of the Century." Day's *Pacific Rim* director pal Guillermo del Toro portrayed McPoyle patriarch Pappy as the McPoyles sued Bill Ponderosa for spiking the milk at his sister's nuptials in season 8's "The Maureen Ponderosa Wedding Massacre," leading would-be groom Liam to lose an eye. Bill, totally skint after the breakup of his family, hired Uncle Jack as his attorney, with Charlie assisting the defense with his expertise in "bird law." The height of absurdist comedy, and reminiscent of the Three Stooges short *Disorder in the Court*, the episode once again pitted The Gang and friends against the Lawyer. But on this occasion, the Lawyer was not only bested for the first time in their rivalry, but Pappy McPoyle's bird, Royal, attacked the Lawyer and may have left him as visually challenged as Liam McPoyle. Thanks to Charlie's bird theory, which suggested Royal was also responsible for the attack on Liam—and, more importantly, the chaos that fueled the proceedings—the frustrated judge (*Family Matters* and *Die Hard* star Reginald VelJohnson) threw the case out. Charlie and Jack, who was proudly wearing his giant fake hands, claimed the trial's conclusion as a victory.

The episode, sadly, has so far remained the last time we've seen the Lawyer, one of the audience's most favorite recurring characters. Brian Unger hopes a reunion with The Gang is in his future, and he even pitched a spin-off idea to Rob McElhenney. It would feature him and Andrew Friedman as the Lawyer and Jack Kelly, and the premise is that, after some particularly bad lawyering on Jack's part, a judge orders him to go work with the Lawyer at his firm.

"Basically, he's forcing Jack to become a real lawyer, and I'm the one who has to do it, be the teacher. He's stuck with me, and I'm stuck with him, and from there, the hilarity ensues.

"We'll call it *We're Lawyers!*" Unger says.

McElhenney was interested in the idea, but Unger began work on another project, and *We're Lawyers!* got lost in his busy schedule.

He does wonder, as do viewers, what state the Lawyer will be in if he does return to *Sunny*, given what appeared to be a serious eye injury from Royal McPoyle. Will we learn his association with The Gang left him permanently scarred, emotionally and physically?

Not long after his move from the West Coast to the farm he bought in Georgia, the actor had a similar scare himself. "I was mending a horse fence in my yard, and I struck a nail; the nail ricocheted off the post and hit me in the eye," he says. "It lacerated my eye. I went to the emergency room, and the only thing I could think of the whole time was, 'Am I actually going to lose my eye in real life?'"

P.S. He did not. But the Lawyer might be wearing an eye patch now, which would complement Uncle Jack's giant-hands gloves if they ever get that spin-off going.

RCG pulled out all the stops for "McPoyle vs. Ponderosa: The Trial of the Century"—it's not often you get a multiple Oscar winner guest-starring as a man carrying a big bird around under his hat—and the character at the center of the legal showdown between the Lawyer and Uncle Jack and Charlie was Bill Ponderosa, Dee's former lover, Dennis's former brother-in-law, and another fan favorite among the crew of recurring associates of The Gang.

Bill, or "Pondy" as he would be nicknamed by Frank, is played to perfection by *Young Sheldon* star Lance Barber. The actor was recruited for the role after RCG saw him on *The Comeback*, the HBO comedy starring Lisa Kudrow as a former sitcom star trying to return to sitcom fame. Barber played Paulie G., the cocreator of the series-within-the-series sitcom Kudrow's Valerie Cherish starred in, for the show's debut season in 2005. Paulie G. was memorable for his obnoxious, rude, crude behavior toward Valerie, so it's not difficult to understand why RCG could picture him bringing Bill to equally obnoxious, rude, crude life in Sunny's sixth season. They didn't even ask him to audition, but simply offered him the part. He accepted even though he hadn't yet seen an episode of *IASIP*.

"Honestly, I didn't know expectations were for [him] to be recurring," Barber says. After his first episode, "Mac Fights Gay Marriage," he immediately caught up with the show. "I became a fan after my introduction to it. And they brought me back for a number of seasons, which was a joy and a stroke of good luck."

His role as George Cooper, Sheldon's tough but caring football coach dad on the *Big Bang Theory* prequel series, didn't begin until 2017, so Barber spent a few years having a lot of fun playing Pondy, one of the few characters whose passion to party hearty has even outpaced the sloppy vulgarity of Frank at his most unsober.

Bill was among the invitees to the "who's Dee's baby's dad?" party in season 6's "Dee Gives Birth," which began Bill's bond with Frank, leading him to become sex-and-drug-addict Bill's sponsor.

"Bill shows up with some cocaine, and he's trying to get the guys to do some with him." Barber laughed. "And at the end of the scene, my favorite line is when Bill says, 'You guys wanna do a bump or what?' and Frank says, 'I'll have a bump.' That was the point where they connected, and it went pretty dark from there."

Bill would go on to visit Paddy's, in a tuxedo, and share with The Gang his plan to drink himself to death (only to be convinced to live by Frank's *Life Is Happy* T-shirt), and then, in the "a day in the life of Frank" episode "Being Frank," drive around in a drug-fueled haze with a gun blazing and a group of angry men pulling him out of his car because he hit on an underage girl at a roller rink.

"That was one of the most fun to do, because I got to spend so much time with Danny," Barber says. "We had defined our friendship as 'Frank and Pondy,' and Frank keeps saying, 'Pondy is the coolest.' I even get a thing from that with the fans. I get a lot of shout-outs in public. [People] want to get a picture with Pondy.

'Pondy is the coolest,' they'll say. I love that that stuck. It's not my catchphrase, but the catchphrase for my character, and I think that's terrific."

Barber, who coincidentally was friends with the McPoyle brother actors Jimmi Simpson and Nate Mooney before they all worked together on *It's Always Sunny* and still gets together with them for game nights, completed work on *Young Sheldon* in May 2024 when the spin-off aired its series finale, and last appeared on *Sunny* in a pair of season 13 episodes in 2018. He's ready to return.

"Just to be inside that sandbox and play with those guys is so easy," he says. "It's so second nature and still seems to be so much fun for them. The atmosphere at that job is . . . I've only felt nothing but pure joy and fun, and occasionally I get some good stories from Danny DeVito about *One Flew Over the Cuckoo's Nest*."

☀ ☀ ☀

The Gang kicked off season 12 with "The Gang Turns Black," the follow-up musical episode fans had been asking for since "The Nightman Cometh." This was a decidedly more divisive effort, however. While watching *The Wiz* together at Dee's apartment, The Gang was struck by a surge of electricity than ran through their electric blanket. When they looked at themselves in a mirror, they appeared to have swapped bodies with a group of Black people. Charlie appeared to be a Black tween, for instance, after the electrical shock.

Almost immediately, The Gang broke into a song about the fact that they were suddenly breaking out into song. "When you just turned Black, and you can't switch back, well ya gotta go and find out the rules," Dennis notes.

RCG had been working on the idea of the episode as a more straightforward storyline, but it wasn't coming together in a way they were happy with. Then Day and Ellis saw *Hamilton* on Broadway, and Day was hit with the idea that the episode could work as a musical. In a very short time, he wrote ten songs and sent them off to his composer pal Cormac Bluestone, who recorded the music and the instruments by the following Monday.

Another element of the episode: guest star Scott Bakula, who Dee first mentioned when The Gang was trying to figure out what happened to them. She suggested they might be in the midst of a *Quantum Leap* situation, where they'd jumped into other people's bodies, just as Bakula did as time traveling scientist Sam Beckett in the original 1989–1993 NBC science fiction drama. A singing Bakula pops up in a most unexpected place....

The Gang hit the outside world to learn more rules and find out who they'd body-swapped with. Old Black Man (the late Wil Garret), who Frank found under a bridge and introduced to The Gang in season 11's "Mac & Dennis Move to the Suburbs," had been watching *The Wiz* with them. But he disappeared when the electric blanket zapped them, and Frank thought he might have something to do with their mystery.

Meanwhile, in this *IASIP* exploration of social and racial inequality, Dennis, Charlie, and Mac tried to get into Dennis's car, but

Dennis didn't have his keys. When cops arrived and found the three of them, who appeared to be Black, rocking the car, the officers assumed they were trying to steal it and arrested them. At the police station, Charlie answered questions about his friends and referred to them as "The Gang," and a social worker assumed he was in an actual gang. He broke into another song to try to explain his life, but details about sleeping in a Section 8 apartment and sharing a bed with an old man who slept with his mother, a prostitute, made the situation go from bad to worse, quickly.

Frank and Dee found Old Black Man and learned his name was Carl. He had gone missing from the nursing home he lived in with his wife, and when Frank and Dee took him back there, his wife recognized them as their children. They also ran into Scott Bakula, who was mopping the floor at the home. He was frustrated when Dee approached him with *Quantum Leap* talk, and her speculation that he had run out of television residuals and hit hard times. He pointed out that he had been working nonstop for thirty years and was at the home researching a role. Just a little reminder that The Gang makes assumptions about everyone, no matter their race. They are equal-opportunity offenders, and their getting an up-close-and-personal experience with what being on the other end of assumptions and stereotypes can feel like was the point of the episode.

In an abrupt moment while they were trying to get Dee's VCR repaired in the hopes it would allow them to get back into their own bodies, cops were called on The Gang, and when Charlie, still appearing to be a Black tween, held up a toy train the cops had given him earlier, they assumed it was a gun and shot him several times.

As Charlie lay on the sidewalk bleeding, The Gang clicked their heels together and sang a song about having learned their lesson and wanting to go home. And suddenly, they were back in Dee's apartment, waking up Old Black Man and kicking him out. He told them he'd had the strangest dream—they were all in it, and they were singing. Their body swap was Old Black Man's dream!

Or was it? As he walked by a mirror when leaving Dee's home, Old Black Man saw the reflection of Scott Bakula staring back at him. Bakula had earlier belted out a tune at the nursing home about being stuck in a leap and missing his old, prosperous life, the one he hadn't lived since his wife left him and took his money. "I miss my old Camaro, and my mansion in Van Nuys, wish I still hung with Nash Bridges, played poker with the Fall Guy," he sang, in one of the all-time most delightful *It's Always Sunny* guest appearances.

Whether or not the episode was clever and entertaining in making its points about the Black experience is a matter of varying opinions. Vox.com called the episode a "surface-level experiment" because "the best they can do is highlight the basic inequality they see ... because they can't feel it," while a Pastemagazine.com review headline read, "Hey, *It's Always Sunny in Philadelphia*, Maybe Don't Joke About Black Kids Getting Shot." The review was written by a critic who called herself one of the show's biggest fans but who was left "shaken and deeply unsettled" by, as the headline highlights, the depiction of a Black child being shot as mined for laughs.

Both are fair comments on a hot-button topic that has become even more so throughout the years since "The Gang Turns Black" originally aired in 2017. The writers of the episode—McElhenney, Day, and Howerton—touched on some racial injustices that can have very different, dangerous consequences than the ones The Gang experienced in the episode.

But the flip side of the charge that the writers can't make an impactful episode because they don't feel the inequalities is that the characters were forced to feel the injustices, the harassments, and sometimes the dangers of everyday life as a Black person in America. It was a commentary; actually, lots of commentaries, and maybe they didn't all land. Maybe, for some viewers, none of them landed. Day was inspired by *Hamilton* to make "The Gang Turns Black" a musical, and for some, this is a subject that's maybe too personal, too raw, and too constantly experienced to be accompanied by catchy little ditties about rules and a desire to say verboten offensive words (that was a Frank song, of course). But many viewers found the episode to be clever, funny, and a pithy entry into a tough topic. *Sunny* viewers trust it was well-intentioned; The Gang is a collection of degenerates, while the series creators are not.

"I'm thankful that we've been able to continue to make these big swings and that we have a platform for doing it and that we have an audience that understands our intentions," Day told *Entertainment Weekly*.

From the point of view of making compelling television, "The Gang Turns Black" is the exact kind of swing-for-the-fences episode the *Sunny* gang should be making for however long the already record-holding comedy airs on FXX. Even the occasional whiff is worth the attempts that lead to the stellar episodes that have become *IASIP* classics. And why would they want to pursue anything less?

☼ ☼ ☼

A far sillier high point, and a major treat for fans of the moms, Mrs. Mac (Sandy Martin) and Mrs. Kelly (Lynne Marie Stewart), was season 12's "Old Lady House: A Situation Comedy," in which The Gang set up a surveillance system in Charlie's mom's house to determine which of their mom roommates may have been torturing the other (spoiler: both). They became so obsessed with the mom mischief that they began editing the footage and turned Charlie's and Mac's mommies' antics into their own personal sitcom, watching for hours in the Paddy's Pub office while snacking on bags of potato chips. Most cleverly, they continued their *It's Always Sunny* series objective of deconstructing traditional sitcom conventions by adding traditional sitcom conventions, like playful music and a laugh track, to "Old Lady House." Said Frank, "Having those other people laugh tells me when I should laugh."

Season 12 also saw *Sunny* plot a sharp send-up of true-crime docuseries, like Netflix's *Making a Murderer*, with "Making Dennis Reynolds a Murderer." While spoofing the murder case of Stephen Avery in the Netflix series, the *Sunny* episode explored Dennis's predatory behaviors with women when his ex-wife, Maureen Ponderosa, turned up in an alley with a broken neck after almost completing her transformation into a cat woman named Bastet. Dennis was the prime suspect, with Frank and Dee telling investigators how he snapped the neck of a crow when he was younger; Dee demanded to portray Bastet in the reenactments; Mac showed off his terrible impersonations while being videotaped; and Charlie spilled the secrets of incriminating evidence in Dennis's safe (where he hid cat toys, yarn, a laser pointer, and cat tranquilizers). In the end, Dennis was cleared of Maureen's murder (she allegedly fell off a roof while acting like a cat), but we'll never really know, because the producers of the docuseries... were Mac and Charlie.

During season 13, RCG and company continued to keep the quality high as they marched toward record-breaking longevity and answered years of *Sunny* comparisons to *Seinfeld* with "The Gang Does a Clip Show." They did, in fact, compile The Gang's best moments, beginning with Frank's naked couch birth from the Christmas special and a montage of the many times Dee got hurt (running headfirst into a car door kicked it off). There was also Charlie taking a big bite out of Santa's neck (also from the Christmas special); Dennis's "because of the implication" speech; a steroid-drunk Dee threatening to punch a hole in Charlie's face; the Birds of War; the high school reunion dance performance; a medley of "What is happening?" utterances; and "The Contest," where The Gang "remembered" themselves in the roles of Jerry, George, Elaine, and Kramer in that classic *Seinfeld* episode about masturbation (or lack thereof). Frank was George, both Mac and Dennis were Jerry (extra cheeky since they each see themselves as the leader of The Gang), and Charlie, complete with tall hair and a vintage shirt, was Kramer, sliding into Jerry's apartment, slapping cash on the counter, and proclaiming,

"I'm out!" Dennis had to buzzkill them all and point out they never lived in New York City and didn't have a laugh track... instead, they were remembering an episode of *Seinfeld*, he told them.

It was a fine tribute to *Seinfeld* and its influence on culture, television, and specifically the show dubbed "*Seinfeld* on crack," but sadly Jerry Seinfeld himself has never seen "The Gang Does a Clip Show." The comedian confirmed as much in an interview with a *Philadelphia Inquirer* editor in 2023, explaining he doesn't watch much TV. Curious, then, that he has some strong opinions on the current state of television comedy. In an April 2024 interview with David Remnick in *The New Yorker*, Seinfeld essentially declared the sitcom dead, or at least on life support. "It used to be, you would go home at the end of the day, most people would go, 'Oh, *Cheers* is on. Oh, *M*A*S*H* is on. Oh, *Mary Tyler Moore* is on. *All in the Family* is on.' You just expected, There'll be some funny stuff we can watch on TV tonight. Well, guess what—where is it?" Seinfeld asked. "This is the result of the extreme left and P.C. crap, and people worrying so much about offending other people."

He went on to say stand-up comics are where people go for humor now (a not untrue but not entirely un-self-serving thought, either, from a *stand-up comic* who is believed to earn $20 million per tour, and who frequently talks about surrounding himself with stand-up comic friends). But it's his diss of the current lineup of comedy on television, and the alleged lack thereof, that sparked headlines of "Okay, boomer" about Seinfeld's interview. Seinfeld brought up what he considers another standard of classic television comedy, alongside those aforementioned 1970s and '80s hits: *Seinfeld*.

Fair enough; no one is disputing *Seinfeld*'s forever spot on the list of the greatest sitcoms of all time. He also namechecked Larry David, his *Seinfeld* cocreator (whose *Curb Your Enthusiasm* was called "the first sitcom about an asshole" by writer and cultural critic Joel Stein), as being "grandfathered in" by the TV comedy community and audience to tell groundbreaking, often politically incorrect stories. He went on to tell Remnick he believes *Seinfeld* plots like Kramer (Michael Richards) and Newman's (Wayne Knight) season 9 rickshaw business, in which they employed homeless people to pull passengers throughout New York City, because "they're outside anyway," would never make it to air today.

Back to Seinfeld's self-serving talk, at the beginning of 2024, Bloomberg included Jerry Seinfeld on its Bloomberg Billionaires Index for the first time, meaning they officially determined he has a net worth of at least $1 billion (it's okay to hold your pinky finger up to your mouth and adopt the Dr. Evil voice when you read that figure). It's estimated that the initial 1989–1998 NBC run of *Seinfeld* earned him roughly $60 million in salary; the past twenty-seven years of multiple syndication deals, streaming rights, and merchandising have earned Seinfeld enough money to make him the billionaire he is now (and that's just *his share* of *Seinfeld*'s earnings).

The point: there's no reason for false modesty; he, David, and their show (*both* of David's shows) are comedy icons, and Seinfeld has earned the right to respect for his opinions on the subject. But with that comes the responsibility to understand what is going on currently with the topic, and to suggest that he and David were the last ones to make great and innovative comedy that is not concerned with ruffling feathers makes him out of touch, at the least. Especially since, by his own admission, his TV-watching habits are limited to sports, Bill Maher, and Jimmy Fallon. When he made those comments to David Remnick, a common response was "What about *It's Always Sunny in Philadelphia*?" The series had been on for sixteen seasons at that point... it's as firmly planted in TV history and our general pop culture as *Seinfeld* is. And he had never even watched the episode of that cultural touchstone that is an elaborate, clever nod to his own cultural touchstone.

Rob McElhenney had thoughts about Seinfeld's stance, too. In replying to a post on the social media platform formerly known as Twitter that asked if people thought Seinfeld would be able to get the episode "The Bookstore," with Kramer and the homeless-driven rickshaws, on the air today, McElhenney responded thusly: a photo of beleaguered, scar-covered Rickety Cricket, the priest driven to drug addiction and homelessness by The Gang, with the word "Probably" next to it.

Sunny, obviously, is not the only series that's aired post-1998 and could be described as a smart, funny comedy without concern about offending viewers and whose characters are sometimes unlikeable and do terrible things. *Veep*, *The Mick*, *Reno 911!*, *Eastbound & Down*, *Community*, *Letterkenny* and its spin-off *Shoresy*, *The League*, *My Name Is Earl*, *You're the Worst*, *Workaholics*, *Girls* ... the list goes on, especially if you add in animated comedies like *Archer*, *South Park*, *Rick and Morty*, and *Family Guy*.

Even in the category of current network TV, which, in general, bears little resemblance to the quality of series in recent decades past, both *Abbott Elementary* and *Ghosts* are awards-worthy comedies. In the *New Yorker* piece, Seinfeld also said that none of the broadcast networks had greenlit a single comedy for their 2024–2025 fall seasons, which isn't true. NBC alone, his old stomping grounds, ordered *St. Denis Medical*, a mockumentary workplace comedy starring Wendi McLendon-Covey and David Alan Grier, and *Happy's Place*, a multi-cam comedy featuring Reba McEntire's return to a television sitcom.

Perhaps Jerry Seinfeld was too quick to sound the death knell for the TV comedy. We all have to acknowledge the format and temperature of the genre has changed, but maybe for Seinfeld it's just about needing to change the channel once in a while.

※ ※ ※

Throughout the most recent seasons of *It's Always Sunny*, The Gang has again tackled the topic of abortion, via short haircuts and pregnant dogs in season 14's "A Woman's Right to Chop"; finally revealed the identity of Charlie's dad during a four-episode arc set in Ireland in the second half of season 15; set up another magnificent and fearless physical performance by Olson, who spent a very cold and uncomfortable night filming in a swamp in Santa Clarita in "Dee Sinks in a Bog"; and brought in RCG's pals Bryan Cranston and Aaron Paul, *Breaking Bad* stars and Dos Hombres mezcal entrepreneurs, as guest stars in season 16's "Celebrity Booze: The Ultimate Cash Grab." RCG, of course, has launched their own celebrity liquor with Four Walls whiskey, which was not mentioned in the episode. Nor were the real names of Cranston and Paul; instead, Cranston was referred to as "Mr. Middle," and Paul was called "Malcolm."

"Mac Finds His Pride," the most critically lauded, fan-appreciated episode of the series after "The Nightman Cometh," aired as the season 13 finale. The storyline was hinted at in the very first season, and played out across the twelve seasons that followed: Mac's sexuality. He dated Carmen off and on; he was vehemently anti–gay marriage. But he also was obviously in love with roommate Dennis, something Dennis had been aware of (and that was before the introduction of the Dennis sex doll in season 13). Mac also declared Carmen's husband, Nick, who she married after her transition operation, was gay because he slept with someone who was born male, ignoring the fact that Mac himself also slept with Carmen. On "Mac Day" in season 9, the rest of The Gang said, "I know we've never said this as a group, but Mac's gay." Then, in the two-episode season 11 finale, "The Gang Goes to Hell: Part One" and "The Gang Goes to Hell: Part Two," Mac came out as gay while The Gang was on a cruise . . . but by the end of the cruise, after The Gang survived a near-death experience, Mac said he was no longer gay. The fact that they were saved meant there was a God, and God, "in his infinite wisdom," would not allow him to be gay, according to Mac.

But in season 12's "Hero or Hate Crime?" The Gang gets into a dispute over which one of them is the rightful owner of a scratch-off lottery ticket. Mac, per the arbitrator they've hired to decide who should get it, wins. The bigger news is that he has come out again, and this time it's for good. And he's going to use his $10,000 lottery booty to start a business with his invention—the Ass Pounder 4000, an exercise bike that he has outfitted with a fist that pops in and out of the seat when it's pedaled (a props department creation that easily tops even the Dennis sex doll for unique projects).

The only thing left for Mac at this point was to come out to his father, which he did in "Mac Finds His Pride." It was the only way he'd ever feel secure with himself, Frank convinced him. To make the episode, and Mac's momentous communication with his father, as impactful as Mac intended, McElhenney embarked on an intense six-month training project. It made his regimen to gain fifty pounds to portray "Fat Mac" in season 7 seem like a piece of cake (and a lot of doughnuts). To portray Buff Mac, McElhenney cut out alcohol, sugar, and carbs, ate nothing after seven every evening, lifted weights six days a week, ran three miles a day every day, slept nine hours a night, and stretched for an hour a day, all just to be strong and supple enough for two hours of dance training every day.

The five-minute modern dance Mac performed for his father, Frank, and all the inmates where his father is incarcerated was choreographed for Mac to show, instead of tell, his dad how he's always felt.

"There's like this storm inside of me, and it's been raging my whole life," Mac explained to Frank. "And I'm down on my knees, and I'm looking for answers, and then God comes down to me, and it's a very hot chick, and she pulls me up and we start dancing."

McElhenney was aware that this emotional dance, performed with ballerina Kylie Shea, would be an unusually serious expression, especially from this character, and would come as a shock to viewers. It could seem completely off-tone for the series. And he was okay with that. He felt he owed it to the LGBTQ+ audience, who had been very supportive of *Sunny* and the Mac character. But they had expressed to him on social media how hurt they were when Mac came out in "The Gang Goes to Hell" but denied who he was again by the end of the episode. Their response made McElhenney realize how much the character and this storyline meant to them. That gave him a reason to devote months of hard work and preparation to the dance, even if not everyone loved it.

"It was both negative and positive, which is one of those things we talked about," McElhenney said. "It's great to surprise people and have them not have any idea what we're doing and why we're doing it. I have people saying, 'Oh my God, I love this, it's one of the best things you've ever done,' and then I have other people saying, 'You've destroyed my show, you've ruined it.' And I'm like, 'Great!' That's exactly what we should be doing on the show ... we should be destroying somebody's idea of what *Sunny* is on a regular basis ... a lot of people felt like it didn't fit into the lexicon of what the show is. And I can't say that they're wrong, but the difference is that I get to dictate what the lexicon is and they don't, and that's a part of the experience."

Todd Biermann, McElhenney's longtime friend and the director of "Mac Finds His Pride," was involved in the episode's evolution, from getting the call from McElhenney to come watch one of the earliest rehearsals of the dance, to watching his friend and Shea perform the routine more than a dozen times, with the rain effects, on the day of production.

"It was just a testament to his maniacal level of discipline and diligence that he rehearsed that dance for however many months he did and got his body in that level of shape to pull off something that was really spectacular," Biermann says. "That was the first time that an episode of that show really, I think, stepped outside of just being. . . . That was the first time that Rob had the idea to challenge himself to try to make an audience laugh and cry in the same episode."

Chapter Twelve

INTO THE RECORD BOOKS, INTO THE FUTURE

So, now what?

Ever since being advised by one of his television heroes, Larry David, that he should never quit making *It's Always Sunny in Philadelphia*, McElhenney has taken the counsel to heart. He has shared on numerous occasions since that exchange with David that he understands and very much appreciates the unique situation he and Day and Howerton enjoy with continuing to make *It's Always Sunny* at FXX, where their creative freedom continues to be largely unrestrained. The comedy has endured for seventeen seasons and counting because of the quality writing and performances they are still sharing with their audience. It's a gift to have a home base where they can gather each new season, reunite with *Sunny*'s troupe of recurring guest stars, and put their distinctive spin on whatever chaos is going on in our world and theirs.

It would seem then that RCG, rewarded in 2020 with a renewal through at least season 18, has no reason to ever even consider ending *Sunny*, packing up shop, and taking their considerable talents and experience elsewhere.

But a funny thing happened on the way to infinity: RCG's hero himself quit his show. Larry David announced at the end of 2023 that his twelfth season of *Curb Your Enthusiasm*, which aired on HBO from February to April in 2024, is the end of the line for the Emmy- and Golden Globe–winning comedy. *Curb*'s dozen seasons had unfolded in an unusual way; the series premiered in October 2000 and ran through season 8, which wrapped in September 2011. Then . . . nothing. Then, after a six-year break, it was back. In October 2017, David returned with season 9, followed by three more in (relatively) quick succession.

Like RCG with FX, David had also been fortunate in his relationship with his network, which essentially allowed the star to come and go as he pleased in terms of when they, and audiences, would be graced with a new season. *Curb*, which has shockingly won just two Emmys, earned an incredible fifty-one nominations (including ten for Outstanding Comedy Series). HBO was overjoyed with having David and his misanthropic adventures on their network whenever he was inspired to drop another ten episodes in their laps. But with his deal at the prestigious network ending in 2023, he decided not to leave executives, and fans, hanging anymore, and announced the series finale would air in April 2024.

His reason for saying goodbye: Exhaustion? Lack of inspiration? More money already than he can spend? Maybe some of those things, or maybe his seemingly tongue-in-cheek answer was fully sincere.

"As *Curb* comes to an end," David said in a statement, "I will now have the opportunity to finally shed this 'Larry David' persona and become the person God intended me to be—the thoughtful, kind, caring, considerate human being I was until I got derailed by portraying this malignant character."

☀ ☀ ☀

And what now for RCG and their castmates and crew? With even Larry David deciding to bid his signature primetime baby *Curb Your Enthusiasm* (well, one of his signature primetime babies) adieu in 2024, will this prompt further reflection, or reflection anew, for RCG? As they head into what is the final two years of their current deal with FX, will they decide to make season 18 their sunset with *It's Always Sunny in Philadelphia*?

It's not as if they aren't still telling compelling, provocative stories that make us laugh and think about the world with their own special insights. Viewers need look no further back than the season 16 finale to see The Gang, and most specifically Howerton's resident rageaholic Dennis Reynolds, to see one of the freshest, funniest, and most of all relatable takes on how simple technological "advances" of the modern world often bring us the most intense stress.

It's not as if the series is not still performing well, in number of viewers and in its widespread influence. During July 2023, in data collected from Parrot Analytics about the most in-demand comedy shows, *It's Always Sunny in Philadelphia* was 37.65 percent more in demand than the average nonanimated television comedy. That put *Sunny* second only to *The Office*, which was 38.92 percent more in demand than the average comedy. The rest of the top five most in-demand comedies: *Ted Lasso*, *What We Do in the Shadows*, and *The Bear* (the last two both also from FX). In IMDb user ratings, season 16's finale, "Dennis Takes a Mental Health Day," received a 9.2 average rating, the highest score for an episode since season 13 and a number that puts the episode in the category of similarly rated *Sunny* classics like season 2's "Mac Bangs Dennis' Mom" (9.2), season 3's "Sweet Dee's Dating a Retarded Person" (9.2), season 5's "The D.E.N.N.I.S. System" (9.3), season 6's "A Very Sunny Christmas" (9.2), season 7's "CharDee MacDennis: The Game of Games" (9.2), and "Mac & Dennis Move to the Suburbs" (9.4) from season 11. And on Rotten Tomatoes, the series is carrying an average audience score of 92 percent for its first sixteen seasons.

As for *IASIP*'s cultural influence, it's everywhere, from social media (where the five cast members had around thirteen million followers across X.com and Instagram at the end of 2023), to memes (people who've never even seen the series use Pepe Silvia to react to something bewildering) to politics (after John Fetterman defeated former TV doctor Mehmet Oz to win a US Senate seat in 2022, he talked about how his campaign had "jammed them up," which *Sunny* fans assumed was a reference to a favorite Dennis line from "Bums: Making a Mess All Over the City"). The official *Always Sunny Podcast*, launched in November 2021 with Megan Ganz as the producer, knocked reigning podcast host Joe Rogan off the top of the Spotify charts during its debut week. Fans have flocked to listen to (or watch on YouTube) RCG break down production scoops, behind-the-scenes reveals, and even personal details, like a January 2023 episode, "Femail Bag with Kaitlin Olson," in which Olson and McElhenney opened up about the beginning of their dating relationship while working on *Sunny*, and how marriage is sometimes a lot tougher than the picture their Instagrams paint. The podcast truly is a companion to the TV show.

The podcast has also sent RCG and Ganz all over the world, with live tapings of episodes in Philadelphia, New York, and Dublin and at the Royal Albert Hall in London, where The Gang was welcomed with packed audiences, some in *IASIP* cosplay.

The Gang had gone international before the podcast, though; a Russian version of the show premiered in 2014, called *It's Always Sunny in Moscow*, and revolved around a group of friends who own a bar in Moscow called "Philadelphia." The redo's storylines were largely based on the scripts of the original series, but the humor and cast chemistry couldn't be duplicated, and *It's Always Sunny in Moscow* lasted just one season. In Japan, meanwhile, a 2013 video went viral of an adorable group of Japanese kindergartners singing "Dayman," the infectious tune from *The Nightman Cometh*.

Most importantly to the continuation of the series, the cast still has a lot of fun making the show together. And after twenty years of working side by side, from the homemade pilots to turning *Sunny* into a hit by almost any measure of success . . . they still like one another. They're still friends who support one another on the *Sunny* set and, in the off-season, cheer on one another's side projects.

☼ ☼ ☼

About those side projects . . .

McElhenney bought the world's third-oldest professional soccer team—the Wrexham Dragons—in Wales, with friend Ryan Reynolds, and costars in *Welcome to Wrexham*, the FX docuseries that follows the new owners and their efforts to improve the team and, by extension, the community where the Dragons are beloved (*Wrexham*'s first two seasons earned seven Emmy Awards). He also stars in *Mythic Quest*, the Apple TV+ comedy he cocreated with Charlie Day and Megan Ganz; and he and Reynolds purchased a stake in the Alpine Formula One international auto racing team.

Named as the greatest living Philadelphian by *The Philadelphia Inquirer* in 2017 ("For years to come, people will watch his heartfelt, cutting ode to our city and immediately attach the word '*Philadelphia*' to the feeling of joy"), McElhenney has publicly declared his desire to Philadelphia Eagles owner and friend Jeffrey Lurie to become a minority stakeholder in his beloved team. Also on the sports front, RCG's Four Walls whiskey is now sold at Citizens Bank Park in Philly (as a drink called "The Man," after McElhenney pal—and Mac's baseball hero—Chase Utley). And, under McElhenney's 2024 launch of More Better Industries, a media conglomerate with a title that's a nod to one of Mac's favorite sayings, the actor teamed with Major League Baseball, Utley, and current Philadelphia Phillies star Bryce Harper in a viral video to promote the Phillies' first-ever international series—two games the Phillies played against the New York Mets in London in June 2024, with Philadelphia winning the June 8 game, and the Mets winning the June 9 contest.

The creation of More Better Industries, with branches for creative executions, strategic investing, and production, led to McElhenney being named *Adweek*'s 2024 Media Visionary, complete with a cover story in the trade magazine. An umbrella under which his many diverse projects will live, the More Better Productions division includes future TV series, movies, and podcasts with collaborators like Netflix, HBO, Elliot Page, Ryan Reynolds, and, in yet another dream come true, Larry David.

The company, most of all, is McElhenney's statement that even with the massive, ongoing success of *It's Always Sunny*, he's continuing to bet big on himself, just as he did when RCG forged the partnership with FX twenty years ago.

Olson has a recurring role in Max's dramedy *Hacks*, as the tormented daughter of lead Jean Smart's legendary Las Vegas comedian (a performance that has earned Olson a pair of Emmy nominations for Outstanding Guest Actress); costars with Bobby Cannavale in the Netflix teen comedy *Incoming*, a movie written and directed by former *Sunny* writers and producers John and Dave Chernin; and is the star of ABC's 2024 breakout hit drama *High Potential*, about a single mom and custodian with a genius IQ who becomes a police department consultant when she organizes evidence in a way that allows her to help solve the most challenging cases. Olson is also a producer on the series, which costars Garret Dillahunt and Daniel Sunjata.

Day's scene-stealing voicework as Luigi in *The Super Mario Bros. Movie* helped the animated flick stack up more than $1 billion in global box office earnings, the first movie based on a video game to hit the billion-dollar mark.

But not everything he touched in 2023 turned to gold. After years of writing and reworking the script (with advice from his mentor Guillermo del Toro), Day released his directorial debut, *Fool's Paradise*, an absurdist-humor poke at Hollywood. The story centered on a case of mistaken identity that leads a mute former mental health patient to take over the life of a difficult actor (both played by Day), with fortune-changing benefits for an ambitious publicist (Ken Jeong). Even with an all-star cast—Kate Beckinsale, John Malkovich, Adrien Brody, Jason Sudeikis, Ray Liotta, Jason Bateman, and Edie Falco, as well Day's *Sunny* cohorts Howerton, Ellis, and others—the passion project Day worked on for almost a decade was a critical and box office failure. Made on a reported $30 million budget, *Fool's Paradise* earned only $464,259 its opening weekend and ended its brief theatrical run with a dismal global box office take of $881,743.

The movie received a mere 18 percent approval rating on Rotten Tomatoes' Tomatometer round-up of reviews. The critics' consensus was that "*Fool's Paradise* suggests Charlie Day may have a bright future as a director, but he'll need to find smarter and more consistently funny scripts," while the *New York Times* critic Nicolas Rapold wrote, "One wishes Day had looked further afield than Hollywood for inspiration."

In fact, the original script, written by Day, was a satirical effort that dealt largely with issues of race, which Day has certainly helped address throughout *It's Always Sunny*'s run. It's the script he filmed in 2018 (when the movie was still titled *El Tonto*), but after race-related events during the pandemic and Black Lives Matter protests, Day felt he was no longer the person to tell that story. The script underwent a major rewrite that required reshoots of scenes he'd already filmed; unwilling to ask his cast to work for free, Day funded the do-overs with cash he'd earned as the spokesman for Mountain Dew in a year-long advertising campaign.

The amount of time, effort, and resources he dedicated to the project made the rejection of *Fool's Paradise* by audiences and critics feel especially harsh. Yet Day said he's already looking ahead to another movie project. Next time, he might tackle something a little more accessible and commercial, but he isn't willing to make a movie without his idiosyncratic point of view.

"Which isn't to say, on the next go-around, I would challenge the audience even more," he said. "Probably I would back off a little bit, and say, 'Okay, okay, okay. This time we'll give you a plot.'"

And though there is a Harpo Marx–ish charm in his mostly wordless performance as the mute character Latte Pronto, especially combined with the innocence and facial expressiveness that makes his Charlie Kelly the most endearing member of The Gang on *IASIP*,

Day should probably commit to using his voice in all future endeavors. The uniqueness, playfulness, and occasional Bobcat Goldthwait–ness of his voice is a signature of Day's humor, and something that was MIA from *Fool's Paradise*.

Another film released on May 12, the same day Day's movie hit theaters, has possibly changed the future for another *Sunny* star's career. Howerton, the Juilliard-trained actor who, while as funny as any of his costars, always intended to pursue a career as a more dramatic actor, had finally found the meaty role that would allow him to show Hollywood exactly what kind of performance he was capable of, how versatile he could be. Howerton starred in *BlackBerry*, a fictional dramedy account of the creation and wild success and fall of Research In Motion (RIM), the Canadian company that launched the titular cell phone.

Howerton, summoning every drop of Dennis Reynolds raging know-how he's perfected across twenty years of playing the character, packed all that into his performance as Jim Balsillie, a real-life investor with a Harvard MBA who became the co-CEO of RIM. With his (allegedly) aggressive, arrogant, and manipulative style, Balsillie helped lead RIM to $20 billion worth of BlackBerry sales before legal woes and market share loss accelerated BlackBerry's downfall. In addition to his stellar performance as Balsillie, Howerton went to great lengths to mirror Balsillie's physical appearance, shaving his head without guarantee, of course, that it would grow back once filming was completed in 2022. But no fear for Dennis: the locks came back.

Howerton almost immediately sparked Golden Globe and Oscar

nomination talk for his performance and did receive supporting actor nominations from the Chicago Film Critics Association, Gotham Awards, Las Vegas Film Critics Society, Independent Spirit Awards, Toronto Film Critics Association, and North Texas Film Critics Association. The movie, which costarred Jay Baruchel, director Matt Johnson, Saul Rubinek, Rich Sommer, and Cary Elwes, was named one of the top ten independent films of 2023 by the National Board of Review. It would seem Howerton is destined to have more such projects to come his way.

And then there's DeVito, whose dance card is always intentionally full. Since 2022, he has starred in television commercials as the first celebrity spokesperson for Jersey Mike's, a national chain of submarine sandwich shops. He also starred in three movies in 2023: *Haunted Mansion*, a supernatural horror comedy with Jamie Lee Curtis, LaKeith Stanfield, Owen Wilson, Dan Levy, Rosario Dawson, and Tiffany Haddish; the comedy mystery *Poolman*, Chris Pine's directorial debut (which he also cowrote and stars in), about a pool guy who uncovers a huge Los Angeles water heist, also featuring Annette Bening; and the Mike White–penned animated comedy *Migration*, about a family of mallards who plan to migrate to Jamaica for vacation. DeVito provides voicework, along with Kumail Nanjiani, Elizabeth Banks, Carol Kane, and Awkwafina.

The Tony-nominated actor also hit Broadway at the end of 2023, costarring with daughter Lucy in the play *I Need That*, about a reclusive hoarder threatened with eviction who has to decide what, and who, is really important in his life.

DeVito has also completed production on *St. Sebastian*, an apocalyptic thriller that is his first feature-length directorial effort since 2003's *Duplex*. Starring the late Lance Reddick, William Fichtner, Constance Zimmer, and Lawrence Gilliard Jr., *St. Sebastian* proves DeVito is still trying to innovate, as the movie will be the first thriller he has directed. Meanwhile, among his other future plans, he wants to reunite with *Twins* costar Arnold Schwarzenegger for a new movie, and to collaborate with Billy Crystal on a *Throw Momma from the Train* sequel, called *Throw Papa from the Train*.

Now, here's the question about all those side projects: Do they make the *Sunny* crew more or less likely to continue making the series?

It might seem like they're so busy with the other projects that leaving the show would be the easiest thing to do. But quite simply, they've gotten to a place where making those eight-episode seasons together is pure joy. With a writing staff that's now a mix of *Sunny* veterans who know the show and characters so well, and younger writers who bring fresh perspectives and ideas, the production has continued to flourish creatively.

"It's a blast out there when we go to work," DeVito said. "Sometimes we'll take a year off and we go back to work and it's like we just saw each other four minutes ago."

Having made it through those years of low budgets and spending most of a year writing, producing, editing, and acting in one season, creating *Sunny* episodes now is a smoother, healthier ride. The days when McElhenney says he practically lived on coffee and cigarettes are far behind him.

Now, instead of being the job that they worry holds them back from pursuing other opportunities, *Sunny* is the familiar place they return to, the place where they've already proven themselves to a fan base always waiting to see what new debauchery The Gang will deliver next. There's a freedom in that.

And RCG and the cast still have things on the table with *Sunny*. Will that "The Nightman Cometh" sequel happen, the one the writers and the cast have been asked about practically since the moment the live sold-out mini tour ended? What about taking *The Nightman Cometh* to Broadway, an idea *Hamilton* playwright and *IASIP* fan Lin-Manuel Miranda has encouraged the cast to do?

And what about the big-screen *Sunny* movie, or the additional holiday episodes, that viewers have asked for and cast members have talked about? (A suggestion: combine them both with "The Nightman Cometh" for a *Sunny* holiday movie, *The Nightman Before Christmas*.)

What about the *Sunny* guest stars still on the cast's wish list? Some names were checked off during season 16: *Breaking Bad* stars Bryan Cranston and Aaron Paul finally appeared and spoofed themselves, while DeVito's estranged wife and *Cheers* legend Rhea Perlman became the final *Sunny* cast spouse to appear on the series. But ever since McElhenney and Ryan Reynolds became pro soccer moguls together, *Sunny* fan chatter has included discussion about Reynolds, a longtime *Sunny* fan before his Wrexham partnership, guest-starring on the show. During a joint interview with *BuzzFeed*, McElhenney even shared a specific suggestion about who Reynolds could play in a cameo appearance: Mac's boyfriend. (And, obviously, with the last name, he might have some relatives around Paddy's Pub.)

There are no breaks in the national and international news cycle, and no lack of cultural shifts, which means, as challenging as it can be to come up with new storyline ideas after seventeen seasons and twenty years' worth of episodes, there is no lack of material to be spoofed, ridiculed, commented on, and viewed through the singular *It's Always Sunny* lens.

And though the writers and The Gang have already addressed this topic in a clever season 9 episode, there is one thing that remains a glaring omission in the *It's Always Sunny in Philadelphia* universe: industry awards.

The longer the series runs without them, the less likely it seems that any Emmy or Golden Globe nominations are forthcoming. Not that there haven't been plenty of episodes and performances worthy of the formal recognition of those awards in the later seasons of *Sunny*. But when the show failed to receive nominations back in the early seasons, when it was at the height of its cult-hit status and the writing was consistently as good, smart, and funny as anything on television, it became less likely *Sunny* would ever get its richly deserved industry accolades.

The continuous snubbing hasn't gone unnoticed by the *Sunny* gang; McElhenney, Day, and Howerton have all voiced disappointment in the show being the subject of interviews and features inside entertainment media like *Rolling Stone* and *Entertainment Weekly*, for instance, but never being featured on the covers of those magazines.

And while they were consistently being approached by fellow television writers and producers and showrunners—like *Mad Men* creator Matt Weiner, *Lost* cocreator Damon Lindelof, and *Game of Thrones* creators David Benioff and D. B. Weiss—it became frustrating for them to not feel any industry love from the Television Academy and Golden Globe voters.

Hence season 9's "The Gang Tries Desperately to Win an Award," in which The Gang tried to win the local Restaurant and Bar Association's Best Bar Award. Charlie, Dee, Dennis, and Mac dismissed the accolade, pretending they didn't care about awards and the fact that they'd never been nominated for one. They weren't interested in playing the game of seeking recognition; Dennis admitted he was curious about why they were annually snubbed, but, as Mac insisted, they didn't care, because awards are stupid. It felt almost aggressive that they'd been so ignored, but really, they didn't care. Awards are lame, they said.

Frank's response: "You know what's lame? Being around this long and never gettin' an award. Makes you look like a bunch of assholes."

So The Gang tried, in what passed for The Gang trying, which meant they could pretend not to be horrible, try not to treat people in an insane way, and avoid saying offensive, completely inappropriate things for only so long. Charlie even wrote a special song for the industry event they hosted at the bar; it's an infectious, Randy

Newman-esque song, because awards shows always have songs, Charlie said. But he got high in the basement during the party at Paddy's and sang a song that essentially instructed all the awards voters to leave. So along with the fleeing voters went The Gang's chances for bar award recognition.

And while Day obviously never got loaded and insulted a room full of Hollywood industry people, he acknowledged a dearth of promotion may have hurt the series' chances at an Emmy. Maybe they didn't know how to play the game of schmoozing at the right parties; maybe they just didn't want to, or didn't think they should have to, in order to have their fine work acknowledged.

No matter, Day said. It may have been a blessing in disguise that the Little Show That Could (and Did) has flown under the radar all these years, with nothing but viewer appreciation and loyalty, financial gain, career opportunities, and making television history to show for it.

"For years, we were upset that the show wasn't getting the media recognition or the acknowledgement of how popular and, I think, good it is," Day said. "But then I really do start to wonder if in some ways we dodged a bullet. We get to reap all the benefits of the show being successful and having great fans. We don't have any little golden trophies, but I think that's not really the point."

During the cast's press panel at the Television Critics Association in 2013, before season 9, McElhenney said, "I also think it's a function of us being off the radar for the first four years, and it being such a word-of-mouth show, and it took a good four seasons for us to get an audience. And I think, because we were off the radar for so long, by the time that it became a little bit part of the national, at least, television consciousness, we were already in our fifth season, and I think by that point, any Emmy voter might be thinking, 'Well, that's not the new show. That's the old show,' because it's five years in. And I think, once you find yourself in that category, it's really tough to push back in. Honestly, we haven't made a concerted effort to do so, and that's also something we address [in 'The Gang Tries Desperately to Win an Award']."

For the record, *It's Always Sunny in Philadelphia* has received three Emmy Award nominations: not for acting or writing, but all three for the very deserving work of Marc Scizak for Outstanding Stunt Coordination for a Comedy Series or a Variety Program.

But as long as *Sunny* is still airing on FXX, there is always the chance the Emmy folks will acknowledge what they've been overlooking this whole time.

In a minor twist in the Emmy saga, McElhenney, Day, Howerton, Olson, and DeVito were invited to appear as presenters on the telecast for the 75th annual Emmy Awards in January 2024. It was The Gang's first time putting on their formal wear to present the nominees for an Emmy (Outstanding Talk Series in this instance), and it wouldn't have been on brand if they didn't spend their first time officially in front of the industry crowd to remind them they've never been on the receiving end of a nomination presentation.

They acknowledged DeVito's past win for *Taxi*, which had received thirty-four nominations in its five seasons. "Okay, thirty-four nominations in five years versus zero nominations in sixteen years? That math is bad!" Olson said.

On the other hand, even on the evening of January 15, 2024, as McElhenney sat in the audience of the Peacock Theater in Los Angeles, his tuxedo steamed and his seat rightfully assigned, finally, to put him among his television-creating brethren, his focus was ultimately more on the sports world. Olson had taken a photo of the city of Philadelphia's most famous and devoted professional sports fan, in his Emmy seat, watching his beloved Eagles play the Tampa Bay Buccaneers in a 32–9 playoff game loss for the Eagles. McElhenney shared the photo himself on X.com, with the caption, "Who schedules the Emmys the same night as the @eagles #gobirds #FlyEaglesFly."

Maybe, in a television landscape where that year's Emmy for Outstanding Comedy Series was awarded to a series that isn't really a comedy (FX's indeed outstanding, but not a comedy, *The Bear*), it is more likely that Rob McElhenney will realize his dream of becoming an owner of his hometown NFL team than it is for *It's Always Sunny in Philadelphia* to be acknowledged with an Emmy statue.

Maybe The Gang's mutual crossover with fellow Philadelphia-set comedy *Abbott Elementary* (a frequent Television Academy nominee and winner) in the ABC sitcom's most recent, fourth season will lead to a guest statue for *Sunny*. . . . Does Emmy karma rub off in a crossover between two outstanding series?

McElhenney, in a sentiment that seems to speak for how the whole cast feels about their show, plans to give the Television Academy plenty more opportunities to correct its error.

"I truly believe we can do the show forever," Rob McElhenney says.

ACKNOWLEDGMENTS

Every book project is a reminder that though writing can be a solitary experience, writing a book takes a village of people who help the author bring it all together, sharing their time, memories, kindnesses, and encouragement.

Endless gratitude to my always wonderful and supportive agent, Laurie Abkemeier, and equally supportive, encouraging, and enthusiastic editor, Ed Schlesinger, and his team, Sarah Schlick and Drew Jubera. The inspiring and entertaining story of *It's Always Sunny in Philadelphia*'s journey to history-making success is one I've wanted to tell for a long time, and it wouldn't have been possible without Laurie and Ed, at every stage and through some unexpected challenges.

And thank you to the whole Gallery Books team: cover designer Rinee Shah, interior designer Julia Jacintho, copyeditor Erica Ferguson, indexer Joan Shapiro, production editor Christine Masters, production manager Chloe Gray, marketing whiz Kell Wilson, and super publicist Lauren Carr. Truly, thank you for your work in helping to get the book out into the world in a state of which I am immensely proud.

294 | ACKNOWLEDGMENTS

The most fun aspect of writing the book was the chance to have some terrific, engaging conversations with the charming actors, writers, and directors who've been part of making us laugh for twenty years of antics with The Gang. I've never talked to any other group of creatives who are prouder or more excited to talk about the work they've done on a series. It truly does look like they're having so much fun, because they are having that much fun. Thank you for sharing that with me, Andrew Friedman, Artemis Pebdani, Brian Unger (Go Bobcats!), Brittany Daniel, Conor Galvin, Cormac Bluestone, Dan Attias, Gregory Scott Cummins, Jerry Levine, Jimmi Simpson, Judy Greer, Kimberly McCullough, Kimberly Shannon Murphy, Kyle Davis, Lance Barber, Luvh Rakhe, Lynne Marie Stewart, Marc Scizak, Mary Lynn Rajskub, Michael Naughton, Rob Rosell, Sandy Martin, Scott Cobb, Sean Clifford, Thesy Surface, Todd Biermann, and Wade Boggs (Wade Boggs!). And to Matt Weiner, not a *Sunny* writer (yet?), but an RCG(KD) friend and *Sunny* fan who so graciously and profusely praised all that makes the comedy so great.

And I could not be more grateful to all the reps who helped make those interviews happen: Naomi Odenkirk, Jeffrey Chassen, Stephanie Pfingsten, Aron Giannini, Melanie Murphy, Tyler Reynolds, Will Altemeier, Lauren Gibson, Monica Barkett, Ashley Partington, Katherine Aranda, Jennifer Hyde, Pamela Lin, Hannah Berkowitz, Ryan Glascow, Alex Franklin, Erik Benjamin, David Gardner, Ryan Flaherty, Maddy Schmidt, and Cassie Arvay.

Many thanks to the delightful Jeff Probst and Karyn Bryant for their tales of the early days of FX and the New York City apartment that was the network's broadcast home. (Karyn, I think of you every time I hear the Goo Goo Dolls now.)

Allison Closs generously shared the details of her Danny DeVito cardboard cutout prom date (and the one-good-turn trip to Paddy's Pub Rob McElhenney and Danny arranged for cardboard cutout Allison), which led to national media coverage and Allison's *Sunny* fandom. This will not be the last we hear about budding producer Allison. Thank you to Deke Cameron, the multitalented artist who found his way to *It's Always Sunny* via the many Ongo Gablogian stained glass figures he's created for his clients. The stained glass commission of Dee and Dennis on the stoop Deke created for me is a treasure. Shout-out to my OU buddy Rick Morris for sharing his enthusiasm for and knowledge of *Sunny*; thank you, Rick!

And thank you isn't enough to John Muraro, my husband, best friend, sounding board, in-house editor, listener of endless *Sunny* stories, supporter of every writing project, insister that empanadas are not a proper meal every day when writing takes over the rest of the universe. I love you, and you're right about the empanadas.

SOURCES

Below is a list of the wonderfully kind individuals who were generous in sharing their time, memories, and experiences of their association with *It's Always Sunny in Philadelphia*. It is clear they are proud of their *Sunny* connections, and it was one of the best aspects of writing this book to hear them talk about it.

I've also included a list of sources I referred to while researching and writing the book, organized by chapter. Few television comedies of the last twenty years have made those of us who count ourselves *IASIP* stans laugh harder, louder, or more consistently. But while everything that has happened on-screen made *Sunny* a beloved, bona fide success, the series' behind-the-scenes timeline—from its storied do-it-yourself pilot to its addition of a certain Emmy-winning veteran actor to its innovative, fearless, and enduringly demented storytelling—unfolds the journey of a series that has gone from cult hit to record-breaking television classic. The materials cited here helped paint that tour of The Gang's ascension. Long may it continue to get even more better.

INTERVIEWS CONDUCTED BY THE AUTHOR

Dan Attias

Lance Barber

Todd Biermann

Cormac Bluestone

Wade Boggs

Sean Clifford

Allison Closs

Scott Cobb

Gregory Scott Cummins

Brittany Daniel

Kyle Davis

Andrew Friedman

Conor Galvin

Judy Greer

Jerry Levine

Sandy Martin

Kimberly McCullough

Kimberly Shannon Murphy

Michael Naughton

Artemis Pebdani

Mary Lynn Rajskub

Luvh Rakhe

Rob Rosell

Marc Scizak

Jimmi Simpson

Lynne Marie Stewart

Thesy Surface

Brian Unger

Matthew Weiner

CHAPTER 1: IT'S ALWAYS SUNNY ON TV

Backstage staff. "Sunshine Boys." *Backstage*, November 4, 2019. https://www.backstage.com/magazine/article/sunshine-boys-15958/.

Day, Charlie, Glenn Howerton, and Rob McElhenney, hosts. *The Always Sunny Podcast.* "Charlie Has Cancer," episode 4, November 22, 2021.

Gabert, Shelley. "It's Always 'Funny' in Philadelphia: Into the Writer's Room with the Stars and Creators of FX's Outrageous Cult Comedy." *Creative Screenwriting* 15, no. 5 (September/October 2008).

James, Meg. "'It's Always Sunny in Philadelphia': A Low-Budget Hit." *Los Angeles Times*, September 25, 2010. https://www.latimes.com/archives/la-xpm-2010-sep-25-la-fi-ct-sunny-20100926-story.html.

Lawrence, Derek. "The Gang Makes History: *It's Always Sunny in Philadelphia* Cast on Their Record-Tying Run." *Entertainment Weekly*, September 23, 2019. https://ew.com/tv/2019/09/23/its-always-sunny-in-philadelphia-cast-interview-season-14-record/.

Maron, Mark, host. *WTF with Marc Maron*, podcast. "Charlie Day and Glenn Howerton," episode 209, September 12, 2011.

Maron, Mark, host. *WTF with Marc Maron*, podcast. "Rob McElhenney," episode 582, March 5, 2015.

Masters, Kim, host. *The Business*, podcast. "John Landgraf, Rob McElhenney, and Glenn Howerton." KCRW, October 29, 2012.

O'Connell, Mikey. "'It's Always Sunny' Cast Talks Near Cancellation, Cult Status and Deciding an Endgame." *The Hollywood Reporter*, October 9, 2013. https://www.hollywoodreporter.com/tv/tv-news/sunny-cast-talks-cancellation-cult-645164/.

Odom, Julia. "'It's Always Sunny in Philadelphia': Glenn Howerton Says Show's Title Was Loosely Based on This A-Ha Song." *Showbiz Cheat Sheet*, April 13, 2022. https://www.cheatsheet.com/entertainment/its-always-sunny-philadelphia-glenn-howerton-shows-title-loosely-based-a-ha-song.html/.

Reddit AMA with Glenn Howerton. August 28, 2013. https://www.reddit.com/r/IAmA/comments/1la53f/i_am_glenn_howerton_aka_dennis_from_always_sunny/.

Santino, Andrew, host. *Whiskey Ginger*, podcast. "Charlie Day & Rob McElhenney," July 30, 2021.

CHAPTER 2: THE SUN ALWAYS SHINES ON SUNNY

"Audition for *It's Always Sunny in Philadelphia*." YouTube video, posted by sanstyler, January 26, 2009. https://www.youtube.com/watch?v=iXswKryavxM.

Collis, Clark. "'It's Always Sunny in Philadelphia' Soundtrack: Star Charlie Day Explains Why Listening to the Show's Music Is Like 'Huffing Paint through Your Ears.'" *Entertainment Weekly*, September 16, 2010. https://ew.com/article/2010/09/16/its-always-sunny-in-philadelphia-soundtrack/.

Hibberd, James. "FX Primed to Double Series." *TelevisionWeek*, December 6, 2004. https://www.tvweek.com/in-depth/2004/12/fx-primed-to-double-series/.

La Rosa, Erin. "Kaitlin Olson and the Perils of Being a (Funny) Woman in Hollywood." *BuzzFeed*, January 13, 2015. https://www.buzzfeed.com/erinlarosa/kaitlin-olson-its-always-sunny-in-philadelphia.

McElhenney, Rob. "'It's Always Sunny's' Rob McElhenney Reveals His Original, 'Disturbing' Pitch." *The Hollywood Reporter*, May 16, 2014. https://www.hollywoodreporter.com/news/general-news/sunnys-rob-mcelhenney-reveals-his-703512/.

Miller, Julie. "*It's Always Sunny in Philadelphia* Star Kaitlin Olson on Comic-Con, Season Nine, and Her Drink of Choice to Accept from Fans." *Vanity Fair*, July 2013. https://www.vanityfair.com/hollywood/2013/07/it-s-always-sunny-in-philadelphia-star-kaitlin-olson-on-comic-con-season-nine-and-her-drink-of-choice-to-accept-from-fans.

Multichannel News. "Dancing on the Edge." February 28, 2005.

Reid, Jordan. "The (Real) 'It's Always Sunny in Philadelphia' Origin Story." *Observer*, July 29, 2016. https://observer.com/2016/07/the-real-its-always-sunny-in-philadelphia-origin-story/.

Spencer, Ashley. "It's Always Sunny with Rob McElhenney." *The New York Times*, November 26, 2021. https://www.nytimes.com/2021/11/26/arts/television/its-always-sunny-in-philadelphia-rob-mcelhenney.html.

Television Critics Association. Annual winter press tour, *It's Always Sunny in Philadelphia* cast session. Ritz-Carlton Hotel, Pasadena, California. January 13, 2006.

CHAPTER 3: AND THEY'RE OFF!

Acuna, Kirsten. "'This Is Us' Star Sterling K. Brown Prepped for 'SNL' by Asking a Good Friend and Former Host for Advice—and the Source May Surprise You." *Business Insider*, May 1, 2018. https://www.businessinsider.com/sterling-k-brown-snl-hosting-advice-charlie-day-2018-3.

Anderson, Neal. "FX's 'Sunny' Follows in 'Seinfeld's' Footsteps." *Albuquerque Journal*, August 2, 2005.

Brownfield, Paul. "New FX Comedy Series Offers Something Fresh." *Los Angeles Times*, August 4, 2005. https://www.latimes.com/archives/la-xpm-2005-aug-03-et-alwayssunny03-story.html.

Day, Charlie, Glenn Howerton, and Rob McElhenney, hosts. *The Always Sunny Podcast*. "The Gang Gets Racist," episode 1, November 18, 2021.

Day, Charlie, Glenn Howerton, and Rob McElhenney, hosts. *The Always Sunny Podcast*. "Charlie Has Cancer," episode 4, November 22, 2021.

Day, Charlie, Glenn Howerton, and Rob McElhenney, hosts. *The Always Sunny Podcast*. "Gun Fever," episode 5, November 29, 2021.

Derakhshani, Tirdad. "Local Talent Sells a Phila. Sitcom." *The Philadelphia Inquirer*, February 19, 2005.

Garron, Barry. "It's Always Sunny in Philadelphia." *The Hollywood Reporter*, August 4, 2005.

Gerhart, Ann. "FX's 'Starved' Is a Bit Too Much to Stomach." *The Washington Post*, August 3, 2005. https://www.washingtonpost.com/archive/lifestyle/2005/08/04/fxs-starved-is-a-bit-too-much-to-stomach/c8bb2e56-427b-4a55-9f17-298d6ebdce13/.

Gilbert, Matthew. "Guy Sitcom 'Sunny' Has Its Bright Spots." *Boston Globe*, August 4, 2005. https://archive.boston.com/ae/tv/articles/2005/08/04/guy_sitcom_sunny_has_its_bright_spots/.

Goodykoontz, Bill. "FX Turns Innovation Loose on 2 Sitcoms." *Arizona Republic*, August 3, 2005.

La Rosa, Erin. "Kaitlin Olson and the Perils of Being a (Funny) Woman in Hollywood." *BuzzFeed*, January 13, 2015. https://www.buzzfeed.com/erinlarosa/kaitlin-olson-its-always-sunny-in-philadelphia.

302 | SOURCES

Lowry, Brian. "A Super Slacker Laffer." *Variety*, August 1, 2005. https://variety.com/2005/film/awards/it-s-always-sunny-in-philadelphia-3-1200524154/.

Martin, Denise. "FX Fete a Mouthful." *Variety*, July 20, 2005. https://variety.com/2005/scene/vpage/fx-fete-a-mouthful-1117926286/.

Purchase, Rob. "Eating Disorder Groups Angry over 'Starved.'" Inside Pulse, August 3, 2005. https://insidepulse.com/2005/08/03/39961/.

Richmond, Ray. "Commentary: Bright Days for 'Sunny.'" Associated Press, August 3, 2008. https://www.hollywoodreporter.com/business/business-news/commentary-bright-days-sunny-116766/.

Shister, Gail. "FX Sitcom Set in Philadelphia." Knight Ridder Tribune News Service, February 23, 2005.

Storm, Jonathan. "New TV Genre Arising in Philly? Cable Sitcom Shooting Here Is Aiming for Something Fresh." *The Philadelphia Inquirer*, May 5, 2005.

CHAPTER 4: THE GANG GETS A NEW MEMBER

Day, Charlie, Glenn Howerton, and Rob McElhenney, hosts. *The Always Sunny Podcast*. "Mac Bangs Dennis' Mom," episode 11, December 20, 2021.

Day, Charlie, Glenn Howerton, and Rob McElhenney, hosts. *The Always Sunny Podcast*. "Charlie Goes America All Over Everybody's Ass," episode 17, January 31, 2022.

Day, Charlie, Glenn Howerton, and Rob McElhenney, hosts. *The Always Sunny Podcast*. "Danny DeVito, Everybody," episode 60, December 19, 2022.

Kasprak, Alex. "Was 'The Gang Goes Jihad' a Real Episode of 'Always Sunny in Philadelphia'?" Snopes.com, November 9, 2023. https://www.snopes.com/fact-check/gang-goes-jihad-sunny-episode/.

Long, Justin, host. *Life Is Short with Justin Long*, podcast. "Charlie Day," episode 65, August 4, 2020.

Stambler, Lyndon. "Risk and Reward." *Emmy*, September 2005.

Tanenbaum, Michael. "'It's Always Sunny in Philadelphia' Resisted Adding Danny DeVito, Rob McElhenney Tells Stephen Colbert." *PhillyVoice*, February 6, 2020. https://www.phillyvoice.com/its-always-sunny-philadelphia-stephen-colbert-danny-devito-rob-mcelhenney-fxx/.

Television Critics Association. Annual winter press tour, *It's Always Sunny in Philadelphia* cast session. Ritz-Carlton Hotel, Pasadena, California. January 13, 2006.

CHAPTER 5: THE NIGHTMAN COMETH

Day, Charlie, Glenn Howerton, and Rob McElhenney, hosts. *The Always Sunny Podcast*. "Sweet Dee's Dating a (Redacted) Person," episode 30, May 2, 2022.

Gilmar, Greg. "'It's Always Sunny in Philadelphia' Star Glenn Howerton: 6 Things We Learned on Reddit." *The Wrap*, March 10, 2014. https://www.thewrap.com/always-sunny-philadelphia-star-glenn-howerton-reddit/.

Goldman, Eric. "It's Always Sunny in Philadelphia: Live!" IGN, April 20, 2009. https://www.ign.com/articles/2009/04/20/its-always-sunny-in-philadelphia-live.

Itzkoff, Dave. "'Always Sunny,' with Singing." *The New York Times*, September 16, 2009. https://www.nytimes.com/2009/09/16/arts/television/16sunny.html.

Keveney, Bill. "It's Getting 'Sunny' on the Stage." *USA Today*, August 28, 2009.

Legacy.com. "Mae LaBorde." https://www.legacy.com/us/obituaries/latimes/name/mae-laborde-obituary?id=19930723.

Lopez, Steve. "At 93, She's Leaving Old Age in the Dust." *Los Angeles Times*, November 29, 2002. https://www.latimes.com/archives/la-xpm-2002-nov-29-me-lopez29-story.html.

Lopez, Steve. "Getting Paid to Act Her Age: 97." *Los Angeles Times*, December 17, 2006. https://www.latimes.com/archives/la-xpm-2006-dec-17-me-lopez17-story.html.

Mergler, Todd. "The Sporting World Has Gone Green Man." ESPN, October 22, 2009. https://www.espn.com/espn/page2/story/_/page/mergler%2F091022.

Nussbaum, Emily. "Bar None." *The New Yorker*, November 3, 2013. https://www.newyorker.com/magazine/2013/11/11/bar-none.

Pearson, Jesse, and Sarah Soquel Morhaim. "Charlie Day." *Vice*, September 30, 2010. https://www.vice.com/en/article/charlie-day-555-v17n10/.

Potts, Kimberly. "Talkin' with . . . 'It's Always Sunny in Philadelphia' Star Charlie Day." *TVScreener* (blog), September 15, 2009. https://tvscreener.com/2009/09/talkin-with-its-always-sunny-in-philadelphia-star-charlie-day/.

Price, Jason. "Glenn Howerton Talks 'It's Always Sunny in Philadelphia' and More!" *Icon vs. Icon*, September 16, 2009. https://www.iconvsicon.com/2009/09/16/glenn-howerton-interview-2009/.

Roca, Teressa. "Rare Sighting: *7th Heaven* Recluse Stephen Collins, 76, Drives Modest Car & Deposits Bottles Near Iowa Home after Admitting to Sex

Abuse." *The U.S. Sun*, May 1, 2024. https://www.the-sun.com/entertainment/11236299/7th-heaven-stephen-collins-deposits-bottles-iowa-sexual-abuse/.

Rogers, John. "No Fading Star: Actress Gets Roles at 94." Associated Press, March 30, 2007.

Thurm, Eric. "Glenn Howerton on It's Always Sunny: Nothing Is Going Too Far Unless It Doesn't Make Us Laugh." *The Guardian*, January 4, 2017. https://www.theguardian.com/tv-and-radio/2017/jan/04/its-always-sunny-philadelphia-season-12-glenn-howerton.

Wood, Jennifer M. "The Nightman Cometh: An Oral History of *It's Always Sunny in Philadelphia*'s Musical Episode-Turned-Live Show Phenomenon." *GQ*, October 3, 2018. https://www.gq.com/story/the-nightman-cometh-oral-history.

CHAPTER 6: THE HOUSE OF THE RISING SUNNY

Day, Charlie, Glenn Howerton, and Rob McElhenney, hosts. *The Always Sunny Podcast*. "Paddy's Pub: Home of the Original Kitten Mittens," episode 73, June 12, 2023.

James, Meg. "'It's Always Sunny in Philadelphia': A Low-Budget Hit." *Los Angeles Times*, September 25, 2010. https://www.latimes.com/archives/la-xpm-2010-sep-25-la-fi-ct-sunny-20100926-story.html.

Littleton, Cynthia. "FXX Launch Bash Mixes Heat, Hipsters, Hitmaker." *Variety*, September 3, 2013. https://variety.com/2013/tv/news/fxx-launch-bash-mixes-heat-hipsters-hitmaker-1200598084/.

Pearson, Jesse, and Sarah Soquel Morhaim. "Charlie Day." *Vice*, September 30, 2010. https://www.vice.com/en/article/charlie-day-555-v17n10/.

Potts, Kimberly. "Just the FAQs: Everything You Ever Wanted to Know About *It's Always Sunny in Philadelphia*." AOL TV, November 4, 2010.

Television Critics Association. Annual summer press tour, *It's Always Sunny in Philadelphia* cast session. The Beverly Hilton Hotel, Beverly Hills, California. August 2, 2013.

Wood, Jennifer M. "The Nightman Cometh: An Oral History of *It's Always Sunny in Philadelphia*'s Musical Episode-Turned-Live Show Phenomenon." *GQ*, October. 3, 2018. https://www.gq.com/story/the-nightman-cometh-oral-history.

CHAPTER 7: SUNNY DEE

La Rosa, Erin. "Kaitlin Olson and the Perils of Being a (Funny) Woman in Hollywood." *BuzzFeed*, January 13, 2015. https://www.buzzfeed.com/erinlarosa/kaitlin-olson-its-always-sunny-in-philadelphia.

Murphy, Joel. "One on One with Kaitlin Olson." HoboTrashCan.com, September 18, 2008. https://www.hobotrashcan.com/2008/09/18/one-on-one-with-kaitlin-olson/.

Potts, Kimberly. "Just the FAQs: Everything You Ever Wanted to Know about *It's Always Sunny in Philadelphia*." AOL TV, November 4, 2010.

Potts, Kimberly. "9 *Sunny* Revelations from Kaitlin Olson." Yahoo TV, September 11, 2013.

Potts, Kimberly. "*Always Sunny*'s Kaitlin Olson on Season 15, Her Favorite Dee Moments, & Running Headfirst into a Car." TheDipp.com, October 19, 2020. https://thedipp.com/its-always-sunny-in-philadelphia/always-sunny-kaitlin-olson-season-15.

Tanenbaum, Michael. "Kaitlin Olson 'Ran into a Wall,' Got Black Eye on First Day of Filming for 'It's Always Sunny in Philadelphia.'" *PhillyVoice*, January 26, 2023. https://www.phillyvoice.com/kaitlin-olson-always-sunny-philadelphia-black-eye-filming-season-16/.

Zemler, Emily. "Kaitlin Olson Picks Sweet Dee's 10 Best 'It's Always Sunny' Moments." *Elle*, January 6, 2016.

CHAPTER 8: PHILADELPHIA FREEDOM... TO GET REAL WEIRD WITH IT

Day, Charlie, Glenn Howerton, and Rob McElhenney, hosts. *The Always Sunny Podcast*. "Sweet Dee's Dating a (Redacted) Person," episode 30, May 2, 2022.

Nagelhout, Ryan. "Rob McElhenney Admits That Some Episodes of 'It's Always Sunny in Philadelphia' Haven't Aged Very Well." *Uproxx*, February 22, 2020. https://uproxx.com/tv/rob-mcelhenney-its-always-sunny-in-philadelphia-aged-poorly/.

O'Connell, Mikey. "'It's Always Sunny' Cast Talks Near Cancellation, Cult Status and Deciding an Endgame." *The Hollywood Reporter*, October 9, 2013. https://www.hollywoodreporter.com/tv/tv-news/sunny-cast-talks-cancellation-cult-645164/.

Price, Jason. "Glenn Howerton Talks 'It's Always Sunny in Philadelphia' and More!" *Icon vs. Icon*, September 16, 2009. https://www.iconvsicon.com/2009/09/16/glenn-howerton-interview-2009/.

Sinclair, Chloe. "Here's Why These 'It's Always Sunny' Episodes Aren't Available to Stream." Collider, December 10, 2023. https://collider.com/its-always-sunny-in-philadelphia-episodes-not-on-streaming/.

CHAPTER 9: SUNNY STANS

Day, Charlie, Glenn Howerton, and Rob McElhenney, hosts. *The Always Sunny Podcast*. "The Nightman Cometh (with Lin-Manuel Miranda and Cormac Bluestone!)," episode 58, November 28, 2022.

Day, Charlie, Glenn Howerton, and Rob McElhenney, hosts. *The Always Sunny Podcast*. "Danny DeVito, Everybody," episode 60, December 19, 2022.

Dowd, Maureen. "It's Delightful, It's Delicious, It's DeVito." *The New York Times*, March 23, 2019. https://www.nytimes.com/2019/03/23/style/maureen-dowd-danny-devito.html.

Greene, Andy. "Last Word: Danny DeVito." *Rolling Stone*, November 2019.

Gruttadaro, Andrew. "Danny DeVito, Never Retire (Bitch)." *The Ringer*, September 25, 2019. https://www.theringer.com/tv/2019/9/25/20881295/danny-devito-its-always-sunny-in-philadelphia-profile.

"How Hamilton's Lin-Manuel Miranda Inspired It's Always Sunny's The Wiz Episode." YouTube video, posted by CinemaBlend, January 4, 2017. https://www.youtube.com/watch?v=Hbe9uzd8ghw.

Hueso, Noelo. "Danny DeVito: The Master of Every Medium." *The Hollywood Reporter*, August 26, 2011. https://www.hollywoodreporter.com/tv/tv-news/danny-devito-master-medium-223201/.

Ritschel, Chelsea. "Danny DeVito Takes Cardboard Cutout of Teenager to Set After She Took One of Him to Prom." *The Independent*, November 23, 2020. https://www.independent.co.uk/life-style/danny-devito-prom-teenager-cardboard-cutout-tweet-its-always-sunny-in-philadelphia-allison-closs-a8385206.html.

Schwartz, Drew. "We Found the Teen Behind That Secret, Viral Shrine to Danny DeVito." *Vice*, November 16, 2018. https://www.vice.com/en/article

/danny-devito-shrine-school-bathroom-interview-guy-who-made-it-suny
-purchase-vgtrn/.
Spitznagel, Eric. "Danny DeVito on Booze, Nude Scenes, and S&M Sex at the White House." *Vanity Fair*, December 4, 2009.
Television Critics Association. Press tour, *It's Always Sunny in Philadelphia* cast session. Virtual via Zoom, November 30, 2021.
VanHooker, Brian. "I Took a Cardboard Cutout of Danny DeVito to Prom." *Cracked*, November 15, 2022. https://www.cracked.com/article_35984_i-took -a-cardboard-cutout-of-danny-devito-to-prom.html.
Wally, Maxine. "It's Always Sunny for Cristin Milioti." *W*, August 17, 2021. https://www.wmagazine.com/culture/cristin-milioti-made-for-love-interview.

CHAPTER 10: THE GANG'S ALL HERE … INCLUDING THE MAYOR OF TELEVISION

Chavez, Danette. "The *Always Sunny* Team Thinks the Show Can (and Should) Go on Forever." *AV Club*, September 24, 2019. https://www.avclub.com /the-always-sunny-team-thinks-the-show-can-and-should-1838414387.
Fox, Jesse David. "Our Better Episodes Are the Ones That We Fight Over." *Vulture*, January 20, 2022. https://www.vulture.com/article/its-always-sunny-charlie -day-glenn-howerton-good-one-podcast.html.
Gray, Ellen. "'It's Always Sunny in Philadelphia': 'Good Chance' It Could Continue Past Next Season, Says FX Chief." *The Philadelphia Inquirer*, February 4, 2019. https://www.inquirer.com/entertainment/tv/tv-its-always-sunny-in -philadelphia-season-chances-20190204.html.
Gregory, Alice. "FX President John Landgraf Is the Quiet Genius Inside Your TV." *GQ*, September 8, 2016. https://www.gq.com/story /fx-president-john-landgraf-is-quiet-genius-of-peak-tv.
Murray, Noel. "*It's Always Sunny in Philadelphia*'s Rob McElhenney, Glenn Howerton and Charlie Day." *AV Club*, September 16, 2008. https://www.avclub .com/its-always-sunny-in-philadelphias-rob-mcelhenney-glenn-1798214800.
Philip, Tom. "Glenn Howerton Won't Stop." *GQ*, September 2019. https://www .gq.com/story/glenn-howerton-interview-2019.
Potts, Kimberly. "TV Tattler: Danny DeVito." AOL TV, September 6, 2007.

Potts, Kimberly. "Just the FAQs: Everything You Ever Wanted to Know About *It's Always Sunny in Philadelphia*." AOL TV, November 4, 2010.

Robinson, Joanna. "What's So Special About FX President John Landgraf?" *Vanity Fair*, September 8, 2016. https://www.vanityfair.com/hollywood/2016/09/john-landgraf-fx-emmy-awards-people-v-oj-americans-fargo.

Thorp, Charles. "Q&A: Glenn Howerton on Getting Handed Lead Roles but Not Emmys." *Rolling Stone*, July 21, 2013. https://www.rollingstone.com/tv-movies/tv-movie-news/qa-glenn-howerton-on-getting-handed-lead-roles-but-not-emmys-202669/.

CHAPTER 11: STILL SUNNY AFTER ALL THESE YEARS

Foreman, Alison. "'Beef' Creator Lee Sung Jin Thanks Real-Life Road Rage Nemesis as He Accepts Award at IndieWire Honors." IndieWire, December 7, 2023. https://www.indiewire.com/news/events/beef-creator-lee-sung-jin-thanks-road-rage-nemesis-indiewire-honors-1234932913/.

"How Hamilton's Lin-Manuel Miranda Inspired It's Always Sunny's The Wiz Episode." YouTube video, posted by CinemaBlend, January 4, 2017. https://www.youtube.com/watch?v=Hbe9uzd8ghw.

Lawrence, Derek. "The Gang Makes History: *It's Always Sunny in Philadelphia* Cast on Their Record-Tying Run." *Entertainment Weekly*, September 23, 2019. https://ew.com/tv/2019/09/23/its-always-sunny-in-philadelphia-cast-interview-season-14-record/.

Lin, Patty. "Writing for *Friends* Was No Dream Job." *Time*, August 22, 2023. https://time.com/6306278/friends-patty-lin-end-credits/.

Massa, Annie. "'Get Out!': Jerry Seinfeld Is a Billionaire." Bloomberg, March 22, 2024. https://www.bloomberg.com/news/articles/2024-03-22/jerry-seinfeld-net-worth-tops-1-billion-thanks-to-sitcom.

Remnick, David. "The Scholar of Comedy." *The New Yorker*, April 28, 2024. https://www.newyorker.com/culture/the-new-yorker-interview/the-scholar-of-comedy.

Sepinwall, Alan. "Was This Glenn Howerton's 'Always Sunny' Farewell? 'It's a Little Complicated,' He Says." *Uproxx*, March 8, 2017. https://uproxx.com/sepinwall/its-always-sunny-in-philadelphia-finale-glenn-howerton-leaving-dennis/.

Stern, Marlow. "Glenn Howerton on Leaving 'Always Sunny': 'It's Time for That Character to Change.'" *Daily Beast*, March 22, 2018. https://www.thedailybeast.com/glenn-howerton-on-leaving-always-sunny-its-time-for-that-character-to-change.

Wood, Jenn. "How *It's Always Sunny in Philadelphia*, the Longest-Running Sitcom on the Air, Keeps Up." *Vanity Fair*, October 14, 2019. https://www.vanityfair.com/hollywood/2019/10/its-always-sunny-in-philadelphia-politics.

CHAPTER 12: INTO THE RECORD BOOKS, INTO THE FUTURE

Bang Showbiz. "Charlie Day Experienced 'Highs and Lows' with Fool's Paradise." August 5, 2023. https://nz.news.yahoo.com/charlie-day-experienced-highs-lows-180349661.html.

Bradley, Bill. "Rob McElhenney Is Doing 'More Better' and Knows Exactly How Always Sunny Will End." *Adweek*, March 19, 2024. https://www.adweek.com/convergent-tv/rob-mcelhenney-more-better-always-sunny-end/.

Chuba, Kirsten. "Larry David on Ending 'Curb Your Enthusiasm': 'People Think I'm Lying—I'm Not a Liar.'" *The Hollywood Reporter*, January 31, 2024. https://www.hollywoodreporter.com/tv/tv-news/larry-david-insists-end-of-curb-your-enthusiasm-1235811180/.

O'Callaghan, Quinn. "Rob McElhenney Is the Greatest Living Philadelphian. Let's Build a Monument to Him." *The Philadelphia Inquirer*, August 24, 2017. https://www.inquirer.com/philly/opinion/commentary/rob-mcelhenney-its-always-sunny-in-philadelphia-20170824.html.

Paiella, Gabriella. "Danny DeVito Has Never Heard the Term 'Short King.'" *GQ*, November 3, 2023. https://www.gq.com/story/danny-devito-i-need-that-interview-2023.

Pearson, Jesse, and Sarah Soquel Morhaim. "Charlie Day." *Vice*, September 30, 2010. https://www.vice.com/en/article/charlie-day-555-v17n10/.

Television Critics Association. Annual summer press tour, *It's Always Sunny in Philadelphia* cast session. The Beverly Hilton Hotel, Beverly Hills, California. August 2, 2006.

INDEX

A

Abbott Elementary (TV show), 292
Alazraqui, Carlos, 57
All the Wilderness (film), 232
Alpine Formula One, 280
Altman, Robert, 39
The Always Sunny Podcast
    on Anheuser-Busch pulling signage from Paddy's Pub, 51
    on controversial content, 81–82, 113, 183–84, 278
    Day on song and dance of Frank Reynolds, 73
    "Femail Bag with Kaitlin Olson", 279
    on filming, 9
    Howerton on naming Guigino's, 39
    live tapings of, 202, 279
    McElhenney on Lil' Kev character, 81
    popularity of, 279
    on writers of *It's Always Sunny in Philadelphia*, 109
Amazon Video, 181
Anderson, Neal, 49–50
Aniston, Jennifer, 232
A.P. Bio (TV show), 244, 245
Apple TV+ (streaming network), 181, 226, 243, 280
Archer, Anne, 63, 97. *See also* Barbara Reynolds (character)
Artemis Dubois (character), 43–44, 115, 120, 124, 146, 148–49
Arthur, Bea, 172
Ass Pounder 4000 exercise bike, 272
Attias, Dan, 40–41, 75–76, 78, 252
Awkwafina, 285

B

Baccarin, Morena, 14, 218
Backus, Christopher, 3
Bakula, Scott, 83, 261–62
Balsillie, Jim, 284
Banks, Elizabeth, 285
Barbara Reynolds (character)
    contested paternity of Dennis and Dee, 73
    death and inheritance for family, 94–97, 147
    Frank divorcing, 63, 67
    Mac, having sex with, 69, 71, 170
Barber, Lance, 252, 258–60
Barrett, Malcolm, 42, 180–81
Baruchel, Jay, 285
Bateman, Jason, 232, 282
Beckinsale, Kate, 282
Beef (TV show), 243
Bening, Annette, 285

Benioff, David, 211, 229, 252
Berg, Alec, 5
Bergeron, Tom, 22
Bergeron, Vic, 47
Berkow, Jordan Reid, 11–12, 28–29
Berlanti, Greg, 17
Bertha Fussy (character), 219
Biermann, Todd, 41, 220–26, 255–56, 273–74
Bill Ponderosa (character), 252, 256–60
BlackBerry (film), 284–85
blackface, 92, 166–67, 171–73, 174–78, 181–82
block-shooting method, 63–65, 80, 231
Bluestone, Cormac
    as composer for *It's Always Sunny in Philadelphia*, 27, 261
    as guest star in season 1, 42, 218
    The Nightman Cometh musical and, 114, 119, 124–25, 128–29
board games, 207
Boggs, Brett, 255
Boggs, Wade, 225, 253–55
Bomer, Matt, 23
Bonnie Kelly (character), 46, 103, 265
Bower, Tom, 32
Braugher, Andre, 83
Brody, Adrien, 282
Brown, Sterling K., 49, 52
Brownfield, Paul, 50
Bruce Mathis (character), 72–73, 95–96
Burns, Edward, 8

C

Campfire Stories (movie), 5
Cannavale, Bobby, 281
Carlock, Robert, 176
Carmen (character), 14, 101, 157, 184–88
CBS (network), 19
Charlie Kelly (character)
    at armed robbery of convenience store, 252–53
    body-swapping with Black person, 260–64
    in Chemical Toilet (musical group), 86–88
    in Christmas special, 192–93
    in citizen watch program, 105–6
    Dee, trying out life of, 151
    Dee's pregnancy and, 155–57
    Dennis as murder suspect and, 266
    drug debt to mob, 104–5
    in Electric Dream Machine (musical group), 89–91
    fight club match, 75–77
    Frank moving in with Charlie's mom and, 102–3
    Frank's affair with Charlie's mom and paternity question, 78
    getting run over by Dennis and Dee, 67
    as Green Man (green-spandex-clad mascot), 94
    human meat, addicted to, 152
    intelligence pill experiment, 252
    McPoyle brothers and, 45
    Mr. Covington character played by, 173
    The Nightman Cometh musical, writing, 114–15, 118–19
    N-word and, 180–81
    Paddy's Pub, attempting to win award for, 289–90
    Paddy's Pub, dance contest at, 107–8
    Paddy's Pub health inspection and, 255–56
    personality of, 204–5
    purchasing gasoline to sell later, 147
    "Rock, Flag, and Eagle" song, 77
    as school janitor, 173–74
    selling Kitten Mittens at Paddy's Pub, 135
    sewing skills of, 101
    sexual harassment seminar and, 249, 251

taking LSD and dressing as Green Man, 93–94
tricking Dee into stand-up comedy scheme, 161–62
Uncle Jack, assisting in court, 256
visiting Mac's father in prison, 72
Wade Boggs drinking record and, 253–54
Waitress, crush on, 11, 44–45, 129–30, 137
Cheers (TV show), 70
Chemical Toilet (musical group), 88–89
Chernin, Dave and John, 242–43, 281
Cherniss, Matt, 23
Chiklis, Michael, 23
Cindy (character), 244
Clifford, Sean, 127–28
Close, Glenn, 23, 55–56
Closs, Allison, 198–201
Cobb, Scott, 119, 124
Colbert, Stephen, 9
Collins, Stephen, 72–73, 95–97
Comedy Central (network), 19, 57–58, 134, 191
Comic-Con (San Diego, 2008), 209
continuity errors, 64–65
controversial content in *It's Always Sunny in Philadelphia*
  cast addressing, 176–80, 182–83
  creative freedom in season 1 and, 32–33
  in "The Gang Goes Jihad", 75
  lack of cancellation for, 189–90, 203–4
  N-word, 180–81
  racial issues, 166–67, 171–73, 174–78, 260–65
  R-word, 80–82, 183–84
  streaming services removing, 171–73, 176, 181–82
  transgender character, 184–88
  T-word, 186–87
Cooper, Bradley, 252

Cranston, Brian, 270–71, 287
Crashtones (musical group), 111, 218
Crawford, Lavell, 162
Crystal, Billy, 286
Cummins, Gregory Scott, 72. *See also* Mr. Mac "Luther MacDonald" (character)
Curb Your Enthusiasm (TV show), 4, 30–31, 234–35, 276–77
Curtis, Jamie Lee, 285

D

Daniel, Brittany, 157, 184–89
Danny DeFeetos (slippers), 201
Danny Packs (fanny packs), 201
David, Larry
  career advice for McElhenney, 234, 275
  Curb Your Enthusiasm, 4, 234–35, 276–77
  McElhenney compared to, 24
  More Better Productions, 281
  Seinfeld episode "The Contest", 184
  Seinfeld on, 268–69
Davidson, Pete, 209
Davis, Kyle, 83–86. *See also* Lil' Kev (character)
Davitian, Ken, 160–61
Dawson, Rosario, 285
Day, Charlie. *See also* Charlie Kelly (character)
  acting career, 5–6, 52, 58, 71, 210, 232, 280, 282–84
  amateur sketch videos of, 5–7
  on block shooting, 65
  Sterling K. Brown, friendship with, 52
  casting friends and family, 42, 218
  on controversial content of *It's Always Sunny in Philadelphia*, 189–90
  creative control of, 25, 32–33, 40–41
  Kyle Davis, casting, 84
  "Dayman" song, writing, 112

Day, Charlie (*cont.*)
    on DeVito joining *It's Always Sunny in Philadelphia*, 59–60
    on Dick Towels, creation of, 136–37
    exhaustion and burnout of, 227–32
    fans and, 208–9
    filming in Philadelphia, 43
    on "go for it" song and dance of Frank, 73
    Howerton and McElhenney, meeting, 5, 7–8
    on industry awards, 288–90
    It's Always Sunny in Philadelphia pilot, 8–15, 24–25
    Sandy Martin, casting, 71
    The Nightman Cometh musical and, 114, 119, 121, 124–30
    "Nightman" song, writing, 112–13
    pitch meetings for *It's Always Sunny in Philadelphia*, 15–20, 23–25
    profitability of *It's Always Sunny in Philadelphia*, 135
    recognized at *Hamilton* by Miranda, 208
    "Rock, Flag, and Eagle" song, writing, 77
    on R-word use, 183–84
    on theme music for *It's Always Sunny in Philadelphia*, 27
    writers, hiring, 109–11
    writing contributions to *It's Always Sunny in Philadelphia*, 32–35, 38, 65–66, 227
"Dayman" (song)
    Charlie and Dennis writing and performing, 89–92
    creation of, 111–12
    in live performances of *The Nightman Cometh* musical, 124–25, 129
    popularity of, 109, 113, 121–22, 208
    Portugal. The Man arrangement of, 211
    viral video of Japanese kindergartners singing, 279
Dead End (play), 71
Deandra "Sweet Dee" Reynolds (character), 141–68
    Artemis Dubois, friendship with, 43–44
    back-brace scam, 67–68
    body-swapping with Black person, 260–64
    Charlie, trying out life of, 151
    Charlie's intervention for being molested and, 46
    in Christmas special, 192–94
    in citizen watch program, 105–6
    clothing design rivalry with high school friend, 100–101
    contested paternity of, 72–73, 77–78
    dance imitating inflatable dancing guy, 164
    dating Lil' Kev, 80–82, 85, 91
    Dennis as murder suspect and, 266
    Dennis mistaken for sex offender and, 102
    drug debt to mob, 104–5
    father, reuniting with, 63, 67–68
    getting cursed, 219
    Josh Groban storylines, 149–50
    human meat, addicted to, 152
    in *Lethal Weapon* remakes, 165–67, 177
    Martina Martinez character played by, 172–73
    at Philadelphia Eagles open tryouts, 93
    in *The Nightman Cometh* musical, 115, 118
    Olson hired for role of, 30–32
    Olson's input on Sweet Dee role, 32, 37–38, 143–44, 167
    origins of nickname, 153–54
    Paddy's Pub, attempting to win award for, 289
    Paddy's Pub, dance contest at, 108

personality of, 205–6
pregnancy of, 155–57, 186
Reid fired from role of, 28–29
respect of The Gang, desire for, 202
running over Charlie, 67
scam marriage to father, 95–96
seduction of a priest, 69–70
self-defense lessons and fight, 75–77, 149
sexual harassment seminar and, 249, 251
stand-up comedy attempts, 151, 159–63, 172–73
stripper and, 158–59
as substitute teacher, 173
Taiwan Tammy character played by, 172–73
tripping and running into car door, 144–46
unemployment scam, 74, 154–55
Waitress, relationship with, 45
waterboarding scene, 147–48
wheelchair scam, 67–68
Delaney, Rob, 2
del Toro, Guillermo, 210, 256
Dennis Reynolds (character)
body-swapping with Black person, 260–64
buying a boat, 163–64
Charlie's intervention for being molested and, 46
in Chemical Toilet (musical group), 89–90
in Christmas special, 192–93
in citizen watch program, 105–6
contested paternity of, 72–73, 77–78
Crazy Paddy character, 173
on Dee dating Lil' Kev, 81
Dee's pregnancy and, 155–57
Dee tricked into stand-up comedy scheme and, 161–62
designing a dress, 101
divorcing Maureen Ponderosa, 99

drug debt to mob, 104–5
in Electric Dream Machine (musical group), 89–91
father, reuniting with, 63, 67–68
finding boyfriend for Dee, 160
inheriting mansion from mother, 95–96
leaving and returning to "The Gang", 244–46
in *Lethal Weapon* remakes, 166–67, 174–75, 177–79
mental health issues, 242
mistaken for sex offender, 102
as murder suspect, 265–66
at Philadelphia Eagles open tryouts, 93
in *The Nightman Cometh* musical, 115, 118–19
Paddy's Pub, attempting to win award for, 289
Paddy's Pub, dance contest at, 108
personality of, 205
purchasing gasoline to sell later, 147
in rehab with Rob Thomas, 214
Rickety Cricket character and, 69–70
running over Charlie, 67
seducing Mac's mom, 71–72
seduction method mnemonic device, 137–38
selling pens at Paddy's Pub, 135
sexual harassment seminar and, 249–50
unemployment scam, 74, 154–55
Waitress, relationship with, 45
Dent, Catherine, 23
Desai, Shelly, 252
Deschanel, Emily, 139
Deschanel, Zooey, 233
DeVito, Danny. *See also* Frank Reynolds (character)
acting career, 59, 232, 233–34, 285–86
Biermann directing and, 225
block shooting and, 64–65
Boggs and, 225

DeVito, Danny (*cont.*)
   casting friends and family, 219–20
   on Christmas special, filming, 193–94
   on Frank character, 194
   on inventiveness of season 2, 70
   It's Always Sunny in Philadelphia fans and, 196–201, 214–15
   Jersey Television, cofounder of, 58
   joining *It's Always Sunny in Philadelphia*, 58–62, 68–69, 78, 132, 194–95, 239–41
   Landgraf on talent of, 194–95
   on McElhenney, 61–62
   meeting Kyle Davis, 83–84
   merchandise sales and, 201–2
   New York Times profile on, 196
   The Nightman Cometh musical and, 127–30
   support for *It's Always Sunny in Philadelphia*, 241
   on *Taxi*, 59, 291
   Trollfoot Twitter posts, 195
   Vanny DeVito vans named for, 196–97
   on working on *It's Always Sunny in Philadelphia*, 286
DeVito, Lucy, 219–20, 285
Dick Towels, 136, 163
Dillahunt, Garret, 282
Donna (character), 169
Dowd, Maureen, 196
"Drug Lord" (amateur sketch video), 6
Dunn, Nora, 169

E

Electric Dream Machine (musical group), 89–91
Ellis, Mary Elizabeth. *See also* Waitress (character)
   in *Fool's Paradise*, 282
   meeting Olson, 41
   The Nightman Cometh musical and, 124, 128
   Pebdani and, 43, 146
   recognized at *Hamilton* by Miranda, 208
   in *Reno 911*, 58
   in Taylor Swift music video, 211
Elwes, Cary, 285
Emmy Awards (2024), 291–92
Entourage (TV show), 40
Espinola, Ray, 27
Esposito, Joe, 76
Eve, 200
Extreme (musical group), 74

F

Falco, Edie, 282
Falconer, Eric, 65
Fallon, Jimmy, 254
fans. *See also* controversial content in *It's Always Sunny in Philadelphia*
   Bill Ponderosa character and, 259–60
   celebrity, 208–14, 234
   college students, 80, 132–33, 197–98
   "Dayman" song, popularity of, 109, 113, 121–22
   DeVito and, 194–201, 214–15
   Green Man and, 93–94
   the Lawyer character and, 99–100
   Lil' Kev character and, 83, 85–86
   merchandise sales and, 77, 135–37, 201–2, 207–8
   The Nightman Cometh musical and, 121–30, 132, 191–92
   requests for movie, 287
   season 1 and, 44
Fatty Magoo (character), 100–101
Favreau, Jon, 8
Fetterman, John, 278–79
Fey, Tina, 176
Fichtner, William, 286
Foley, Dave, 174, 212–13
Followill, Nathan, Caleb, Jared, and Matthew, 210
Fool's Paradise (film), 282–84
Fortenberry, John, 40

INDEX | 317

Four Walls whiskey, 271, 280
Fox (network), 3, 19, 56, 133
Fox Home Entertainment (FHE), 132
Foxworthy, Jeff, 40
Foxx, Jamie, 25
Frank Reynolds (character)
    affair with Charlie's mom and paternity question, 78
    at armed robbery of convenience store, 253
    Barbara's death and, 94–95
    Bill Ponderosa and, 259–60
    body-swapping with Black person, 260–64
    on censorship of racially insensitive content, 176–77
    in Chemical Toilet (musical group), 86–91
    in Christmas special, 192–94
    in citizen watch program, 105–6
    contested paternity of Dennis and Dee, 73, 77–78
    Dennis as murder suspect and, 266
    divorcing Barbara, 63, 67
    drug debt to mob, 104–5
    Gail, having sex with, 169–70
    on gay marriage, 186
    getting weird for *It's Always Sunny in Philadelphia*, 169, 194–96
    "go for it" song and dance of, 73
    human meat consumption, lying about, 152
    joining *It's Always Sunny in Philadelphia*, 63, 68–69, 78
    in *Lethal Weapon* remakes, 177–78
    Mac in *Lethal Weapon* remakes using blackface, 174–75
    Martina Martinez character played by, 173
    merchandise sales and, 201–2
    moving in with Charlie's mom, 102–3
    in *The Nightman Cometh* musical, 115, 118
    Paddy's Pub, attempting to win award for, 289
    personality of, 207
    reuniting with Dennis and Dee, 63, 67–68
    scam marriage to daughter, 95–96
    seeking relationship with children, 67
    selling hard-boiled eggs at Paddy's Pub, 135
    sexual harassment seminar, 249–50
    sweat shop of, 101
    taking LSD, 93
    teaching Dee self-defense, 75, 149
    Trash Man character, 197
    tricking Dee into stand-up comedy scheme, 161–62
    Waitress, having sex with, 69
    waterboarding Dee, 147–48
    wheelchair scam, 67–68
Frenkel, Nick, 3, 7, 13, 15, 23–24
Friedman, Andrew, 46, 99–100. *See also* Jack (character)
Friends (TV show), 21, 50, 77, 228, 247
Funko Pop! figurines, 207
FX (network)
    changes to *It's Always Sunny in Philadelphia*, 25–27, 33, 56
    comedy block, development of, 25–26, 51–52, 138
    Comedy Central's purchase of *It's Always Sunny in Philadelphia* syndication rights, 134
    diversity campaign, 246
    evolution of, 21–23
    It's Always Sunny in Philadelphia merchandise sales, 135–37, 207–8
    Landgraf as president of entertainment at, 55–56
    pitch meeting for *It's Always Sunny in Philadelphia* at, 20, 23–25
    production costs for *It's Always Sunny in Philadelphia*, 33

318 | INDEX

FX (network) (*cont.*)
   The Shield, 23
   success and support for *It's Always Sunny in Philadelphia*, 79–80, 182, 191, 235
FXX (sub-network), 138–39

G

Gail "Gail the Snail" (character), 169–70, 252
Galvin, Conor, 242
Ganz, Megan, 248–51, 279–80
Garant, Robert Ben, 57–58
Garret, Wil, 261–62
Garron, Barry, 49
gay marriage, 185–86, 271
Gerhart, Ann, 50
Gervais, Ricky, 9
Gibson, Mel, 166, 174
Gilbert, Matthew, 50
Gilbert, Sara, 200
Gilliard, Lawrence, Jr., 286
Gillooly, Jeff, 108
Gladys (character), 116–18
Glazer, Ilana, 226
Glover, Danny, 166, 174, 254
Goggins, Walton, 23
The Golden Girls (TV show), 172
Goodykoontz, Bill, 50
Grad, Nick, 23
Greenburg, Ari, 15, 17–18
Green Man (Charlie's green-spandex-clad mascot), 93–94
Greer, Judy, 100–101
Grenier, Adrian, 40
Grier, David Alan, 270
Groban, Josh, 149–50
Groundlings (improv troupe), 30, 46, 142
Gugino, Carla, 39
Guigino's (fictional restaurant), 38–39, 73, 219–20
Gurland, Andrew, 25
Guzmán, Luis, 42

H

Hacks (TV show), 142, 243, 281
Haddish, Tiffany, 67, 285
Harmon, Dan, 250
Harper, Bryce, 281
Harris, Aisha, 181–82
Harris, Marcuis W., 178
Haskins, Dennis, 33
Haunted Mansion (film), 285
Hauser, Paul Walter, 174
HBO (network), 19, 40, 142, 234–35, 276
Hearst, William Randolph, 38
High Potential (TV show), 281–82
Hornsby, David, 6, 11–12, 65–66, 69–70, 138, 242. *See also* Rickety Cricket (character)
Horrible Bosses 2 (film), 232
Hotel Artemis (film), 52
Howard, Ryan, 218
Howerton, Glenn. *See also* Dennis Reynolds (character)
   acting career, 2–3, 232, 233, 244, 282, 284–85
   on Barbara's death in *It's Always Sunny in Philadelphia*, 97
   casting friends and family, 218
   on controversial content of *It's Always Sunny in Philadelphia*, 189–90
   in Crashtones (musical group), 111, 218
   creative control of, 25, 32–33, 40–41
   Day and McElhenney, meeting, 3–5, 7–8
   "Dayman" song, writing, 112
   decision-making process for writing, 227
   on DeVito joining *It's Always Sunny in Philadelphia*, 59–60
   exhaustion and burnout of, 227–32, 243–44

INDEX | 319

on FX's support of *It's Always Sunny in Philadelphia*, 182
on Ganz's writing talent, 248
on industry awards, 288–89
It's Always Sunny in Philadelphia pilot, 8–15, 24–25
marriage to Jill Latiano, 126–27
naming Guigino's, 39
The Nightman Cometh musical and, 114, 119, 124–30
on Olson for Sweet Dee role, 31
pitch meetings for *It's Always Sunny in Philadelphia*, 15–20, 23–25
profitability of *It's Always Sunny in Philadelphia*, 135
title of *It's Always Sunny in Philadelphia*, inspiration for, 15
on using R-word in *It's Always Sunny in Philadelphia*, 82
writers, hiring, 109–11
writing contributions to *It's Always Sunny in Philadelphia*, 32–35, 65–66
Hulu (streaming network), 133, 172–73, 176, 179–81
Hwang (character), 252

I

Imagine Dragons (musical group), 213
IMDb user ratings, 278
Incoming (film), 281
I Need That (play), 285
Ingrid Nelson (character), 100–101
Insane Clown Posse (musical group), 174
It's Always Sunny in Moscow (TV show), 279
It's Always Sunny in Philadelphia (TV show). *See also The Always Sunny Podcast*; *individual seasons and characters*
  actors' other projects and, 286–87
  controversial content of. *See*
  controversial content in *It's Always Sunny in Philadelphia*
  creators' exhaustion and burnout, 227–32
  as deconstructed sitcom, 21, 82, 228, 235–36, 241, 247
  DeVito joining, 58–62, 68–69, 78, 132, 194–95, 239–41
  diversity of writers, 246–49
  DVD release, 132
  fans of. *See* fans
  friends and family of creators, casting, 41–42, 218–26
  FX changes to, 25–27, 33, 56
  FX support for, 79–80, 182, 191, 235
  industry awards and, 288–91
  merchandise sales and, 77, 135–37, 201–2, 207–8
  opening credits and theme song, 26–27, 43, 226
  original storyline and title, 10–11, 25–27
  personality summaries of cast, 204–7
  pitch meetings for, 15–20, 23–25
  popularity and cultural influence of, 278–79
  "A Very Sunny Christmas" special on DVD, 192–94, 196, 278
  writers and writers' rooms for, 80, 109–12, 229–30, 242–43, 246–47
It's Always Sunny in Philadelphia (TV show) season 1
  budget and profitability of, 33–35, 38–39, 51
  "Charlie Got Molested", 33, 44, 45–46
  "Charlie Has Cancer", 1–4, 10–13, 37, 41, 43, 187
  "Charlie Wants an Abortion", 41–42
  controversial content in, 32–33
  critical response to, 49–50
  directors and staff of, 39–41
  "The Gang Gets Racist", 37, 41–42, 180–81

It's Always Sunny in Philadelphia (TV show) season 1 (*cont.*)
  "Gun Fever", 39
  opening credits, 43
  pilot and second episode, 8–15, 24–25
  renewed for second season, 52–53
  series premiere, 37, 46–47, 49
  sets and shooting locations for, 38–39, 41–42
  Television Critics Association press tour and, 47–49
  "Underage Drinking: A National Concern", 52
  viewership of, 50–52
It's Always Sunny in Philadelphia (TV show) season 2
  block shooting of, 64–65
  "Charlie Gets Crippled", 67–68, 240
  "Charlie Goes America All Over Everybody's Asses", 77
  "Dennis and Dee Get a New Dad", 72, 77–78
  "Dennis and Dee Go on Welfare", 74, 154–55
  DeVito joining, 58–62, 68–69, 78
  Frank Reynolds character joining, 63
  "The Gang Exploits a Miracle", 65, 69–70, 219
  "The Gang Goes Jihad", 74–75
  "The Gang Runs for Office", 65–66
  "Hundred Dollar Baby", 75–77, 149
  "Mac Bangs Dennis' Mom", 71–73, 110, 219–20, 278
  summary, 68–69
  viewership of, 79–80
  writers and writers' room for, 80, 110
It's Always Sunny in Philadelphia (TV show) season 3
  "The Aluminum Monster vs. Fatty Magoo", 100–101
  "Bums: Making a Mess All Over the City", 105–6, 220, 279
  costumes, 119
  "Dennis and Dee's Mom Is Dead", 94–97, 218
  "Dennis Looks Like a Registered Sex Offender", 101–4
  "The Gang Dances Their Asses Off", 107–8
  "The Gang Exploits the Mortgage Crisis", 133–34
  "The Gang Finds a Dumpster Baby", 79, 92
  "The Gang Gets Invincible", 93–94
  "The Gang Gets Whacked (Part 1 and 2)", 104–5
  on Hulu, 133
  the Lawyer character, 97–100
  "Mac Is a Serial Killer", 101–2, 178, 185
  "Sweet Dee's Dating a Retarded Person", 80–91, 109, 111–12, 183–84
  viewership of, 79
  writers and writers' room for, 80, 109–12
It's Always Sunny in Philadelphia (TV show) season 4
  "America's Next Top Paddy's Billboard Model Contest", 172, 181
  "Dennis Reynolds: An Erotic Life", 151, 213–14
  "The Gang Solves the Gas Crisis", 147–48
  "Mac and Dennis: Manhunters", 152–53
  "The Nightman Cometh", 113–21, 191–92
  viewership of, 121
  "Who Pooped the Bed?", 144–46
It's Always Sunny in Philadelphia (TV show) season 5
  "The D.E.N.N.I.S. System", 116, 126, 137–38, 278
  "The Gang Gives Frank an Intervention", 169

"The Gang Wrestles for the Troops",
    137
"Mac and Dennis Break Up", 137
"Paddy's Pub: Home of the Original
    Kitten Mittens", 135–37
ratings and viewership of, 132–33, 134
"The Waitress Is Getting Married", 137
writers and writers' room for, 137
It's Always Sunny in Philadelphia (TV
    show) season 6
  budget for, 134
  "Dee Gives Birth", 157, 186, 259
  "Dee Reynolds: Shaping America's
      Youth", 173–74
  "Dennis Gets Divorced", 99
  "The Gang Buys a Boat", 163–64
  "The Gang Gets Stranded in the
      Woods", 218
  "Mac Fights Gay Marriage", 185–86,
      258
  "Mac's Mom Burns Her House
      Down", 149–50
  "Who Got Dee Pregnant", 155–57
It's Always Sunny in Philadelphia (TV
    show) season 7
  "CharDee MacDennis: The Game of
      Games", 278
  "Fat Mac", 229
  "The High School Reunion", 210
It's Always Sunny in Philadelphia (TV
    show) season 8
  "The Gang Gets Analyzed", 224–25
  "The Gang Recycles Their Trash", 172
  "The Maureen Ponderosa Wedding
      Massacre", 256
It's Always Sunny in Philadelphia (TV
    show) season 9
  "Flowers for Charlie", 211, 252
  "The Gang Broke Dee", 159–63, 251
  "The Gang Goes to Hell: Part One
      and Two", 271, 273
  "The Gang Makes *Lethal Weapon 6*",
      165–66, 173, 181

"The Gang Saves the Day", 150,
    252–53
"The Gang Squashes Their Beefs",
    225, 251–52
"The Gang Tries Desperately to Win
    an Award", 289–90
"Mac Day", 271
It's Always Sunny in Philadelphia (TV
    show) season 10
  "Ass Kickers United: Mac and
      Charlie Join a Cult", 219
  "Charlie Work", 255–56
  "The Gang Beats Boggs", 225, 253–55
  Howerton on ending series, 231–32
It's Always Sunny in Philadelphia (TV
    show) season 11
  "Being Frank", 232, 259
  "Mac & Dennis Move to the
      Suburbs", 232, 278
  "McPoyle vs. Ponderosa: The Trial of
      the Century", 256–57
It's Always Sunny in Philadelphia (TV
    show) season 12
  "Dennis' Double Life", 244
  Dennis leaving, 244–45
  "The Gang Goes to a Water Park",
      211
  "The Gang Turns Black", 260–65
  "Hero or Hate Crime?", 271–72
  "Making Dennis Reynolds a
      Murderer", 265–66
  "Old Lady House: A Situational
      Comedy", 265
  "PTSDee", 158–59
It's Always Sunny in Philadelphia (TV
    show) season 13
  Dennis returning to, 245–46
  "The Gang Does a Clip Show", 225,
      266–67
  "The Gang Gets New Wheels", 219
  "The Gang Solves the Bathroom
      Problem", 247
  Mac changing physique for, 230, 272

322 | INDEX

It's Always Sunny in Philadelphia (TV show) season 13 (*cont.*)
   "Mac Finds His Pride", 225, 232, 271–74
   "Time's Up for the Gang", 248–51
   writers and writers' room for, 247–49

It's Always Sunny in Philadelphia (TV show) season 14
   "Dee Day", 172–73, 183, 251
   DVD box set, 183
   "The Janitor Always Mops Twice", 251
   "A Woman's Right to Chop", 270

It's Always Sunny in Philadelphia (TV show) season 15
   "Dee Sinks in a Bog", 270
   "The Gang Buys a Roller Rink", 153–54
   "The Gang Makes *Lethal Weapon 7*", 176–79

It's Always Sunny in Philadelphia (TV show) season 16
   "Celebrity Booze: The Ultimate Cash Grab", 270–71
   "Dennis Takes a Mental Health Day", 242, 278
   "The Gang Gets Cursed", 219
   "Risk E. Rat's Pizza and Amusement Center", 220

"It's Nature, Shit Happens" (song), 129
"I've Got a Troll in My Hole" (song), 129

J

Jack (character), 46, 99–100, 256–57
Jackson, Samuel L., 209
Jacobson, Peter, 161
James, LeBron, 39
Jeong, Ken, 282
Jersey Television (production company), 57–58
Jimmy Doyle (character), 42
Johnson, Matt, 285

K

Kaling, Mindy, 244
Kane, Carol, 285
The Karate Kid (film), 76
Kenney-Silver, Kerri, 57–58, 224
Kiessling, Heinz, 27
Kingsley, Sidney, 71
Kings of Leon (musical group), 210
Kitten Mittens, 135
Knight, Wayne, 268
Kudrow, Lisa, 258

L

Laborde, Mae, 116–18
Landgraf, John
   changes to *It's Always Sunny in Philadelphia*, 25–27, 33, 56
   comedy block for FX, development of, 51–52
   on DeVito joining *It's Always Sunny in Philadelphia*, 58–61, 194–95, 240
   diversity campaign, 246
   early career, 21, 57
   giving creative control to creators of *It's Always Sunny in Philadelphia*, 25, 32–33
   as mayor of television, 237–38
   on "peak TV", 237
   pitch meeting for *It's Always Sunny in Philadelphia*, 20, 23–25
   as *Reno 911!* executive producer, 57–58
   series premiere of *It's Always Sunny in Philadelphia*, 47
   The Shield and, 55–56
   success and support for *It's Always Sunny in Philadelphia*, 52, 191, 235–36
The Late Show (TV show), 9
Latiano, Jill, 126–28
the Lawyer (character), 94–96, 99–100, 133, 256–57

INDEX | 323

Leary, Denis, 22–23, 40
Lee, Sung Jin "Sonny", 242–43
Leggero, Natasha, 67
The Lego Movie (film), 232
Lennon, Thomas, 57–58
Lethal Weapon (movie), 165–66, 173–79
Levine, Jerry, 80, 84, 90, 92, 106, 132
Levy, Dan, 285
LGBTQ+ issues
    gay marriage, 185–86, 271
    Mac's sexuality, 225, 245, 271–74
    transgender character, 14, 101, 157, 184–88
Life Is Short with Justin Long (podcast), 65
Liguori, Peter, 22–23, 56
Lil' Kev (character), 80–86, 91
Liman, Doug, 25
Lindelof, Damon, 209, 229
Liotta, Ray, 282
Live Nation (concert promoters), 125
Lopez, Steve, 116
Los Angeles Herald Examiner building, 38–39, 41
Lowry, Brian, 49
Lurie, Jeffrey, 280
Luther MacDonald "Mr. Mac" (character), 72, 102–4

M

MacIntyre, Carter, 158–59
"Mac" Ronald MacDonald (character)
    at armed robbery of convenience store, 252
    arrest of father, 103–4
    attempt to reunite parents, 103
    Barbara, having sex with, 69, 71, 170
    body-swapping with Black person, 260–64
    buying a boat, 163–64
    in Chemical Toilet (musical group), 86–91
    in Christmas special, 192–93
    in citizen watch program, 105–6
    custom Dennis sex doll and, 245
    Dee's pregnancy and, 155–57
    Dennis as murder suspect and, 266
    drug debt to mob, 104–5
    Gail, attempting to have sex with, 170
    in *Lethal Weapon* remakes, 166, 174–78
    at Philadelphia Eagles open tryouts, 93
    in *The Nightman Cometh* musical, 115, 118
    Paddy's Pub, attempting to win award for, 289
    Paddy's Pub, dance contest at, 108
    personality of, 206
    purchasing gasoline to sell later, 147
    selling Dick Towels at Paddy's Pub, 136
    serial killer, mistaken for, 101–2
    sexual harassment seminar and, 249
    sexuality of, 225, 245, 271–74
    Taiwan Tammy character played by, 173
    Teen Wolf, wearing T-shirt from, 106
    transgender woman, dating, 14, 184–88
    tricking Dee into stand-up comedy scheme, 161–62
    upset for not being molested as child, 45–46
    visiting father in prison, 72
    Waitress, relationship with, 11, 45
    wheelchair scam, 67–68
MacVittie, Bruce, 70–71
Malkovich, John, 282
Maloney, Ross, 242
Mandel, David, 5
Mann, Becky, 134, 242
Marder, Scott, 80, 109–12, 137, 242
Margaret McPoyle (character), 77
Marshall-Green, Logan, 6
Martin, Sandy, 70–71. *See also* Mrs. Mac (character)

Martinez, Benito, 23
Matchbox Twenty (musical group), 213–14
Mather House (TV show), 5
Matthew Mara (character). *See* Rickety Cricket (character)
Maureen Ponderosa (character), 99, 265–66
McClanahan, Rue, 172
McCloskey, Don, 122–25
McElhenney, Axel, 156–57
McElhenney, Bob, 106, 128, 220
McElhenney, Katie, 176, 220, 243
McElhenney, Leo, 220
McElhenney, Patrick, 220
McElhenney, Rob. *See also* "Mac"; Ronald MacDonald (character)
  acting career, 3, 5, 211, 213, 232–33, 280–81
  on *The Always Sunny Podcast*, 279
  casting friends and family, 41, 220–26
  on controversial content of *It's Always Sunny in Philadelphia*, 179–80, 190
  creative control of, 25, 32–33, 40–41
  Larry David's career advice for, 234, 275
  Day and Howerton, meeting, 3–5, 7–8
  DeVito fans and, 199
  on DeVito joining *It's Always Sunny in Philadelphia*, 59–62, 239–41
  on Dick Towels, creation of, 136–37
  dream as inspiration for scene, 1–4, 10–11
  exhaustion and burnout of, 227–32
  filming in Philadelphia, 42–43
  Green Man, idea for, 93–94
  on industry awards, 288–92
  It's Always Sunny in Philadelphia pilot, 8–15, 24–25
  on Lil' Kev character, 81
  marriage to Kaitlin Olson, 148
  The Nightman Cometh musical and, 114, 119, 122–30
  Olson's on-set injury and, 165–67
  pitch meetings for *It's Always Sunny in Philadelphia*, 15–20, 23–25
  profitability of *It's Always Sunny in Philadelphia*, 135
  Reid, breaking up with, 28–29
  on Ryan Reynolds guest-starring, 288
  Erin Ryan, hiring as writer, 246–48
  screenwriting of, 7–8
  season 1 of *It's Always Sunny in Philadelphia*, 32–35
  on Seinfeld's TV comedy comments, 269
  on sexuality of Mac, 273
  on T-word use, 186–87
  Unger, casting, 97–98
  weight gain and loss for *It's Always Sunny in Philadelphia*, 230, 272
  writers, hiring, 109–11
  writing contributions to *It's Always Sunny in Philadelphia*, 65–66, 227
McEntire, Reba, 270
McGinn, Devin, 84
McLendon-Covey, Wendi, 57, 270
McMahon, Julian, 22
McNabb, Donovan, 93
McPoyle, Liam and Ryan (characters)
  casting, 44, 218
  in "Charlie Goes America All Over Everybody's Asses", 77
  false accusations of molestation, 45
  getting Mac to call their sister, 155
  in "McPoyle vs. Ponderosa", 256–57
  at Philadelphia Eagles open tryouts, 93
  Pappy McPoyle and, 210, 256
  Thanksgiving with The Gang, 252
Mekka, Eddie, 75
merchandise sales, 77, 135–37, 201–2, 207–8
Mergler, Toby, 93–94

#MeToo movement, 249–51
Michael Rotenberg (character), 161
Michaels, Lorne, 40
The Mick (TV show), 243
Middlebrooks, Windell, 157, 186
Migration (film), 285
Mike (character), 158–59
Milioti, Cristin, 196
Million Dollar Baby (film), 76
The Mindy Project (TV show), 232–33
Miranda, Lin-Manuel, 208–9, 287
Mooney, Nate, 44, 260. *See also*
  McPoyle, Liam and Ryan (characters)
More Better Industries, 280–81
"More Than Words" (song), 74
Morgan, Julia, 39
Mr. Mac "Luther MacDonald"
  (character), 72, 102–4
Mrs. Mac (character), 70–72, 102–3, 265
MTV (network), 19
Muniz, Frankie, 10
Murphy, Ryan, 22
musical episodes of *It's Always Sunny in
  Philadelphia*
  "The Gang Turns Black", 260–65
  "The Nightman Cometh", 113–21,
    191–92
Mythic Quest (TV show), 226, 243, 247,
  280

N

Nanjiani, Kumail, 285
Nash-Betts, Niecy, 57
New Girl (TV show), 233
Nick (character), 157, 186
Nielsen (TV ratings), 51, 132
"Nightman" (song), 88–89, 99, 112–13
The Nightman Cometh musical
  DeVito's Trollfoot Twitter posts, 195
  future of, 287
  merchandise sales, 207–8
  performed live at Troubadour,
    121–25

  repeat viewings of, 191–92
  season 4 episode of, 113–21, 191–92
  six-city live tour (2009), 126–30
  viral video of singing kindergartners,
    279
Nip/Tuck (TV show), 22
Nussbaum, Emily, 82
N-word use, 180–81

O

Obama, Malia, 212
O'Brien, Conan, 161–62
Ochocinco, Chad, 136
The Office (British TV show), 9, 278
O'Kelley, Tricia, 219
Old Black Man (character), 261–63
Olson, Kaitlin. *See also* Deandra "Sweet
  Dee" Reynolds (character)
  acting career, 142, 213, 233, 281–82
  on *The Always Sunny Podcast*, 279
  on auditioning for Sweet Dee role,
    30–32
  on broken back, 148
  casting friends and family, 219
  on *Curb Your Enthusiasm*, 30–31
  on DeVito in Christmas special, 194
  Ellis, meeting, 41
  on fan base of *It's Always Sunny in
    Philadelphia*, 132
  on FX's support of *It's Always Sunny
    in Philadelphia*, 182
  injuries on set, 145–46, 165–67
  input on Sweet Dee role, 32, 37–38,
    143–44, 167
  on "Mac and Dennis: Manhunters"
    episode, 152–53
  marriage to Rob McElhenney, 148
  The Nightman Cometh musical and,
    122–30
  pregnancy, working it into *It's
    Always Sunny in Philadelphia*,
    156–57, 186
  talent and career of, 141–43

One Direction (musical group), 233
Osbourne, Sharon, 200
Osment, Haley Joel, 10
Owens, Geoffrey, 93, 178

P

Pace, Lee, 23
Pacific Rim (film), 210
Pacino, Al, 106
Paddy's Pub (fictional pub)
    Anheuser-Busch pulling signage from, 51
    branded merchandise from, 135
    Charlie's patriotism and, 77
    dance contest at, 107–8
    Electric Dream Machine performing at, 91
    filming location of, 38
    Frank purchasing land under, 69
    The Gang attempting to win award for, 289–90
    health inspection at, 255–56
    model contest at, 172, 181
    musical performances at, 91–92
    political conversation events at, 245
    safety of women at, 249–51
Paddy's Pub: The Worst Bar in Philadelphia: An It's Always Sunny in Philadelphia Cookbook (Randolf), 207, 242
Page, Elliot, 281
Pappy McPoyle (character), 210, 256
Parrot Analytics, 278
Paul, Aaron, 270–71, 287
Pebdani, Artemis, 43–44, 124, 128, 146, 217. *See also* Artemis Dubois (character)
Penn, Sean, 209
Pepper Jack (character), 178
Perlman, Philip, 219
Perlman, Rhea, 70, 124–25, 128, 219, 287
Peter Nincompoop (horse), 104–5

Philadelphia, Pennsylvania
    chosen as location for *It's Always Sunny in Philadelphia*, 26
    filming in, 41–43, 71
    McElhenney named as greatest living Philadelphian, 280
    in opening credits, 43, 226
Philadelphia Eagles (NFL team), 93–94, 280, 292
Philadelphia Phillies (baseball team), 218, 280–81
Phirman, Dannah, 242
Pine, Chris, 285
Piper, Rowdy Roddy, 137
Piven, Jeremy, 40
Polaha, Kristoffer, 68
Poolman (film), 285
Pop-Pop (character), 32
Portugal. The Man (musical group), 211
Posner, Mike, 210
Pounder, CCH, 23
Principal MacIntyre (character), 174, 213
Probst, Jeff, 22

Q

"Quit Smoking" (amateur sketch video), 6

R

racial issues
    blackface and, 92, 166–67, 171–73, 174–78, 181–82
    Fool's Paradise and, 283
    The Gang body-swapping with Black people, 260–65
Radcliffe, Daniel, 210
Rajskub, Mary Lynn, 30, 169–70. *See also* Gail "Gail the Snail" (character)
Rakhe, Luvh, 242
Rapold, Nicolas, 283
RCG Productions, 34
Reddick, Lance, 286

Reddit, 183, 202
Reid, Jordan, 11–12, 28–29
Reiner, Rob, 233
Reitman, Catherine, 99. *See also* Maureen Ponderosa (character)
Remnick, David, 267–69
Reno 911! (TV show), 57–58
REO Speedwagon (musical group), 6
Rescue Me (TV show), 22–23
Reynolds, Dan, 213
Reynolds, Ryan, 280–81, 287–88
Richards, Michael, 268
Richie (character), 174
Rickety Cricket (character), 69–70, 104–5, 107–8, 252, 269
"Rock, Flag, and Eagle" (song), 77
Romano, Chris, 65
Romano, Ray, 83
Rosell, Rob, 80, 109–12, 137, 242
Roth, Andrea, 223
Rotten Tomatoes, 278, 282
Rubinek, Saul, 285
R-word use, 80–82, 183–84
Ryan, Erin, 246–48
Ryan, Shawn, 23, 56

S

Savage, Fred, 80, 93
Scapin, Anna, 218
Schaeffer, Eric, 25
Schaffer, Jeff, 5
Schneider, Danielle, 242–43
Schrader, Paul, 7
Schrier, Eric, 23
Schwarzenegger, Arnold, 39, 286
Sczak, Marc, 291
Seinfeld (TV show), 184, 266–69
Seinfeld, Jerry, 267–70
Sepinwall, Alan, 237–38
Serpico (movie), 106
Serpico, Frank, 105–6
Shakman, Matt
    Biermann shadowing, 223–24
    directing season 3 of *It's Always Sunny in Philadelphia*, 80, 95
    directing season 4 of *It's Always Sunny in Philadelphia*, 120
    directing season 10 episode of *It's Always Sunny in Philadelphia*, 255
    on Mae Laborde, 117
    The Nightman Cometh musical and, 124–25, 128
Shea, Kylie, 273–74
Shepard, Dax, 219
The Shield (TV show), 23, 55–56
Sielaff, Audra, 134, 242
Simone, Hannah, 233
Simpson, Jimmi, 5–7, 12, 44, 260. *See also* McPoyle, Liam and Ryan (characters)
Sinbad, 213–14
Sklar, Jason and Randy, 107
Smart, Jean, 243, 281
Smith, Kevin, 8
Snopes.com, 75
Snyder (character), 160–61
Solberg, John, 139
Sommer, Rich, 285
Son of the Beach (TV show), 22
"Speedwagon" (amateur sketch video), 6
Spillane, Sherri, 116–17
St. Sebastian (film), 286
Stack, Timothy, 22
Stanfield, LaKeith, 285
Starved (TV show), 25, 46–52
Stein, Joel, 268
Stern, Howard, 22
Stewart, Lynne Marie, 46. *See also* Bonnie Kelly (character)
Storm, Jonathan, 42
Sudeikis, Jason, 232, 282
"The Sun Always Shines on T.V." (song), 15
Sunjata, Daniel, 282
SUNY Purchase, New York, 197
The Super Mario Bros. Movie (film), 282
Surface, Thesy, 77

Swardson, Nick, 139
Sweet Dee (character). *See* Deandra "Sweet Dee" Reynolds (character)
Swift, Austin, 211
Swift, Taylor, 211

T

A Tail's Tale: A Mermaid's Tale (movie script), 201
The Talk (chat show), 200–201
Taxi (TV show), 59, 291
Taylor, Keyonna, 176
Television Critics Association (TCA), 47–49, 61, 139, 290–91
"Temptation Sensation" (main title theme), 27, 43
Terrell (character), 42, 180–81
That '80s Show (TV show), 3, 5, 187
Thicke, Robin, 139
30 Rock (TV show), 176
Thomas, Rob, 213–14
The Tonight Show (TV show), 254
transgender character, 14, 101, 157, 184–88
Troubadour, Los Angeles, 122–25
20th Century Fox, 61
Twitter, 195
T-word use, 186–87

U

Unger, Brian, 94–95, 97–100, 257. *See also* the Lawyer (character)
Utley, Chase, 218, 280–81

V

Vanny DeVito (fan vehicles), 196–97
VelJohnson, Reginald, 256
VH1 (network), 19

W

Waitress (character)
  at armed robbery of convenience store, 252–53
  Charlie's crush on, 11, 44–45, 129–30, 137
  dance contest at Paddy's, 107–8
  Dennis, having sex with, 45
  drunken wipeout in shoe store, 146
  Frank, having sex with, 45, 69
  Mac, having sex with, 11
  The Nightman Cometh musical and, 124, 129–30
Walsh, Dylan, 22
Walsh, Patrick, 242
Weiner, Matthew, 211–12, 229
Weiss, D. B., 211, 229, 252
Welcome to Wrexham (docuseries), 280
Wendell Albright (character), 102
White, Betty, 172
White, Mike, 285
Wiig, Kristen, 30
William Morris Endeavor (WME), 17–18
Williams, Robin, 209
Williamstown Theatre Festival, Massachusetts, 5–6, 11, 27, 44, 71
Willis, Allee, 77
Wilson, Owen, 285
Witwer, Sam, 111, 218
Wolf, Dick, 17
Wrexham Dragons (soccer team), 280

Y

Yarbrough, Cedric, 57
"You're the Best" (song), 76–77
YouTube
  The Always Sunny Podcast, watching on, 279
  Day's amateur sketch videos on, 6
  It's Always Sunny in Philadelphia episodes on, 181, 214
  Olson's audition video on, 31

Z

Zimmer, Constance, 286